STUDENT RESISTANCE IN THE AGE OF CHAOS

Book 1, 1999–2009

STUDENT RESISTANCE IN THE AGE OF CHAOS

Book 1, 1999–2009
Globalization, Human Rights, Religion,
War, and the Age of the Internet

MARK EDELMAN BOREN

Seven Stories Press
New York • Oakland • London

A SEVEN STORIES PRESS FIRST EDITION

Seven Stories Press
140 Watts Street
New York, NY 10013
sevenstories.com

College professors and high school and middle school teachers may order free examination copies of Seven Stories Press titles. Visit https://www.sevenstories.com/pg/resources-academics or email academics@sevenstories.com.

Library of Congress Cataloging-in-Publication Data

Names: Boren, Mark Edelman, author.
Title: Student resistance in the age of chaos / Mark Edelman Boren.
Description: New York, NY : Seven Stories Press, 2021. | Includes
  bibliographical references and index. | Contents: Book 1. 1999-2009 :
  globalization, human rights, religion, war, and the age of the Internet
  -- Book 2. 2010-2020 : social media, women's rights, and the rise of
  activism in a time of nationalism, mass migrations, and climate change.
Identifiers: LCCN 2021008148 | ISBN 9781644210369 (book 1) | ISBN
  9781644211267 (book 2)
Subjects: LCSH: Student movements--History--21st century. | Education and
  globalization. | Social justice and education. | Social media in
  education.
Classification: LCC LB3610 .B666 2021 | DDC 378.1/981--dc23
LC record available at https://lccn.loc.gov/2021008148

Printed in the United States of America

9 8 7 6 5 4 3 2 1

For Averil and Maisie

CONTENTS

Book 1, 1999–2009:
Globalization, Human Rights, Religion, War,
and the Age of the Internet

ACKNOWLEDGMENTS. ix
PREFACE xiii
INTRODUCTION: Student Resistance Drives Social Evolution 1
PRELUDE TO THE CHAOS: Watershed Developments in Student
  Activism and Traditional Strategies of Resistance 9
1 Antiwar Protests, Internet Activism, and the
   Power of Divestment in North America 35
2 War, the Push for Liberalism, and Conservative
   Backlash in the Middle East. 53
3 Educational Reforms, Virtual Activism,
   Anticapitalism, and the Growth of International
   Networks in Europe 75
4 Prodemocracy Revolutions, the Color Revolutions,
   and the Changing Tactics of Activism in Eastern
   Europe and Russia. 107
5 Technological Explosions, Revolutions, and Gender
   Justice Movements in Asia and Australia. 135
6 Student Networking, Violence, and Social
   Upheaval in Africa 189
7 International Networks, Indigenous Peoples'
   Rights, and Economic Justice in Mexico, Central
   America, South America, and Island Nations. 211
THOUGHTS ON THE TRANSFORMATION AND POWER OF
  STUDENT RESISTANCE 235
NOTES 241
BIBLIOGRAPHY 247
INDEX 261

Book 2, 2010–2020:
Social Media, Women's Rights, and the Rise of
Activism in a Time of Nationalism, Mass Migrations,
and Climate Change

ACKNOWLEDGMENTS. ix

PREFACE xiii

INTRODUCTION: Resistance in the Time of Chaos 289

8   Fires of Revolt in the Middle East. 297

9   Authoritarians, Radical Activism, and Social Justice
    in Eastern Europe and Russia 347

10 Nationalism, Antifa, and the Climate Change
    Movement in Europe 383

11 Revolutionizing Street Activism, Women's Rights,
    and the Rise and Fall of Democracy in
    Asia and Australia. 431

12 Tyrants, Violence, and the Struggle for
    Human Rights in Africa. 511

13 The Latin American Spring and the Proliferation
    of Student Movements in Mexico, Central America,
    South America, and Island Nations 547

14 Resistance, Riots, and Black Lives Matter in
    North America. 581

LOOKING FORWARD TO THE FUTURE OF PROTEST 625

NOTES 631

BIBLIOGRAPHY 637

INDEX 651

ACKNOWLEDGMENTS

This book would not exist at all if it weren't for an initial conversation I had with Dan Simon, who suggested I consider following up my first book on the general history of student resistance with one focused on the current historical moment and the immediate years leading up to it. Dan not only encouraged this undertaking but helped make plain the ethical imperative to do this work and to do it now.

Second on my list of thanks are the people who helped me research this project. Lauren Krouse and Andy Tolhurst were invaluable, tireless researchers, and this project could not have been completed without them. The scope of the research was enormous, but despite facing a vast sea of information, the three of us waded through hundreds of thousands of documents, reports, books, and articles, culled from thousands upon thousands of sources. This work was followed up with interviews and further investigations. Thank you, both. Other researchers contributing to the project include Caleb Horowitz, Abby House, and Lilly Craig, who undertook targeted research on specific movements, organizations, and sources. Together, the six of us built what we called the Resistance Archive, a large, organized pool from which the writing of this labor draws. All five researchers have my deepest gratitude for their efforts.

I'm indebted to many people who talked through specific issues with me, offered insights, or pointed out further areas to research. Thank you Philip Altbach, Bill Atwill, Kathleen Berkeley, Todd Berliner, Curt Boren, Doyle Boren, Jan Boren, Dawn Brown, Don Bushman, Michelle Britt, Maia Butler, Sadie Campbell, Nina de Gramont, Venkat Dhulipala, Stephen Duncombe, Kimi Faxon Hemingway, Amy Feath, Lewis Feuer, Bill Germano, David Gessner, Christopher Gould, Kathleen Gould, Tom Hayden, Sarah Hallenbeck, Chip Hemingway, Paula Kamenish, Thea Keith-Lucas, Amy Kirschke, Rory Laverty, Nick Laudadio, Miles Lewis, Sheri Malman,

Vic Malo-Juvera, Michelle Manning, Sue McCaffray, Tonia McKoy, Amol Mehendale, Lynn Mollenauer, David Monoghan, Jacob Montwieler, Marlon Moore, Gabriel Nadeau-Dubois, Rich Ogle, George Pace, Medha Patkar, Srdja Popovic, Anirban Ray, Dana Sachs, Michelle Scatton-Tessier, Amy Schlag, Michael Seidman, Meghan Sweeney, Eric Tessier, Paul Townend, Alice Tucker, Sridhar Varadarajan, Lewis Walker, Yishi Wang, Barbara Waxman, Bob Waxman, and Michael Wentworth.

I am particularly grateful for those who took time to critique the manuscript. Peter McLaren, Cary Nelson, Nancy Montwieler, and Bill Montwieler read early drafts of the manuscript in its entirety—acts of incredible generosity. Although many of the people already mentioned advised me on individual movements and sections of the manuscript, I want to single out Jennifer Baumgardner, Aric McBay, Fatou Jagne Senghore, Inna Shevchenko, and Nadya Tolokonnikova for their generosity, perspective, and suggestions on specific regions and events. My sincere apologies to anyone I may have overlooked. I also wish to thank those who spoke to me who wished not to be identified, for modesty or fear of reprisal, but who had the courage to trust enough to share their stories.

At Seven Stories Press, Lauren Hooker has been delightful to work with, and she steered this project through dangerous passages of publishing with skill and grace. Molly Lindley Pisani did a wonderful job copyediting the text, and thanks as well to Jon Gilbert, Shayan Saalabi, Eva Sotomayor, and Ruth Weiner for their contributions to the book.

Lisa Coats and Stephanie Crowe at the University of North Carolina Wilmington's Randall Library gave me invaluable advice for compiling data and sifting through international databases, thousands of newspapers, journals, internet sources, and academic studies. Also at UNCW, Aswani Volety, Ron Vetter, Kemille Moore, David Webster, Michael Wilhelm, Jess Boersma, and Tiffany Gilbert facilitated the project by giving me time and funds to do research and hire help. I am indebted to UNCW for a timely research reassignment award, for a summer research development grant, and for supporting research assistants. International research travel grants that allowed for primary and secondary research were provided by UNCW's Office of International Programs, College of Arts and Sciences, and English department. Carie Kempton, Donna Carlton, and Karen Doniere facilitated the clearing of obstacles to make the research possible.

Thanks to indomitable librarians and staff at Alamy; Amnesty International; Arbejdermuseet Museum and the Labour Movement Library and Archives, Copenhagen; Archives Nationales, Paris; Bancroft Library, Berkeley, California; Bibliothèque Nationale de France; Bridgeman Images; CANVAS; Casablanca Occupied Social Center, Madrid; Center for the Study of Political Graphics, Los Angeles; Center for the Study of Social Movements; Charles University, Prague; Columbia University; Daybreak Project; Duke University; Femen; Hamburg Institute for Social Research; Harvard University; Heidelberg University; Hoover Institution Library and Archives; Howard University; Human Rights Watch; Huntington Library, Pasadena; Institute of the Royal Academy of the Netherlands; Center for Artistic Activism, New York; International Institute of Social History, Amsterdam; Interference Archive, New York; KARTA Center Archives, Warsaw; Library of Congress, Washington, DC; National Archives of South Africa; National Archives, United Kingdom; National Library of India; National Security Archive; Archivo General de la Nación, Mexico; New York Public Library; New York University; Oberlin College; Oxford University; People's Archives, Helsinki; Project STAND (Student Activism Now Documented); Spelman College; Sorbonne Library and Archives; Stanford University; State University of New York at Buffalo; Survival International; Swarthmore College; Tate Britain Archive; Taub Center for Social Policy Studies in Israel; Tisch Library, Tufts University; Trinity College Dublin; University of Auckland; University of Bologna; University of Florida; University of Georgia; University of Melbourne; University of Miami Archives; University of Pennsylvania; University of North Carolina at Chapel Hill; University of North Carolina Greensboro; University of North Carolina Wilmington; University of Wisconsin–Madison; University of Toronto; and *Witness*.

I am grateful to Stewart Cauley and Debra Williams for years of friendship that has outlasted two dogs and a cat, for their advice and suggestions, and for a constant supply of curious, sometimes shady, avenues to investigate or explore. Katie Peel has kept me in spirits throughout this project and talked through most aspects of this book in weekly rap sessions. I am particularly indebted to her for her deep knowledge of Eastern European history and the history of LGBTQ and women's movements, and for her sense of humor. Most thanks go to Katherine Montwieler, whose intellectual prowess and perspective on all this have been invaluable and whose unwavering support has kept me, and thus the project, going. And finally, I am grateful to my children, Averil and Maisie, for they provide both reason for and relief from work such as this.

PREFACE

APRIL 20, 2019

Notre Dame Cathedral was still smoldering when I arrived in Paris, and this afternoon a week later other parts of Paris would be on fire. The day had begun for me as typically as any other that week, with research in the morning, though the location for my *déjeuner*—a recommended sidewalk café several blocks removed from the Place de la République—was not among my usual haunts. Five streets came together before the café, and as in most such establishments, the tables and chairs faced outward, giving diners a lovely panorama of the ornate buildings topped with steep slate roofs that lined the streets. It was Saturday; the weather was absolutely beautiful, and the area was bustling. The spot was on the Right Bank, in the eastern part of the city—some distance from the Sorbonne, near where I was based, but I had been alerted to come here by students who were planning to protest the government's attempt to raise tuition fees for foreign students attending university. Their group would be but one faction of what they described as a formidable *gilets jaunes* (yellow vests) demonstration to occur that afternoon. As I waited and enjoyed a double espresso and *plateau de fromages*, people in brightly colored vests began to walk past, and soon one heard chanting in the distance. I had attended a *gilets jaunes* march immediately following the burning of Notre Dame, and it had been a relatively calm affair, nothing at all like the previous month's riots on the Champs-Élysées. The combination of crisp air and sun on this day couldn't have been more delightful, and I thought I would enjoy my repast and then leisurely walk down to snap some pictures of protestors, take notes, and interview demonstrators and police. This was, after all, Paris, and even given recent tussles between police and demonstrators, my expectations for how the day's events would unfold were admittedly different from those I'd held for protests I witnessed in Guatemala, where social unrest was controlled by armed federal police and military units wielding automatic rifles. And although I may have rinsed some clothes that morning in the sink of my hotel room, with its balcony overlooking the Panthéon, I was not in clothes laundered in a Central American lake.

As I finished my Camembert de Normandie, the distant chanting changed in both tempo and intensity, and I thought it time to try to catch the server's eye and signal for the bill. That was when the unmistakable "weeee-waa" of French police sirens suddenly filled the streets, and half a dozen blue-and-white cars with flashing lights sped through the intersection and down the street, the echoes of their sirens reverberating down the canyon of buildings. These smaller cars were immediately followed by a wailing caravan of eight giant dark-blue police transports coming from the same direction, though they veered off and disappeared down another route. A massive armored police tank surmounted by two remote-controlled water cannons rumbled past. I forsook my receipt (and with it any hope of claiming my per diem reimbursement), dumped a pocketful of euros on the table, and stepped out onto the sidewalk.

More police vehicles flew past, and two others screeched to a halt in the intersection, completed quick three-point turns, and sealed it off. Traffic on the three streets to the left was immediately jammed, and angry drivers began honking. It was the day before Easter Sunday, and the *gilets jaunes* had orchestrated the simultaneous occupation of key Métro stations across the city, bringing the entire city of Paris to a standstill. They set fire to vehicles, Vespas, and barricades in targeted locations to shut down all the trains at once and to underscore that the government faced immediate problems other than the restoration of a burned landmark. The demonstration at the Place de la République, a few blocks from where I stood, would in short order escalate into the most violent uprising Paris had seen in some time, with masked rioters throwing pavers and flares at riot police, who repeatedly charged them with batons. The protestors were enraged that a billion euros had, in only a matter of days, been donated by wealthy tycoons and corporations for the restoration of Notre Dame—the pledges being viewed by the protestors as offensive brand-raising PR stunts—while the poor of

France continued to suffer economic hardship. Yes, they wanted the cathedral restored, but they also wanted economic justice.

Demonstrators at the protests carried signs saying things like, "Must I set myself on fire to get the government's attention?" and shouted, "Give us our money back, and we'll rebuild our cathedral!" Many would be injured in the riots, and more than two hundred protestors arrested. Storefront windows would be smashed; cars and motorcycles would be vandalized, and the smoke of burning vehicles would mix with tear gas to choke the air for blocks around. One part of the group would try to force a march to Notre Dame itself, only to be repelled by security troops.

Unknown to the tourists coming to the city that weekend, sixty thousand police had been mobilized in anticipation of the day's demonstrations, which in Paris alone drew close to ten thousand participants. Across France, another twenty thousand demonstrated, in some cases violently. Police I interviewed in the days prior only knew that they had been deployed to maintain order, to prevent vandalism, and to keep people from getting hurt. This was a classic maneuver in the modern counterdemonstration playbook—police were brought in from outlying areas so they would have no personal connection to locals or to the neighborhoods to which they were assigned. Those I had spoken with had been courteous, friendly, and generous—middle-class professionals, many with families at home, doing their jobs—but they also made it clear that when challenged by protestors they would push back. That Saturday, some of them would be firing tear-gas grenades and water cannons at their fellow citizens, and others would be taking part in baton charges, resorting to beating the anarchists and provocateurs among the protestors who escalated the conflict by hurling bricks and stones, as well as others who happened to get in the way.

Even hesitating on the periphery of the Place de la République, as I was doing at the moment, was not safe. As the sounds of fighting increased from down the avenue to my right, a crush of people began fleeing the area on foot. Personal motorcycles and scooters zipped crazily (even for Paris) back up the blocked-off streets, past the police barricades, and through crowds of curious onlookers. All this happened in the first minutes of the conflict. The yelling grew louder, along with the unmistakable sounds of physical violence. More sirens—a different kind, I noted—wailed from my left, accompanied by the high-pitched whine of speed bikes. Parisian bystanders, knowing what was coming, drew back toward the walls of buildings as twenty police motorcycles suddenly appeared in rapid succession, weaving at stunning speed through the jammed cars beyond the barricades to scream past the café one after the other, flying in the direction of the protest. Slaloming through parked cars, around medians, over sidewalks, and in and out through iron lampposts and signs, they shot between the bumpers of the police-car blockade and roared by in a serpentine line, as if the entire formation was a giant snake racing through the cars and obstacles. At incredible speed, each bike trailed the one ahead by only a meter or so, maintaining precise formation and speed, with absolute faith in the path chosen by the lead bike. This, then, was the modern solution to the problem of rapid troop movement in the city, and a much more stylish one than Haussmann's: fleets of strategically placed low-slung motorcycles, each one surmounted by two shock troops—a driver and another clutching him from behind—all in modish, matching black clothes, on black motorcycles, as if they were in some Tarantino remake of *Tron*, a rapid response that delivered forty superbly trained reinforcements to the scene of a riot, in midday traffic through the narrow streets of Paris, in mere seconds.

Of all the protests I've witnessed in my travels and research for this book that I could have used as an introductory example (some larger, some more violent), I chose this one because not only did it include a traditional march and bodies-on-the-barricades aspect but it also suggested how much technology and shifting tactics will play a role in the future of activism. While media coverage focuses on the rock throwing, the tear gas, and the fires, technology is changing both activist strategies and police response. That day, the protestors' overall strategy began with a decentralized social-net-working organization of the protests that allowed the *gilets jaunes* to avoid tipping off the police they knew were monitoring them. Informing people of the coming demonstrations, to get protestors ready for day-of instructions to follow, was done via both websites and social media, but the most sensitive information about the specific locations of demonstrations and who would go where and do what was sent to those on standby through encrypted chat lines. When they struck, they did so at multiple locations at once, with flash mobs..

Organizers sent subnetworks (such as the faction of communist students from the Sorbonne) to specific locations, suggesting needed numbers and needed supplies, and released real-time tactical instructions (the setting of small fires, for example, near key train stations) to effectively sow confusion and paralyze the city's Métro; thus, when the demonstration began, police would have to scramble to multiple locations and spread out their personnel. Knowing media coverage would be intense, organizers co-opted the symbol of fire from the burning of Notre Dame as a theme of the protests. This allowed them simultaneously to draw attention to economic disparity and to criticize the government's policies. The image of fire appeared on a great many of the signs and banners protestors created ahead of time, and thus the fires set throughout the city by protestors were folded into a larger conversation about and critique of government policies in the media.

At the same time, the police response revealed authorities were both using traditional countermeasures (importing troops in overwhelming numbers) and applying new technologies, including cybersurveillance, which alerted security forces to the coming demonstrations and picked up enough social media and online "chatter" to tell them—if not specifics regarding how and where the protests would be launched—at least how big they likely would be and how many troops they'd need. They then stationed troops near likely sites throughout the city. New tactics, aerial surveillance, and dedicated telecommunication strategies allowed for real-time reconnaissance to discern where reinforcements were needed (through both troop reports and surveillance tracking crowd movements) and facilitate quick conventional responses (the street blockades and the deployment of troop carriers and water cannons). They enabled the use of the futuristic rapid-response motorcycle columns to deploy additional reinforcements where needed.

Well before the protests, police had spent time developing urban-capable, heavily armored water-cannon tanks that could not be breached by demonstrators, which clearly were capable of driving over street barricades and stalled vehicles. Each tank was surmounted with multiple remote-controlled water cannons, which could be safely operated from within the vehicle's sealed cab, behind the protection of shatterproof, bulletproof glass. Of course, on the side of security, technological innovations included everything from the tear gas used (intense but rapidly dissipating) to the design of body armor, batons, and transparent full-body shields. There were also those guns that fired rubber-coated bullets intended to incapacitate but not permanently harm. These new measures were all backed up, should things get out of hand, by conventionally armed security forces with semiautomatic weapons. Thus, security forces were deploying sophisticated intelligence operations and had developed a series of response levels and tactics of increasingly firm suppression.

Police troops were trained to be firm but restrained. On this day they used a lot of tear gas, but there was not widespread beating of protestors; the idea was to control unrest but not widen support for the movement, which could happen if they were filmed hurting people—and the media had clearly been made aware of the demonstrations to come by protest organizers. Heavily armed squads of police similar to those seen in French airports were deployed in close proximity to the events, ready should they be needed but held back from the conflict as much as possible. There would be no martyrs to the cause of the gilets jaunes. Groups of police stationed in clumps across Paris who were not tasked with stopping protestors remained friendly toward citizens and tourists, indulgently posing for selfies, and pleasant toward people wearing neon vests who were clearly on their way to or from protests. (The demonstrators I interviewed before and after the protests were also personable, and took time to explain their positions.) Security would undoubtedly analyze surveillance footage in the days to come and seek to identify and arrest participants who had set fires, were violent, or otherwise destroyed property, but everyone involved in the actions seemed acutely aware that they were under constant surveillance (by police, media, protestors with cameras, and bystanders with phones). How people comported themselves would inevitably become part of the messaging by both sides. The protest and countermeasures were thus a complex political-physical media event, one that would be represented, narrated, and interpreted for days, and years, afterwards. It was also a harbinger of the future of demonstration and counterdemonstration strategies, tactics, and technologies. (Complicating this careful dance between the forces of protestors and security was always the threat of anarchists, provocateurs, or unrelated groups that might seek opportune moments to strike other targets in the city or escalate the violence at demonstrations to capture the attention of the media.)

Back to the motorbikes. As quickly as they had appeared, the piggybacking squad of special-forces bikers flew past me again in rapid succession—Voom! Voom! Voom! Voom! Voom! (twenty of them!) to disappear down the now empty street, their bikes screaming as they raced toward another flashpoint in the growing conflict, leaving behind stunned bystanders in the intersection, in a state of terrified awe to have witnessed them. I and two locals (who were clearly trying to make it to their apartments halfway down the block before the expanding riot could cut them off) slipped past the police blockade and hurried down the empty sidewalk toward the increasing sounds of chaos . . .

STUDENT RESISTANCE DRIVES SOCIAL EVOLUTION

This book documents a constant, often spontaneous worldwide struggle of idealism and change against powers of social control and stasis, a multifront, multi-issue battle that over the past two decades has been waged in both new and old forms in every nation on earth, between youth aspiring to power and older generations trying to keep it for themselves. Hundreds of thousands of student resistance actions have occurred since the start of the new millennium—from strikes to marches, petitions to bombings, single defiant stands against injustice to massive social media–driven boycotts. The sheer number of actions and their effects on the course of societies and cultures confirm that in today's modern world, student resistance is defining of, or an integral part of, the evolution of every society in existence today. The myth that the heyday of student activism was in the past—in the 1960s and '70s—is a fiction. Globally, no period has seen more student activism than the past twenty years. And the process has been accelerating. The amount of student activism in the world more or less doubled from the first decade to the second decade of the new millennium—and by all accounts the future holds more.

Since the beginning of the twenty-first century, the world has increasingly been enveloped in turmoil if not outright chaos. Authoritarianism has been on the rise, alliances between nations have been weakened or shattered, and war and famine have caused massive human migrations. Internment camps, slavery, and violence against large groups of people are mundane facts of life, even within developed nations, while many of those in charge of those nations pretend it is not happening. The leaders of nuclear-armed countries have repeatedly challenged and threatened one another, and in 2016, an unpredictable and wholly self-absorbed television personality with no government experience took the reins of the most powerful nation on earth, appointing cronies and corrupt officials to key posts and plunging the world into four years of confusion and instability. While geopolitical and economic storms continue to rage, the planet itself is threatened by pollution and climate change. The stakes for the future of earth and humankind have never been higher than they are today.

Enter the student. She embodies a paradox, having been taught knowledge and strategies for success but also the idea that to gain and accept new knowledge, she must challenge preconceptions, prior beliefs, and authority (the received knowledge of the past). This questing, this cultivation of a "why this and not that?" disposition, makes education, personal development, social growth, and innovation possible, but sooner or later it also may turn her against the forces that control students and their respective societies. Combined with her youthful idealism and the fact that, as is the case with many students, she isn't yet economically or professionally invested enough for opponents or authorities to use leverage to stop her from protesting (she may risk physical suppression and expulsion but doesn't yet have a family to support or a career to protect), many students use their newfound awareness, education, and independence to challenge the status quo.

The student, in her nature, is a political creature, learning to be adept at negotiating channels of power in order to accumulate more power (knowledge, position, status, money, technology, things), and more than a few begin to chafe at the restraints of their societies. Although social activism is certainly not limited to students or the young, the conditions that make for creative, aware, knowledgeable, and socially involved students are also perfect for subsequently inducing them to become social activists. This is why education is often perceived as inherently threatening to conservative forces of authority, and why student activism in the modern world is a perennial threat to repressive societies. In times when social and political chaos reigns, when widespread human suffering is clearly evident, when so many resources are available and so many of them wasted, when extremes in human nature come to the fore, when injustice is rampant and the divide between the haves and the have-nots is great, students are more likely to challenge their societies and raise up their heads and their fists.

Granted, not all students fight for altruistic reasons (witness the recent rise of alt-right student groups in the United States, Germany, Hungary, or Poland and violent "traditionalist" student groups in India), but student activists of every sort believe they are fighting for positive social change and against perceived social or governmental threats. Their belief in their causes and the de facto martial context make for a volatile mixture. And since the deck is always stacked against protestors (they do not have well-trained, armed security forces with conflict experience and tactics based on known demonstration practices on their side), students must constantly invent new ways to challenge authority. Usually physically, financially, and legally disadvantaged from the start in their quest, they increasingly resort to guerilla-style tactics (even if they are carried out through peaceful or legal means), trying to stay one step ahead of more powerful opponents and police. They must constantly open new fronts against entrenched power before stronger physical responses can be launched against them. And when they do march in force, they characteristically try to spark larger movements before administrations or governments can assert control or counterattack with direct, overwhelming physical force. In terms of social power, the struggle between the forces of change and forces of stasis is what defines all of our societies, and it is what forces societies to evolve or to entrench and calcify. In this context, student and youth resistance drives social evolution.

Student activism is many centuries old and has always been political in nature—indeed, the first universities were coalitions of student scholars who hired teachers and used collective power to extort concessions from local businesses and towns—and since the Middle Ages, students have repeatedly increased their power and influence on their societies through social, political, and physical engagement with ruling authorities. The types of resistance actions student activists have fashioned are incredibly varied, and while some never rose above fights for personal entitlements or beyond beer-fueled town-and-gown riots, others have sparked dramatic social changes, reformulated national political structures, fomented revolutions, and started or stopped wars.

But the last twenty-five or so years have seen student resistance actions different in kind and magnitude from those at any other time in history. This is due to radical changes in technology and the sophistication of networking, information dissemination, and protest methods through the internet and social media, coupled with widespread geopolitical chaos and a rampant reformulation of national and international power structures throughout the world. What makes this particular moment in time unique, and what makes this book necessary (and even possible), are tremendous technological changes—the access common people now have to information, tactics, images, news, and each other. New tools and strategies available for resistance have augmented traditional protest actions and armed a dizzying number of student resistance movements. The use of phone-driven flash mobbing, the ability to connect with and mobilize thousands, even millions, through the internet and cell phones, the ability to record video on phones and immediately transmit images and events internationally have all put tremendous power in the hands of common people. And more governmental reliance on computer technology has given sophisticated hackers new government targets.

Yet, the prolific cyberlinking of activists has also awarded technologically sophisticated governments access to entire networks of opposition groups, identified potential targets for arrest, and let authorities monitor movements of individuals. Our phones track us, our televisions and computers listen to and watch us, and in cities and transportation hubs we are constantly scanned by facial-recognition software. Satellites and drones observe us from above, and following protests, images of crowds (even when they number in the tens of thousands) are processed through software, face by face, to identify participants. Lists are drawn up, targets are tagged for future surveillance, and in many cases arrests are made. In conjunction with a rash of new and intentionally vague "antiterrorist laws" adopted in almost every country in the world in the last ten years, such antiopposition tools repeatedly have been used to stamp out even moderate opposition, and have served up political networks and opponents to authoritarian regimes. The already central role that technology plays in the perennial battle between activists and entrenched authority, between the forces of change and the forces of repression, only continues to grow.

This two-volume project details student protest actions and technological changes of the last few decades, fleshing out their immediate historical context and their effects upon their societies and the world. It identifies major trends and trajectories. While the scope and details may seem overwhelming at times, describing them—and doing so in some detail—is necessary for the reader to see how incredibly pervasive and important resistance actions have been globally in recent years and, at the same time, how violent the forces of oppression are today throughout the world. Out of the details, pictures and trends emerge, as does a better understanding of what is at stake in these human struggles. The extensive documentation of sexual violence brought to light by protests in India, for example, can be soul crushing, but without seeing their extent and understanding their context, one cannot fully grasp the importance of the protests, in 2019, in which millions of women stood together to form a three-hundred-mile-long human wall in India, courageously demanding an end to sexual violence. The protest would not have been possible without the technology-driven dissemination and discussion of incidents of sexual violence, the context of the #MeToo movement, and the ability, through social media, to announce the demonstration quickly.

In addition to the relevance of historical context, one cannot overstate the importance of the role technology plays in activism today. In comparing maps of student resistance and activist attendance with maps tracking the penetration and use of Twitter in Asia in the late 2000s and early 2010s, for example, one can see distinct parallels. As new technology became available, activists put it to use, experimenting with and refining strategies in their struggles against authoritarian regimes. Unlike in Eastern Europe, where the technology became available almost at once, in Asia its adoption occurred over time, and one can discern more easily how the rise of social media and affordable technology brought with it an explosion in activism. Globally, activism has exploded to the point where an attempt like mine, here, to cover two whole decades between book covers has become a nearly impossible task.

So much has happened and is currently happening that I have had to make difficult decisions as to what to include in this survey beyond the most well-known movements and events (the kind disseminated by the major news media) and those with critically agreed upon historical importance. I've tried to choose demonstrations, strategies, and movements that serve to give a sense of the range and extent of actions undertaken, and I've included ones that were particularly illustrative of certain struggles or issues and the contexts in which they occurred. Whether it's a million people marching in the streets of Hong Kong, two prodemocracy protestors standing on the one spot allowed for demonstrations in Singapore, or a child travelling by sailboat across the Atlantic to fight for action on climate change, the willingness to put one's body and future at risk for social change suggests much about the human character and the values of those challenging authority—and it reveals just as much about the character and nature of the authorities themselves. To understand recent social and global history, and the current moment in which we live, we must understand the pervasive role of activism in defining and shaping national and world events.[1]

Student resistance is an important part of human history. In the twentieth and twenty-first centuries it has increasingly affected societies and played a central role in shaping them. In researching and writing this book, I've come to realize just how much student resistance reveals who we are as humans and—beyond serving as the canary in the coalmine—how much student activism is shaping the present moment and will shape our separate and shared futures. In order to write this book, I and a group of researchers, guided by librarians and archivists and an adept cyberspecialist, culled through thousands of different newspapers, government and NGO reports, articles, accounts, posts, letters, documents, and internet and social-media sources in every form imaginable, and conducted in-person interviews, to build what we called the Resistance Archive. We tracked hundreds of thousands of demonstrations, uprisings, movements, organizations, and materials into a searchable and meaningful form that, even after we had pared it down, still contained tens of thousands of reports of discrete events, organizations, and movements. The sheer number of actions that have occurred recently and that are occurring today as you read this—actions often attended by brutal suppression—reveals the extent to which humans across the planet are locked in this seemingly everlasting struggle between those seeking greater democracy, civil rights, and social justice and the forces of authoritative, entrenched power and social restriction.

The historian's axiom that in order to understand the present we must look to the past has much value, and in the first section of the book I give a brief history of important events of student resistance throughout history to establish a context for the student resistance actions of the new millennium. While current resistance fits into a long tradition of actions and common strategies, looking at the history also serves to underscore exactly how unique and pervasive recent actions have been, why they've proliferated, and how much technology has changed the nature of resistance. By the end of this book, I hope it will be clear to the reader that in order for societies to continue to evolve, to move beyond the constricting forces of social injustice, repression, brutality, cynicism, and entrenched power, young people need to fight against the status quo, to strike for social change, to push for laws that are just and justly enforced, and to hold those in positions of authority accountable. They are in a unique position to do so, and when they take up the challenge of wielding social power directly, they have access to power that can, and does, bring about lasting change. Student resistance shapes the future.

PRELUDE TO THE CHAOS
WATERSHED DEVELOPMENTS IN STUDENT
ACTIVISM AND TRADITIONAL STRATEGIES
OF RESISTANCE

Many societies have ancient traditions and histories of formal education, but the most common systems of higher education around the world today evolved from medieval European universities, originally formed by scholars and students as collectives. These collectives gave scholars the means to pool resources to hire lecturers and to wield economic power (the way a trade guild would). They could threaten to leave a town unless they received concessions on rent or taxes. In 1220, students picked up and left Bologna until the city submitted to economic demands and the masters at the university pledged to follow rules of behavior. Often populated by the children of the wealthy, early universities also received special protections from leaders of European states, and land grants (which, while giving the collectives status, also gave birth to university administrations and a certain level of oversight—thereby foiling future threats to relocate). University attendance swelled as well-off parents realized universities were excellent places to put (and monitor, at a safe distance) their maturing but still rambunctious offspring.

Many of the earliest acts of student collective resistance in Europe were town-and-gown melees after violence between students and locals escalated into riots, and many of the recorded early struggles began not on campus but in local taverns. But from such ignoble origins, in most cases where brouhahas escalated into violent riots, the long-term outcomes of these conflicts favored universities, which through student body and patronage had direct connections to aristocracy and those in power. In 1354, the Saint Scholastica's Day Riot occurred at Oxford, in which locals fed up with privileged students attacked the school and slaughtered many. In response, the university was by royal decree given power over the town and its market. The political and ideological struggles within European societies were reflected in their student populations, with students forming competing groups within and between universities. When, for example, Martin Luther travelled to debate with scholars at universities in other cities, he was escorted by a student guard armed with battle axes.[2] The recognition that collectives were a source of power was present from the beginning, and that awareness grew as groups and associations proliferated and jostled for power. Teachers formed their own groups, or "colleges," to wield internal power. As universities expanded and formalized their practices through administrations, those administrations slowly became bureaucracies and powerful entities of their own, mediating between students and local towns and benefitting economically and politically from their unique position as middlemen. Universities sprang up all over Europe, becoming economically and politically integrated with their host cities and states.

The colonial exportation of European institutions around the world in the eighteenth and nineteenth centuries would include pedagogical models, and "modern" educational systems replaced older systems in subjugated lands. In terms of student collectives, however, it would be the German *Burschenshaften* of the early nineteenth century that would revolutionize student power. The *Burschenshaften* were political student groups formed expressly to fight apathy and to agitate for educational and social reforms among the various German states. Some worked for moderate reforms, but others, led by charismatic revolutionaries such as Karl Follen (his compatriots were called "Schwartzen") and Karl Sand, challenged separate state authorities, argued for a greater German patriotism and German unification, mobilized thousands, and attempted to spark revolts in German cities such as Göttingen, Hambach, and Frankfurt.

The 1820s and '30s German uprisings were repeatedly, violently suppressed by professional troops, with leaders killed, or arrested and sometimes executed. Although they failed, and their actions resulted in greater governmental control over universities, they nevertheless revolutionized student organization. Students for the first time formed large-scale national organizations based on political ideas and the idea of social reform, generating a certain cultural cachet and fashion around the figure of the student revolutionary. Student groups modeled on the *Burschenschaften* would rise in France (under Louis-Auguste Blanqui), in Poland, in England, in the Americas, and around the world. In pitting idealistic, explicitly political students against their institutions and states, the *Burschenschaften* also drew generational lines that would be replicated wherever student groups arose, setting the stage, and countercultural fashion, for the European revolts of 1848 to come.

France's 1848 revolution was followed by attempted revolts in Berlin, Munich, and other German cities, and in Austria, students briefly liberated Vienna and installed their own government. While short-lived, these student-led uprisings asserted a new scale of student power in Europe, energizing students to form more and more coalitions—many with their own fashions, slogans, and ideologies (whether formalized or not)—and a fever for student organizations spread throughout the world. By the end of the century, large student organizations formed in the Americas, the Middle East, Eastern Europe, Russia, Asia, Africa, and India. China, which had not yet changed over to Western-style educational systems, was in the midcentury dealing with its own large-scale student movements that repeatedly forced concessions from their rulers.

In Russia in the 1860s, massive student protests against restrictions blossomed in Moscow and Saint Petersburg and were brutally suppressed by whip-wielding Cossacks. Students went on strikes, staged protests, and were arrested and imprisoned. Hunted by security and forced off campuses, student revolutionaries went underground, became more extreme, and began terrorist campaigns, attempting to assassinate officials. Even small student groups were subsequently outlawed and broken apart by government troops (which paradoxically made belonging to a student group more fashionable). Effectively suppressed on campuses, many committed student activists left schools to work among peasants. Political students who remained on campus found themselves charged by mounted Cossacks.

Although they couldn't force substantial reforms in czarist Russia, the Russian student strikes and protests that occurred defined Russian students as being in opposition to the state and made them see the need to forge alliances with peasants and workers to increase their strength (thus setting the stage for the Russian revolutions to come). They forced the students to articulate their ideologies more clearly and to work, so as to avoid provocation, in small groups. (Thus, they were in form and tactics harbingers of recent Russian activist-provocateurs who use media-based guerilla distribution strategies against brutal authoritarianism, groups such as Pussy Riot and Voina. In the first years of the twentieth century, Russian students would again attempt to hold massive protests, would again be suppressed, just as in the 1905 Bloody Sunday Massacre, and again would be forced into hiding.)

Following the 1908 annexation of Bosnia-Herzegovina by Austria-Hungary, Bosnian students protesting against Austro-Hungarian control were repeatedly, viciously suppressed by troops and, like their Russian counterparts, forced to go underground, where they were radicalized, forming groups and alliances with other dissidents and workers. The most infamous of these was the Black Hand, which began a terrorist campaign of murdering officials and setting off bombs. In 1912, students occupied government buildings in Zagreb and demonstrated in Sarajevo before being routed. Student radical Gavrilo Princip and a small group of Black Hand members succeeded in assassinating Franz Ferdinand in Sarajevo in 1914, setting off a series of events that would spark the First World War.

At Beijing University in 1919, the May Fourth Movement began with massive protests by thousands of students against both Japan and their own government's unwillingness to stand up to Japan.

The students were attacked by Chinese security forces; they subsequently declared a national strike and were joined by students across China, as well as workers and business owners in Shanghai, forcing the government to take a stand against Japanese imperialism. The success of the May Fourth Movement (which ended the strikes but kept up the boycotts of Japanese goods) was profound, for it pushed social and political reforms that fueled a radical modernization of China and Chinese culture. In the decades to follow, leading up to the war with Japan, China would see more anti-Japanese and anti-imperialist student demonstrations in the May Thirtieth Movement, and then in the December Ninth Movement, as the Guomindang government under Chiang Kai-shek was increasingly pushed to deal more forcefully with Japan (which was making incursions into Mongolia). The Chinese leader was at the time purging China of Chinese Communists, struggling with Mao Zedong's Red Army in northern China, and facing challenges by his own generals. The student uprisings were used as leverage by him against Japan, but when activists began to challenge his authority, he suppressed them, having police, for example, overrun Tsinghua University. Leaders of the December Ninth Movement, such as Lu Ts'ui, that weren't arrested in the crackdowns escaped to join Mao's forces.

After the turn of the twentieth century, a fever for student groups swept Latin America, from Argentina to Mexico, with students successfully agitating for reforms from Chile to Ecuador to Peru. Many of these groups formed alliances with groups in neighboring nations, beginning international support coalitions that would be a hallmark of postwar twentieth-century Latin American student movements. Other non-student alliances such as the Alianza Popular Revolucionaria Americana (APRA, or Apristas) also agitated for reforms. In the 1920s, massive student demonstrations directly challenged authoritarian leaders in Peru (and were suppressed), the Venezuelan president (suppressed as well), and Argentina's ruler (here they were successful, but then lost the government to a military takeover). A similar revolutionary spirit would sweep the continent a hundred years later, in the 2019 Latin American Spring uprisings.

In the United States, students formed campus groups and national organizations, including the National Student League and the Student League for Industrial Democracy, which together in 1934 led an antiwar strike that drew tens of thousands of participants. In 1935, the action was repeated, this time with over a hundred thousand students. Columbia University and the University of California, Berkeley were hotbeds of activity. The NSL and SLID subsequently fused into the American Student Union, and in 1937 staged an antiwar protest that garnered three hundred thousand participants. That same year saw the establishment of the Southern Negro Youth Congress. Thus, just prior to the Second World War, students across the globe were organizing for peace and pushing for social and cultural changes on an unprecedented scale.

As the European conflict expanded, student activism spiked, and then plummeted as more and more youth were drawn into the war, though in those countries not decimated by fighting and in those in which infrastructure survived or was quickly rebuilt student activism returned in force in the fifties. In Europe and the United States, for example, domestic issues and struggles came to the fore. In Eastern Europe, student resistance to the Soviet occupation was intense, with the Soviet state suppressing demonstrations in a host of nations. An attempt at revolution in Hungary was viciously put down, as were student challenges to authority in Poland that resulted in riots. In Asia in the fifties, students began forming large networks. In Japan, students formed the national Zengakuren, which successfully staged national strikes that lasted weeks and drew hundreds of thousands of participants opposing proposed educational reforms. Their success dramatically increased their popularity and membership, and by 1957 they were able to launch demonstrations attended by hundreds of thousands in Tokyo, force changes to national security policy, and compel the resignation of Japan's prime minister.

By this point in history student activists on every continent had plenty of examples of the successful power of collective, organized action, and they realized that with enough support they could affect institutional, state, and national governance. For their part, authorities and authoritarian governments clearly realized the power that students could wield in modern societies if they were allowed to build large collectives, and many countries began restricting student demonstrations and infiltrating them in order to monitor their activities.

Immediately after the war, in China, most students not drawn into the struggle between Mao's Communist forces and the Guomindang remained nationally apolitical (though they did agitate against Japan), but that changed when the Guomindang began violently suppressing peaceful anti-Japan student demonstrations, pushing students to be more sympathetic to Mao's forces when his army moved south. Following his rise to power, Mao tried to win over demonstrating students but eventually employed force to stop protests. During the Cultural Revolution, the most bizarre acts of student resistance occurred in Wuxuan, in the far southern region of Guangxi, where students reportedly killed, dismembered, barbecued, and ate the bodies of their teachers and others accused of being counterrevolutionaries. The students' cannibalism—whether an atavistic act fueled by hunger, factionalism, and class hatred or just plain opportunistic revenge against teachers—was not in that time and place unusual, for numerous similar atrocities were occurring in the region, but these actions were certainly rich metaphors to describe the brutal appetite for change sweeping the country.[3]

Of more concern for greater China was Mao's closing of schools and enlisting the country's youth in an unprecedented cultural purge that overturned the government and effectively destroyed both artifacts of and links to China's past, and resulted in the deaths of hundreds of thousands of people. The Cultural Revolution was extremely effective, though by 1967 the zeal of the conscripted youthful revolutionaries for destruction and violence began to be a liability for the government, and the roaming Red Guard units were disbanded and schools reopened.

During the Second World War, students in India formed large national federations and organizations. These in turn gave way to groups such as the All India Students Congress, which began agitating for national independence. Student demonstrations and actions were often more extreme and uncontrollable than those of Gandhi's independence movement, and many of these turned to sabotage and violence against the British occupiers. Following independence, the fever for student activism in India broke and students became more apolitical for a while.

A rage for student groups in the forties and fifties swept across Africa, with students organizing and demonstrating from Algeria to Kenya, from Tunisia to South Africa. Many of these movements had to do with pushing back against colonialist governments or colonially inherited systems of government and societies. They had anti-imperialist parallels in former and current colonial nations across Europe and in the United States (Puerto Rican students, for example, held massive anticolonial demonstrations in the fifties). Along with government and education reforms, other issues such as civil rights, desegregation, and antiracism were issues that began to push to the fore of student activist efforts in Africa, in Europe, and in the United States.

In the 1940s and '50s in Latin America, student activism soared, forcing many governments in Central and South America to institute reforms. Actions ran the gamut from massive peaceful protests (in Guatemala, they set the stage for a revolution) to uncontrollable riots (in Rio de Janeiro, Brazil) to aiding larger revolutions (such as Castro's eventual overthrow of Batista in Cuba). Students directly challenged authority (and were violently attacked for doing so) in Argentina, Brazil, Colombia, Paraguay, and Venezuela. But even if unsuccessful at the moment, their struggles against their respective leaders precipitated the formation of international alliances among student groups, which in the coming years would be instrumental in coordinating reform efforts and strategies. By the 1960s, student networks of both small and massive organizations crisscrossed the globe, with students sharing information, tactics, and support in ways that would have profound effects in the coming decade.

In 1960, massive Korean student demonstrations followed the corrupt reelection of President Rhee Syngman in South Korea and escalated into a full-blown revolt after the military personnel dispatched to suppress the students switched sides. Instead of blasting the revolutionaries, they spun the guns of their tanks around and trained them on government buildings. The president fled the country, and for a while student demonstrations brought enough bodies into the streets to influence the course of the new government, though as their numbers waned so too did their influence. A military coup in 1961 put the government in the hands of a new authoritarian regime that immediately outlawed student groups.

In Indonesia, following a failed communist coup attempt against the government of President Sukarno, a massive anticommunist student organization formed called the Action Command of Indonesian Students (KAMI) and began assailing the Indonesian Communist Party (PKI) during demonstrations, which gave way to armed riots against the PKI. KAMI students identified communists and communist students for arrest, imprisonment, and extrajudicial execution. Following the demise of the PKI, a strong, well-organized KAMI began agitating for government reforms. When Sukarno tried to suppress them by enlisting and arming mobs to attack the University of Indonesia, the students convinced the military to defend them. Enormous student-led anti-Sukarno protests rocked Jakarta, and Sukarno abandoned the presidency. General Suharto stepped into the power vacuum in 1967, took over the nation, and began a purge of the country, arresting, imprisoning, or killing tens of thousands of communists and political opponents.

In West Germany in the early sixties, student activism again spiked, in the context of a growing political divide between the left and the right, and both student demonstrations and police suppression became increasingly violent. Politically slanted news media heightened the conflicts between the government and students agitating for political reforms, social liberalization, international politics, and anti-imperialism, but it was the execution of a student

17

who had already been kicked unconscious by police at a demonstration against the visiting shah of Iran that gave the nation's students a martyr and galvanized them. A cycle of protests, police violence, and more protests continued, and as the decade wore on the focus of the students shifted to include the government's silence on the Vietnam War and thus its tacit support of the war's brutalities.

In 1967, a student march in Prague was suppressed by police, and in response, students in Czechoslovakia began a public media campaign, plastering the city with posters depicting the police violence and calling for changes. The massive demonstrations that followed called for government reforms and the restoration of civil liberties, and challenged Soviet control of the country. Supported by Prague's citizens, the government made some reforms. The "Prague Spring" was short, though, as Soviet troops subsequently crushed student demonstrations. Student activists expanded their activities to include acts of terrorism against the communist regime, sabotage, and more guerilla-style actions.

Student actions in the United States in the early sixties focused mostly on civil rights, desegregation, and voting drives in the South. Nonviolent desegregation sit-ins in Greensboro, North Carolina, garnered national attention, made national news, and inspired students to organize on campuses across the country. In 1964, students formed the Student Nonviolent Coordinating Committee (SNCC) to link together the disparate student groups fighting for social justice and began to pressure Washington for federal protections and reforms. Following a vicious mob attack on buses of volunteers going to Alabama to help register African American voters and set up educational and medical programs locally (the "Freedom Riders" program of the Congress of Racial Equality, or CORE), SNCC helped to publicize and condemn the violence and coordinated campaigns urging the federal government to step in, which it did by desegregating all interstate travel and travel facilities. SNCC went on to coordinate the "Freedom Summer" in 1964 in Mississippi, in which many students were bussed to the state to help with voter registration, hold marches, and set up medical and educational programs. They were often attacked. After three volunteers were murdered by the Ku Klux Klan, public outrage across the United States forced more government intervention and more desegregation efforts, and helped push through the Voting Rights Act of 1965.

Students for a Democratic Society (SDS) was the largest leftist student organization, and it supported and coordinated campaigns ranging from anti–Vietnam War protests to the larger Free Speech Movement. The latter began with the student occupation of buildings at Berkeley following the university's banning of political and free speech from public spaces in 1964 and its decision to prosecute an activist who handed out CORE pamphlets and was arrested for his efforts. The subsequent demonstrations forced the resignation of the university president and sparked occupations in other universities. The Free Speech Movement would soon spread across the nation.

By far the biggest subject of student demonstrations in the United States in this time was the war in Vietnam, with demonstrations and marches taking place on campuses across the country and massive antiwar demonstrations occurring in Washington, DC. Police often used suppression tactics, though this would eventually backfire when images of police attacking unarmed youth began appearing on television. But students also became violent, frustrated by the relentless suppression even of peaceful protests. Members of some groups, like CORE, became more radical, fearing government intelligence agencies, and paranoia among students grew as security agencies began monitoring and infiltrating campus organizations. The Pentagon was attacked on numerous occasions (both in large demonstrations and secretly, by small groups using bombs), and the more radical student groups went underground.

In Latin America in the sixties, many young people, inspired by the revolution in Cuba led by Che Guevara and Fidel Castro, joined student groups in droves and agitated for reforms—and sometimes revolution—in Brazil, Colombia, the Dominican Republic, Ecuador, Guatemala, Haiti, Mexico, Nicaragua, and Peru. Holding strikes and staging marches, groups formed alliances with student groups in neighboring countries. As in the United States, most of the really large Latin American demonstrations and marches were at least initially peaceful, though participants were sometimes violently attacked by local police. And throughout the region, university officials often called local police to break up smaller demonstrations on campuses, even when they amounted to peaceful calls for education reform. Under the more repressive regimes, after protests were put down, organizers were often arrested, imprisoned, and tortured. Extrajudicial killings of student leaders were sufficiently common that, as was happening elsewhere in the world, as student groups politicized they also increasingly radicalized. Extremists incited riots, blocked or sabotaged transportation, bombed government facilities, and attempted to assassinate government officials.

By the mid-1960s, student networks crisscrossed the globe, and it was recognized that student activism played a significant part in social change throughout the world. But the student demonstrations that occurred in 1968 and 1969 were of an entirely different magnitude than those that came before. They marked a new pinnacle of student protest actions globally and underscored the power of students to challenge authority in even the most powerful of nations. They also exhibited an evolution in the tactics used by students and the types of networks available to them. Demonstrations large enough to challenge state and national governments or cause massive riots occurred in France and Italy, in numerous nations in the Middle East and Latin America, and in the United States. In France, a small group of edgy activist students inspired by Situationist-style "interventions" began countercultural anarchistic "disruptions" on French campuses, calling for everything from educational reforms to anti-imperialism to the destruction of the bourgeoisie. Inspired by Castro's Cuban revolution, the student groups called for a new French Revolution (of sorts), occupied a building at Paris Nanterre University, and demonstrated at the Sorbonne. They were set upon by police. Protesting the police violence, the Union Nationale des Étudiants de France and other large student unions and organizations called for a massive student strike. Two days later, a demonstration at the Sorbonne was attacked by police, but students had arrived prepared; they were wearing wet rags over their faces to protect themselves against tear gas and carrying sticks to fight back. They erected makeshift barriers and tore up cobblestones to hurl at police, forming cobblestone supply lines for blocks behind the front-line barricades where students manning the fortifications battled troops for hours.

On the following day, May 7, 1968, forty thousand students marched on the Champs-Élysées in Paris, and for the next few days students took over the streets of the Left Bank, erecting giant barricades across the narrow avenues and stockpiling weapons—cobblestones, bottles, and Molotov cocktails. President Charles de Gaulle sent in thousands of police on May 11 to clear out the students, and the Left Bank erupted in riots and running battles between police and students. The students were overmatched, but they had the sympathy of residents and the attention of the world. Factory workers, labor unions, and public service workers saw the moment was ripe to push for their own reforms, and millions of workers went on strike. De Gaulle left Paris but refused to give up power. The strikes ground on, week after week, but they did so without unity or a leader who could challenge de Gaulle (who used the time to shore up his control of the military and to plan how to regain control while police continued to suppress the demonstrations). De Gaulle called for new elections and, with the support of conservative nonurban citizens, was reelected, taking the steam out of the striking workers and the protesting students. The May '68 Revolution in France, although ultimately unsuccessful, shocked Western nations. It inspired students throughout the West, who were as surprised as everyone else at the power they could potentially wield, and it struck fear into Western authorities who had up until then seen students in their own respective countries as more annoyance than threat.

In Italy, students who had long been agitating for education reforms joined workers striking at the Turin Fiat factory calling for labor reforms. They swelled the workers' numbers and also began a media campaign, printing posters and flyers and networking with other students and labor groups to encourage them to join. After they were attacked by police, university students called for a national strike and occupied their respective campuses. They were joined by secondary schoolers who began monthlong campaigns, occupying their own schools. Workers from other factories started strikes, as well. Seeing the moment was suitable for negotiating from a position of strength, labor cut a deal with the government for reforms and cut the students loose, leaving them without their strongest ally and precipitating the collapse of the Italian student movement.

The year of the student continued in other regions as well. In Pakistan, 1968 saw a series of student reform demonstrations that, like those in France, elicited suppression by police (who managed to kill a student), and this led to larger anti–police violence demonstrations (which were also attacked). These escalated into antigovernment demonstrations that were suppressed, but which sparked more unrest. Fearing growing resistance, President Ayub Khan began rounding up political opponents and hammering protests with suppression by both police and military troops. Labor unions united behind the students, called nationwide strikes, and took to the streets, pushing the country into turmoil and forcing Khan to flee. Thus, what had begun as small student demonstrations quickly grew into a massive general uprising that toppled the government.

In Japan, students repeatedly demonstrated and occupied the University of Tokyo in 1968. Armed fights between rival groups occupying different buildings broke out, however, and in 1969 Japan's government ordered troops to remove all the occupiers. The students didn't go willingly, forcing security to fight for every building. A similar occupation and building-by-building battles with police occurred at Nihon University. In 1969, the government reformed the higher-education system and made it clear to the students that occupations would not be tolerated and that future uprisings would be suppressed. The larger protests fizzled, and the more politically extreme students left the campus to operate underground, several of them turning to what today would be called domestic terrorist tactics.

Student uprisings were sweeping Central and South America as well. In Mexico City in 1968, police, who by now were used to violently suppressing demonstrating students occupying city high schools, resorted to brutal force, including murder. Students and residents poured into the streets to protest. With the 1968 Summer Olympic Games to be held in Mexico City, and fearing the embarrassment of student demonstrations, the government shut down the sprawling National Autonomous University (UNAM) system, ejected students from campuses, and posted military troops to protect university facilities. Incensed students called national strikes and took to the streets of the capital by the tens of thousands, bringing traffic and commerce in the capital to a grinding halt. The damage to services and the nation's economy was severe. Campuses not yet closed saw large student occupations, with students barricading themselves in buildings against military assault. The National Polytechnic Institute was held for half a day, even after military troops began an attack, with the students throwing Molotov cocktails at the advancing lines and soldiers shooting back.

In the Tlatelolco neighborhood of Mexico City, ten thousand students and residents, including children, gathered on the Plaza de las Tres Culturas to hear speakers who were decrying police violence, President Díaz Ordaz's repressive policies, and the profligate expenditures on the forthcoming Olympics when so much of the city was mired in poverty. Trucks and armored government vehicles arrived, and the agitating crowd found itself surrounded by five thousand armed soldiers. Snipers stationed on building rooftops opened fire from above, and the troops surrounding the groups began shooting, some using machine guns. The October Massacre, which went on into the night with troops searching apartments nearby, arresting and beating any students they found, left close to four hundred dead and thousands of people injured. The bodies of the slain were hauled off in trucks and secretly buried. Suppressing the numbers killed and injured, the government weathered the subsequent international condemnation, and only decades later revealed the extent of the violence and killings, a cover-up that, given recent advances in social media and recording technology, is hard—though not impossible—to imagine today. Every October since 1968, on the anniversary of the Tlatelolco Massacre, an annual march to the square is led by the surviving family members of those slain, a march which still draws tens of thousands of participants.

In the United States, desegregation efforts continued, and in 1968 civil rights protests on campuses soared, especially after a violent confrontation between demonstrators and police at South Carolina State University, in Orangeburg, ended with three students killed and close to thirty wounded. Large demonstrations for greater representation, for the establishment of race centers, and for civil rights occurred at HBCUs Howard, Fisk, and Bowie State, and at Columbia University, with students adding the occupation of administrative buildings to their tactics. At Columbia, students led by the Student Afro-American Society occupied buildings to protest the university's planned development of a Harlem neighborhood park, issuing a list of demands and holding a dean hostage. Security forces surrounded the occupiers, and a week of negotiations (resulting in the scrapping of the development plans) ensued, convincing some students to surrender. Others refused, and outside the held buildings students, teachers, and local residents formed barriers between massing police forces and the occupiers within to prevent what was clearly coming. Afraid the standoff would incite the neighborhood around the university to riot, on April 30 more than a thousand New York police troops were given permission to raid the buildings in what became known as the Battle of Morningside Heights. Media coverage was intense, and the reports of police brutality found an international audience. The events sparked further occupations and threw wider public support behind students.

US activists learned a valuable lesson in these actions (which they incorporated into future activist training workshops). If they could generate media interest, articulate a clear platform, and delay any coming onslaught until news media was present to record it, they realized that though they might lose the battle they could still widen, and perhaps win, the larger war. They began to see the usefulness of media in spreading images of police brutality, that doing so garnered sympathy and public support for their causes.

Another massive demonstration (much of it centered on an antiwar platform) erupted in violent clashes with police outside the 1968 Democratic Convention in Chicago, where a countercultural event was organized in which tens of thousands gathered and occupied the city's public parks. Participants travelled from all over the United States and ranged from students (SDSers, CORE members, and others) to families with children. Here again, excessive police brutality on US soil stunned national television viewers as police indiscriminately clubbed protestors, bystanders, and journalists.

At Berkeley, free-speech activists again challenged bans on campus demonstrations, and national guardsmen under Governor Ronald Reagan were ordered to secure the campus. They attacked the demonstrators, shooting them with birdseed-laden shotguns, blinding some and killing one. This sparked more demonstrations and campus occupations, and further troop and police suppression—and all of it was televised. The suppression increased, and the officials who ordered it were clearly out of touch with the younger generation and how the violence was being received by those watching it on their televisions at home. As in other countries, frustrated activists radicalized, formed underground terrorist groups such as the Weather Underground, and took more extreme measures of resistance. The less radical staged occupations and demonstrations, including massive marches in Washington and San Francisco against the war.

With the widening of the Vietnam War into Cambodia in 1970, antiwar demonstrations on college campuses in the United States soared, and police and National Guard troops were often called in to suppress them. At Kent State University, the National Guard opened fire on a demonstration, killing four protestors and turning public opinion against the use of the National Guard to control civil disobedience. At the same time, radical groups continued efforts to bomb government facilities engaged in defense research and war efforts. The Pentagon was bombed repeatedly, though news of this was kept from the public for years. Fed up with their treatment as second-class citizens (even within progressive social movements), women forged feminist groups and started agitating for social equality. Seeing that suppression was not the smartest way to handle all the protests they faced, university administrations began co-opting issues, creating, for example, women's-studies centers and race centers on campuses and designating special "free-speech zones," away from administrative buildings, for protestors to vent their issues. They began refining university regulations and institutionalizing codes of conduct as conditions of enrollment for newly matriculating students.

Native American groups began agitating as well, with students and activists staging numerous protests, including taking over Alcatraz Island (home to the abandoned prison) and offering the government twenty-four dollars' worth of beads for it. And for months they occupied the Pine Ridge Reservation, near the site of the 1890 Wounded Knee Massacre, in which hundreds of Sioux men, women, and children had been slaughtered by the US Cavalry.

In Europe, protests in the seventies often focused on the Vietnam War, anti-imperialism, and whether or not students' respective nations were doing enough to end physical and economic colonialism. Students in Germany continued to form groups and agitate for national reforms, but with the official formation of the Green Party, on the one hand, and more extreme groups conducting their terrorist campaigns off campus on the other, student activism on campus was siphoned off and levels died down. Similar diminishment of levels of intense student activism trended across Europe.

With the world in geopolitical turmoil, student demonstrations and riots were common in the early seventies, with massive demonstrations in Mexico City, Bangkok, and Jakarta sparking brutal suppression. Management of media coverage was beginning to be a factor for both the protestors and authorities in terms of strategies of action and suppression. In Mexico City, for example, the mayor tried enlisting right-wing mobs to put down protests so police wouldn't be filmed, but this ended badly, as the paramilitaries were uncontrollable in their violence. Images of the brutality circulated widely, and the media had a field day at the government's expense. In Asia, many student efforts were focused on anti-Western imperialism, an end to the Vietnam War, and reforms within national borders. In Iran, anti-imperialist, anti-shah students surrounded, overran, and occupied the US embassy in Tehran and held the staff hostage. While the world watched the standoff between Iran and the United States, the conservative power brokers of Iran capitalized on the crisis and took control of the government, curtailing the country's shift toward liberalization and Westernization.

Student demonstrations for equality in Rhodesia, which were suppressed, joined a larger drive for independence, leading to a full-blown revolution and the remaking of the country into the Republic of Zimbabwe. In the seventies, the battles followed general trends: smaller demonstrations were ignored or suppressed, but sometimes that suppression then led to larger demonstrations, heightened by the presence of news media where they existed. Subtlety and diplomacy were not widely resorted to as effective ways of resolving these challenges to authority, and the presence of media was often not yet factored in when authorities decided how to handle public protests. This would radically change in the coming decades, with the proliferation of video and the birth of the internet, but already those organizing demonstrations were factoring in media coverage as part of their strategies.

In the eighties, students in the United States began campaigns against international corporations, against apartheid in South Africa, and for related divestment, challenging their universities to pull investments from companies with South African holdings. They also agitated for ethnic-studies centers, LGB centers, and women's-studies centers on campuses. In Latin America, students were realizing they needed strategies other than directly challenging ruthless strongmen like Pinochet in Chile. In Gaza and the West Bank in the early eighties, students repeatedly demonstrated against Israel's occupation of contested territories, resulting in skirmishes, violent suppression, and university closings and campus occupations by Israeli troops. In 1987, the skirmishes between Palestinian youth and Israeli occupational forces became sustained street battles in urban areas. The Intifada lasted for years, but was suppressed wherever it flared by well-armed Israeli troops. Hundreds were killed, thousands were injured, and many were imprisoned.

In South Korea, students protesting the United States and their own government participated in massive demonstrations in the eighties and faced off against South Korean troops sent to quell them. Protests in major cities turned into riots, with soldiers attacking demonstrators, protestors fighting back, and radicals firebombing buildings. The riots were suppressed, but public opinion turned against the government, forcing a transition in the next elections.

In the media in Europe and the United States, though, such foreign events were reported at arm's length. The world was not yet connected through social media and internet networks. For most, there simply was not a widespread, daily awareness of the volatility of geopolitics, the interconnection of international economies, and the concept of a global rather than merely a regional environment. Although students were protesting economic imperialism and the labor practices of international corporations in the eighties, at least in the West, there still remained a feeling of isolation from the rest of the world. When revolutions occurred or were attempted and violently suppressed in distant lands (even if these were not that far away), they only momentarily shocked, for they mostly seemed limited in relevance to their respective regions.

One shock that did ripple throughout the world happened in 1989 in Czechoslovakia, when students gathering to memorialize the Prague Spring were attacked by police, sparking larger demonstrations against police violence. These morphed into widespread calls for government reforms, and hundreds of thousands of citizens spontaneously took to the streets in demonstrations so massive the government resigned rather than try to control them. The Velvet Revolution, as it was called, would be an inspiration to nonviolent revolutionaries in other countries, and many organizers would seek to emulate its success.

But while the Velvet Revolution was a beacon for those aspiring to set off their own peaceful revolutions in 1989, the Chinese pro-democracy student movement that ended in the Tiananmen Square Massacre was a cautionary tale. Throughout the eighties in China, small student demonstrations (and occasionally large ones in cities like Shanghai and Nanjing) increasingly took place, and purges of liberals in the government fueled a prodemocracy movement, culminating in a series of large demonstrations on Tiananmen Square in Beijing in May 1989. The government-controlled media criticized the demonstrators in an orchestrated campaign, but many city residents were sympathetic, and following a hunger strike by the prodemocracy leaders, thousands of students assembled on the square and openly criticized the Chinese Communist Party. Unrest grew, and the protests embarrassed the government during a state visit by Russian leader Mikhail Gorbachev. The occupation of the square continued to swell over the next few days, spreading into neighboring streets, and students erected a giant Goddess of Democracy statue in the center of the plaza, directly across from the plaza's massive portrait of Mao.

Residents and workers joined the demonstrations, increasing the numbers occupying the square and the surrounding streets, directly challenging the CCP's claim to represent the workers of China (and thus the government's legitimacy). Fearing more workers would join, the government dropped a media blackout on Beijing and, in June, sent in battalions of soldiers from distant regions, supported by armored vehicles and tanks, against the demonstrators at night. The state had planned its attack well, and the soldiers were purposefully commanded by leaders without local ties.

Attacked, the workers rioted and threw Molotov cocktails at the advancing troops sent against them. Soldiers bayonetted and opened fire with automatic rifles on demonstrators, relentlessly pushing toward the square from all sides. The workers fought back and captured and beat soldiers who became separated from their companies, but they posed little real challenge to the military. The streets around the square were soon littered with the dead and wounded, and troops started sweeping across the massive square. The government subsequently downplayed the numbers killed, but recently released internal Chinese government documents put the death toll at around ten thousand people. Although some students were killed, they were largely ignored by the soldiers, who focused on the workers occupying the streets and the outer areas of the square.

By the end of the onslaught, the several thousand students still huddled around the Goddess of Democracy—who had watched in horror as the workers were cut down—were convinced to flee after a phalanx of tanks rolled onto the square and thousands of troops surrounded the students. To encourage their egress, the military purposely left one avenue for them to exit through and then fired warning volleys into the monument above them. Following the violence, China's government continued the media blackout until it had removed the bodies of the dead and secured the city with reinforcements and more armor.

International media reported the massacre and documented the violence through smuggled-out video footage; the most famous images of resistance included those of a single man stopping a line of tanks rolling into the city by standing before them. But Chinese media downplayed the event and cast the protestors as instigators of a small riot. Following the event, the government hunted down, arrested, and imprisoned tens of thousands of prodemocracy activists and demonstration participants. It then began a campaign to scrub all references to the event from national media outlets and reports, the Chinese internet, and historical accounts.

The state control of all media was such that for most of China's population, the government effectively contained and covered up the event. This was made possible through the initial media blackout, the decision to attack the demonstration at night, and the effective whitewashing campaign afterwards. Some of the leaders of the movement made it out of the country, but those who stayed were arrested and imprisoned. On anniversaries of the massacre, bans on demonstrations on the square, carefully timed construction projects, and heavy troop presence precluded memorial demonstrations from taking place. Purging the event from media and historical accounts and maintaining active censorship ensured that the future education of China's youth would not include the event, and subsequent generations of citizens grew up not knowing the massacre had ever happened.

That the Tiananmen Square uprising and massacre occurred at all was stunning to many in the West, and in some senses paralyzing—a rude alarm bell that the world was not what many in the West imagined it to be (if they imagined it at all). The call for democracy, the government response, and the violence covered in news media outside China brought tremendous attention to international politics between the East and the West and to the importance of human rights. It signaled in a big way the struggles that would play out in the next two decades in numerous nations, between youth pushing for change and the forces of tyranny. The size and extent of the uprising was important, but so too were the ways in which technology was used both to expose the violence that occurred during it (video smuggled out of the country) but also, by the government, to suppress the movement afterwards. In terms of technologies of resistance and suppression, it was a harbinger of what was to come.

In Latin America in the 1990s, students continued to agitate. In Mexico, UNAM students repeatedly held strikes against reforms that would impose limits on the time students had to earn a degree and charge tuition. Radical students set up semi-permanent camps in occupied university buildings that, without maintenance for months on end, began falling apart. Roofs began to leak, ceilings collapsed, and plumbing failed. In Brazil, one peaceful student-led antigovernment corruption campaign joined forces with labor advocates and was able to field demonstrations numbering into the hundreds of thousands. They grew large enough to pressure Brazil's congress to impeach President Fernando Collor. Afterwards, he resigned.

In Eastern Europe, student activism and agitation for more civil freedoms flared in Albania, Georgia, Romania, Ukraine, and Yugoslavia following the 1991 breakup of the Soviet Union, with students challenging their respective governments to loosen restrictions and to embrace liberalization and Westernization. While some heads of states took a more indulgent attitude and allowed students to demonstrate, others, such as Romania's Ion Iliescu and Yugoslavia's Slobodan Milošević, brutally stamped out dissent. Iliescu, at one point, bused mobs of miners into Bucharest to attack demonstrators on University Square; the miners subsequently overran the University of Bucharest, demolishing property and beating students.

In the Middle East, the Persian Gulf War galvanized students to protest either for or against US actions, depending on the country. Most neighboring nations closed universities to prevent demonstrations that could lead to greater conflicts or riots or complicate international relationships. In the occupied territories, Palestinian youth continued to challenge Israeli authority, and in Turkey and Iran, large demonstrations took place both for increased liberalization and for more fundamentalist conservative reforms; clashes between oppositional groups and between demonstrators and security were violent. In Africa, students agitated for reforms in Kenya, Mozambique, Nigeria, South Africa, Zambia, Zimbabwe, and a host of other nations, though many demonstrations against authoritarian regimes faced vicious suppression.

Indonesian students in the nineties again led protests that grew to massive scale, with demonstrators openly battling police and security forces, and although thousands died, the conflict eventually forced President Suharto to resign after the military threatened to support the protestors. The military then stepped in to control the government and to violently suppress rioting students who had continued to march for democratic reforms. The demonstrations and riots eventually lessened, though, following moderate government reforms in concert with military suppression.

In Europe, as in the United States, the 1990s saw students agitating for social justice and for university reforms. They demonstrated in anti-imperialism and antiwar campaigns and in divestment movements. They protested against nations such as China that were suppressing democratic movements. But as was true in the United States, the percentage of students engaging in social and political protests was down. Most students seemed focused on their careers, and levels of general interest in politics and activism declined. While aged pundits bemoaned the apathy of current students in op-ed pieces or waxed melancholic over the passing of the "golden age of student activism" (meaning the sixties and seventies, when they themselves were young), however, a new wave of tech-savvy activists was already exploring how the internet could be weaponized on behalf of social justice and true democracy, in an age when democracy itself seemed to be flailing amid the onslaught of globalization and corporate hegemony.

Prescient activists around the world saw that the future of social change would be tied to new networking technology, new methods of distributing information virtually, and the ability to reach across national boundaries. Still, they had no idea yet of the extent to which new technologies would transform activism and activist strategies. The age of the cell phone and social media was on the horizon. Soon, millions of people would be able to connect to massive organizations (even anonymously), and everyone with a cell phone would have a video camera at her disposal to record and disseminate information or images of violence. Gone were the days of needing a charismatic leader to hold a movement together; indeed, the more successful movements would often be leaderless, just masses of linked individuals pushing for reforms. Cyber-resistance attacks would be waged on government computers, servers, and websites, and hacked information on politicians, governments, and corporations would be released in doxing campaigns. Physical demonstrations would be necessary still, though, and within two decades the world would see them in unprecedented numbers as region after region would explode in unrest and uprisings.

In addition to continuing physical suppression of protests, authorities would develop countermeasures, including cybernetic infiltration strategies. They would become adept at dropping internet and cell-phone service blackouts on areas of unrest. They would pass antiterrorist laws, under which tens of thousands would be arrested and imprisoned, and impose heavy penalties for those deemed threatening to civil society. Massive surveillance systems would be developed to track individuals and to identify protestors from crowd shots for later arrest. The means and ways of both resistance and suppression would evolve radically, leading to more unrest than ever before to combat a rising trend in authoritarianism. All this would drastically change student resistance over the next two decades—even without factoring in the geopolitical chaos that was soon to envelop the world and the existential threat of climate change that the twenty-first century would bring.

1

ANTIWAR PROTESTS, INTERNET ACTIVISM, AND THE POWER OF DIVESTMENT IN NORTH AMERICA

The first decade of the millennium saw surges of Canadian student activism against US military operations in the Middle East and against the administration of George W. Bush, against Canadian economic and environmental policies, against international corporations, and against oil exploration. Students waded into ongoing conflicts between the government of Canada and the First Nations, criticizing government policies that left indigenous peoples impoverished. The US invasion of Iraq in 2003, and Canada's government's decision to mobilize military support for the occupation, led to tens of thousands of students and workers protesting the occupation. To give one an idea of the seriousness with which Canadian students take their activism, in January of 2003, in Toronto, Ottawa, Vancouver, Halifax, and other cities across Canada, tens of thousands braved frigid temperatures to march on government buildings in protests against the United States, *prior to the actual invasion*—for the US government was clearly pushing for the war, trying to link Iraq to the 9/11 terrorist strikes on the United States. In Montreal, despite sub-zero temperatures, estimates of demonstrators before government buildings nevertheless reached as high as twenty-five thousand.[4] Such rallies—in which participation would continue to swell over the coming months—were often headlined by student leaders and artists, as well as oppositional politicians seeking to widen their support in coming elections. Once the invasion occurred and Canada threw its support behind the United States, student activists turned their attentions from protesting US aggression onto their own government's complicity.

Students soon had more to be upset about. In 2004, the provincial government of Quebec, led by Premier John James Charest, suddenly announced that more than a hundred million dollars would be cut from student grants, turning future disbursements into loans instead. Apart from breaking campaign promises, the plan outraged students and parents because it would financially cripple thousands of students attending colleges and universities—many of them already struggling to get out of poverty. Understandably, student-activist efforts in the region shifted from international policies toward domestic ones, especially those that hurt their own financial situations. In 2004 and 2005, the Fédération Étudiante Collégiale du Québec (FECQ), the Fédération Étudiante Universitaire du Québec (FEUQ), and a newly formed Coalition de l'Association pour une Solidarité Syndicale Étudiante Élargie (CLASSÉÉ), an association of independent unions, staged sit-ins, occupations, and marches. In 2005, they launched massive strikes, marshalling hundreds of thousands of students and supporters (including the leading opposition party in Quebec), and in some cases bringing a hundred thousand marchers onto the streets of Montreal for protests. They took as their symbol a square of red cloth, which they pinned to their shirts or waved as flags, and soon the symbol began appearing all over the region—spray-painted on buildings, bridges and sidewalks, and hung as banners from lampposts and bridges.

Activists realized the power such a symbol had in expanding public awareness of their cause, and they used it liberally. This symbolic tagging of Montreal was inspired in part by tactics used in uprisings against Slobodan Milošević, when the student group Otpor ("Resistance") stenciled their logo of a clenched fist all over Belgrade. Guerrilla activists in Canada scaled the hundred-foot-tall Mount Royal Cross to hang a giant red square from its top. Students repeatedly boycotted classes en masse, and the strikes went on through most of the spring 2005 semester. The tactics of the protests ranged from the symbolic—at demonstrations in front of the offices of education minister Jean-Marc Fournier, to prove their commitment, a group of students stood in wet cement until it hardened—to the economic, as demonstrators camped out across Autoroute 40 to blockade commercial access to Montreal's port.[5]

The massive protests took the government by surprise, and it entered negotiations with the student unions, with FECQ and FEUQ eventually coming to terms with the government (which for the most part agreed to restore the grants for the next four years). CLASSÉÉ and other groups—constituting tens of thousands of students—rejected the terms. Die-hard activists continued to protest, but the splintering of the movement over the arrangement with the government brought an end to the largest demonstrations, and inertia took over; the protests fizzled out as exams approached.[6] The high cost of education in Quebec would continue to be an issue for students, and as the decade closed, student activists began carefully organizing and doing the groundwork for a campaign that would in a few years blossom into what would become known as Canada's Maple Spring.

For Canada's behemoth neighbor to the south, student activism was more diverse both in terms of specific issues and in sustained levels of intensity. Just before the new millennium in the United States, there was a tremendous range of things protested by student and youth organizations, though mainstream US media often decried student apathy and a perceived lack of political awareness. The rising cost of education, the corporatization of universities, the success of neoliberalism, and a generation that seemed particularly capitalistic and narcissist, if not alienated from channels of power, coincided with a low rate of activism (relative to total student numbers). But the generalizations were misleading: there were in fact a dizzying number of local and specific protests taking place in addition to more general national movements. The largest ongoing student efforts at the turn of the millennium were those that fell under the umbrella of the anti-sweatshop movement, which targeted university and name-brand apparel made under unfair labor practices, much of it produced in foreign countries.

Anti-sweatshop protests had been going on for a few years in specific locations but, now taking advantage of the internet to organize, they suddenly went national, with activists from universities across the country volunteering to travel to foreign factories, monitor them, and send reports back. What they reported was horrible factory conditions and child labor used to make products from T-shirts to shoes. University administrations were slow to respond and clearly misjudged the determination of the activists, continuing to choose profits and corporate sponsorship over clear consciences (as with the University of Arizona's decision to partner with Nike despite revelations of horrific abuses).

Students responded by going directly after the corporations themselves; for example, they distributed Nike shoes that came with a list of documented factory abuses and atrocities attached to them in place of typical advertisement labels and tags (a cultural protest tactic called *détournement*, developed by the Situationists in the 1960s). The United Students Against Sweatshops (USAS) coordinated efforts at dozens of universities, published guides discussing effective tactics, and reported successes as they came in, but also listed continuing offenders. Eventually, enough negative publicity resulted in slumps in sales and forced universities and the corporations they purchased from to more closely monitor their own suppliers. Anti-sweatshop campaigns were conducted at every major university from Duke to Berkeley, from the University of Wisconsin to the University of Florida, from the University of Texas to the University of Hawaii. Students at regional campuses organized and held local protests as well.

As the student anti-sweatshop movement, which often focused on specific university contracts locally, gained steam, students began partnering with worker unions and organizations in the United States, moving to tackle sweatshop labor in general and what happened when corporations outsourced production to foreign countries. They exposed, for example, a Levi Strauss factory in Mexico that had been documented with working conditions akin to slavery. They attacked a whole slew of companies, from the Gap to Nike. By 2005, under pressure from students and the news media that had picked up the stories, many of the targeted brands were publishing their own reports on factory abuses and their efforts to prevent them, trying to control the fallout and to recapture lost moral ground (in an effort to recapture lost market share). The winds were indeed changing, but they only changed because US student activists remained committed and relentlessly went after corporations and their own school administrations, developing strategies to imperil the profits of both.

Instead of fighting on what was clearly going to be the losing side economically, corporations began PR campaigns that incorporated so-called humanitarian responsibility in their ads. "Made in America" labels started to catch on as effective marketing tools—both as a moral good and, of course, as patriotic, something that appealed to consumers on the left and the right. By 2006, Levi Strauss was marketing its use of organic cotton, and after Russell Athletic came under fire at campuses across the nation, the company announced in 2009 it would open a new plant in Honduras, staffed entirely by ousted union workers.[7] The anti-sweatshop protests showed student activists that they could indeed effect change in corporate America—which in many ways had begun to seem unassailable.

The attention given by activists to student apparel and university-condoned immorality was not confined to how the apparel worn around campus was made but spread to include the ethics of longstanding university brands. In 1999 in North Dakota, the University of North Dakota Student Political Action Network joined seven Native American tribes in a battle to remove the school's offensive "Fighting Sioux" mascot. But right or wrong, people become invested in their symbols, and the reform efforts met with mainstream pushback. Economically, the boycotts of logo-bearing apparel resulted in alumni threatening to withdraw millions of dollars in funding from schools contemplating logo changes, and the conservative press sided with what it called "harmless tradition" against what would become a stereotype of students who were overly sensitive, politically correct snowflakes. Sports organizations were themselves conflicted, though, and to the surprise of many in the United States, in 2005 the National Collegiate Athletic Association decided to penalize nineteen schools for offensive or abusive logos and mascots. The NCAA's decision was subsequently challenged by state governments in courts and became a central issue in statewide elections and on right-wing talk radio, the issue being used by many to define a threat to what they had decided represented "traditional American" culture and values.

With hindsight, it's easy to see that these types of political and rhetorical maneuvers by politicians and talking heads were early forays into creating the current ideological divide between the right and the left in the United States—and as defenses of socially institutionalized racism that dismissed inequality and the horrors of history in order to maintain the status quo and white dominance. Columnists, right-wing firebrands, and talking heads only knew the arguments encouraged outrage and stirred up the base. Little did they know how effective or far-reaching such strategies would be in the future of conservative ideology and political power in the United States. They had no idea that a populist interloper would soon refine the strategy into a weapon that would ultimately let him take the leadership of the Republican Party out of their hands and land him in the White House.

For their part, students and activists wanting to make their world less racist continued to fight, circulating petitions and holding sit-ins and demonstrations, but even on the left it was difficult getting mainstream media to see the issue as socially serious. The battle over mascots served to help define those on the right much more than those on the left, and although fights were being waged across the United States at many universities with problematic mascots, it would take years for activists to gain any real traction. Almost twenty years later, racist symbols are taken much more seriously by the US media, of course; the surfacing of, say, youthful party photos in blackface can now temporarily derail or permanently damage a political career. But that's largely due to the efforts of civil rights activists, including students, to focus attention on them and to increase cultural awareness. Battles between students and the extreme right over symbols are still being fought in many places in the United States, such as the debate over whether Confederate monuments are markers of Southern tradition and heritage or symbols of racism, slavery, and violence. At Dartmouth College, which has a history of producing outspoken conservatives like Dinesh D'Souza, the *Dartmouth Review*, for example, published an edition in 2006 sporting a cover with an "Indian" holding a tomahawk and essays lambasting political correctness. Promoters of such racism today—whether institutions or individuals—are much more often and easily called out, but the defense by those using racist symbols or rhetoric remains the same: they're harmless fun; those were different times; extremists on the left are oversensitive; or, most often, it's part of some vague tradition. In the case of the "Fighting Sioux," the use of the "Indian head" mascot and logo was only finally discontinued in 2012.

Contrary to the self-interest and apathy of students frequently bemoaned in popular media, many students in the first decade of the millennium were fighting against the institutionalized economic disparity that affected others. In 1999, student members of the Progressive Student Labor Movement (PSLM) at Harvard were already well into the Living Wage Campaign, which was a series of protests, marches, and sleep-ins to get the university administration to raise the hourly pay for janitors and other staff from minimum wage to more than ten dollars an hour. The administration initially ignored the protestors, so they began petitions, signing up hundreds of faculty supporters in addition to thousands of students to their cause, demonstrating during events like Parents' Weekend and holding demonstration concerts. Pickets outside administrative buildings brought as many as two thousand supporters, and candlelight vigils made the news. A tent city was erected in front of the Harvard Club, with protestors waving Living Wage signs and chanting anti-racism slogans.

The PSLM activists' relentless efforts began getting attention, and articles started appearing in journals such as the *Chronicle of Higher Education* and in major newspapers, comparing salaries of top administrators with those earned by university janitors. In 2002, finally embarrassed into doing something, the administration negotiated with its workers and the LWC, bringing the workers' hourly wage to around eleven dollars.[8] Harvard was but one of many campuses embroiled in Living Wage campaigns at the time. Students at Johns Hopkins had been battling for fair wages for employees since 1996. Students at Swarthmore, Wesleyan, the University of Virginia, the University of California, the University of Georgia, and many other schools began their own Living Wage Campaigns that would play out over the next decade.

Related efforts were launched by students across the United States, agitating for the right to unionize for custodial staff, administrative staff, graduate teaching assistants, and part-time teachers. These didn't have the same appeal to news media that the Harvard protests did, and they were fought vigorously and often effectively by university administrations, which were fast becoming more corporate. At Swarthmore, which is a campus known for a rich history of effective activism, for example, the Swarthmore Labor Action Project's repeated attempts to unionize on-campus workers was ignored by the administration and repeatedly failed.[9]

Inspired by divestment campaigns and the effectiveness of the anti-sweatshop movement, US students began looking deeply into the investments their own universities were making, and by concentrating their efforts on their own institutions they helped create an ethical responsibility movement. Members of the Student Labor Alliance (SLA) at Brown University protested against their university's investments in HEI (a hotel management corporation handling hotel brands like Hyatt, the Westin, and Hilton) and target it because of HEI's unfair labor practices. At Vanderbilt, students protested the university's investment in EMVest—an international corporation involved in what was known as the Great Land Grab speculation, in which millions of acres in sub-Saharan Africa and Latin America were purchased following the global rise in food prices after the global recession of 2008. These battles took years to fight, and although they didn't make for great headlines in the media, they often produced results; in the case of Vanderbilt, after fighting students and faculty for years the administration announced in 2013 it would pull its money from EMVest. So, while in the popular media US students were often castigated for being politically unaware and apathetic, there were many student activists hard at work in this period trying to make the country and the world a better, more just place.

And student activists in the United States were hardly inwardly focused. In the first years of the new millennium, there were hundreds of student-led protests against the ramping up of US military, intelligence, and economic support of Colombia's fight against the leftist insurgent Fuerzas Armada Revolucionarias de Colombia (FARC) and Ejército de Liberación Nacional (ELN), which coincided with US efforts in the War on Drugs. Students—such as those from Lewis and Clark College, in concert with other activists in Oregon—began campaigns in 2000 to challenge corporations with investments in Colombia. Beating red plastic buckets, the Oregon students chained themselves inside Fidelity Investments' main office to protest the company's investment in Colombian oil drilling. In 2001, six Oberlin College students protesting US military activities in the country chained themselves in the National Guard Memorial Building in Washington during a conference attended by the makers of the Black Hawk helicopters being used in the South American country to fight insurgents.

Coca-Cola was at this time constantly besieged with student protests, after a worker trying to unionize a Colombian bottling plant was killed by paramilitaries. It was revealed that the company was facing in a lawsuit filed by the International Labor Rights Fund, which charged that not only was the company *not* protecting its employees, it was encouraging paramilitaries to stamp out union-building efforts through intimidation and violence. In addition to beatings, kidnappings, and harassment by paramilitaries, an estimated nine workers by 2004 had been murdered over the previous decade as a result of their unionizing efforts at bottling plants in Colombia.[10] Students picketed Coca-Cola shareholder meetings, boycotted and demonstrated against events sponsored by the company, and pressured their schools to drop contracts with the corporate giant. Bard College and Lake Forest College were two of many schools where students effectively pressured their administrations to end dealings with the company and to stop selling their products on campus.[11] The Coca-Cola protests were just a few of many similar anti-corporate campaigns in the 2000s. By middecade, hundreds of campus groups were targeting their respective universities' investments in corporations with questionable dealings in foreign countries, with students identifying through public records the investments held by their schools and demonstrating against those they found objectionable. These underreported actions had profound economic impacts on universities across the United States and how they invested their funds.

The success of many of these student campaigns had to do with students using the internet to build and connect their networks. In April 2002, student and activist organizers attempted to pull disparate groups together to build coalitions and coordinate actions by sending out a nationwide call to gather at the Washington Monument in the District of Columbia for a massive multi-issue demonstration. The participants waved protest signs regarding a range of issues from the US war in Afghanistan to the US operations in Colombia, promoting opposition to globalization and corrupt multinationals like Coca-Cola, advocating for women's rights and civil rights for minorities. Representatives of the Green Party, Democratic Socialists of America, and pro-Palestine groups attended. Student activists could not yet forge broad alliances or mobilize as large groups in the way that they would in the coming years, but in pulling together they did show there was substantial opposition to the direction the country and mainstream American culture were heading. Notably, they were challenged by a counter protest—the Patriots Rally for America—which was held on the same grounds, sponsored by the Free Republic movement. The demonstrations and the counterdemonstration were prescient of a political left challenging a range of specific social issues and the more unified right wing of self-appointed (though sponsored) representatives of a dominant culture that perceived itself as existentially threatened by the forces of change. They were an early harbinger of the extreme protests and counterprotests between left and right that would come a decade and half later as the political divide in the country opened up.

The importance of that subsequent divide for current levels and intensity of activism cannot be overstated, and it illustrates why coordinated resistance didn't happen in the 2000s. In 2000, when the Green Party rose to national prominence—enough so that some claim it served as a spoiler for Democrats in the 2000 presidential campaign—the left was split by its differences, and due to those differences could not coordinate large-scale efforts for change. By 2020, though, the wide variety of positions Democratic presidential candidates would espouse in debates would encapsulate everything from moderate ones to those touted by the Greens in the early 2000s, a testament to the efforts by the Greens in getting their message and platform into mainstream media.

It was not until the Bush administration's decision to invade Iraq, however, that student activism on the left really galvanized. As US president George W. Bush prepared to take the country to war in early 2003, tens of thousands of students demonstrated in hundreds of US high schools, colleges, and universities in nationally coordinated "Books Not Bombs" campaigns set up by the National Youth and Student Peace Coalition, a consortium of more than a dozen student organizations. Pro-Bush counterprotests, sponsored by College Republicans and other right-wing political organizations, took place on campuses as well.[12] Giant peace demonstrations occurred around the world in February. Immediately after the shock of the invasion in March, antiwar rallies broke out all over the country and quickly morphed into a full-fledged antiwar move-ment capable of pulling together thousands of protestors. By 2005, a national antiwar rally in Washington, DC, would be attended by 150,000 people, with tens of thousands marching in other major cities including San Francisco, Los Angeles, and Chicago. Demon-strations against the war and the subsequent occupation would for years draw massive crowds, coordinated by antiwar organizations and populated by activists, students, parents, and university faculty, with student groups such as the College Democrats of America, Stu-dents for a Democratic Society, and the Young Communist League swelling their ranks.

Major US cities were not the only places targeted by students in the antiwar campaigns. In 2004, more than fifteen thousand stu-dents and activists demonstrated outside Fort Benning's gates in Georgia to protest the School of the Americas (a training facility for soldiers from Latin American countries), or as the govern-ment renamed it, the Western Hemisphere Institute for Security Cooperation. Students from California State University, Ball State University, the University of Wisconsin, Xavier University, and other schools travelled to the protest, joining thousands already gathered from the region. Attending activists waved pages of SoA training manuals outlining military interrogation techniques. As a common cause among activist groups on the left, the antiwar/antioccupation/antimilitary demonstrations provided valuable opportunities for activists to link networks and share organiza-tional strategies and protest tactics. They also diminished feelings of separation and opposition among groups that had up until then found little in common, other than being lumped on the same end of the political spectrum.

Importantly as well, the demonstrations allowed opportunities for students to find their voice. Conflicts on campuses flared when military recruiters set up tables at job fairs or applied for permits to recruit on campus, and recruiters found themselves besieged with angry students when they showed up. Most of these demon-strations were relatively small, but many of them ended in violence as conservative students found their voices too. Anticipating anti-recruitment demonstrations, conservative mobs began attending recruitment events and went on the offensive when the antirecruitment protests occurred.

In numerous incidents, campus security or police would show up to arrest students protesting the military presence on campus, and some who were arrested were harmed by police. Ironically, such violence happened to an air force veteran and sociology major at George Mason University who in 2005 taped a handmade "Recruiters lie" sign to his chest and quietly stood beside the recruiter's table. He was attacked by security and then arrested. By 2006, the counterrecruiting movement was sweeping campuses across the nation, organized by groups such as the National Network Opposing the Militarization of Youth and Students Against War. At big universities—Wisconsin, South Carolina, University of California Santa Cruz, Florida—recruiters faced sizeable counterrecruitment protests; organizers had by then learned that they needed to field large enough numbers to dwarf counterprotests and make suppression by campus security impossible. These protests occurred less frequently at community colleges and smaller schools, and that is where the military shifted the majority of its campus-level recruitment efforts.

There were other fights brewing in the United States as well, revealing the racism and xenophobia that would erupt fully into view a decade later. In 2006, in a foreshadowing of the immigration battles to come, hundreds of thousands of students joined in protests across the country after congressional Republicans began pushing legislation to criminalize and penalize undocumented immigrants. Tens of thousands of students held a day of walkouts. An estimated half a million people marched in Chicago, and more than twice that number marched in Los Angeles.[13] When Columbia University's College Republicans invited Jim Gilchrist, leader of the paramilitary citizens' border-patrol group the Minuteman Project to speak on campus, the Chicano Caucus and the International Socialist Organization coordinated a disruption action. During the talk, a dozen students rushed the stage, chanting for immigrants' rights, interrupting the speaker, and sparking a melee between pro- and anti-immigration audience members. The actions were condemned by news media and the university administration but went unrecognized for what they could offer the right in terms of media airplay; they did not elicit the type of freedom-of-expression complaints or energize the counterprotests that similar actions would ten years later.

Incidents in which right-wing speakers on campuses served as intentionally provocative lightning rods for protests—and there were a number of them at the time—reveal a wider xenophobia and racism in US culture, but simultaneously they show that activists on the left recognized the greater implications of allowing hate speech to become politically acceptable rhetoric. They also illustrate how much has changed on both the left and the right in the last decade or so in terms of developing strategies around such speaking events to spark larger protests. Now, there is an acute awareness from both sides of how controversial media coverage of such events can widen their respective bases. Fourteen years later, right-wing organizations would stage similar events on campuses—aimed at getting attention and airplay when right-wing speakers, including hatemongers like Milo Yiannopoulos, were challenged—under the guise of exercising their speakers' rights to freedom of expression. For their part, protestors against these spectacles would capture and spread images of the neo-Nazis who would inevitably show up to highlight the underlying racism driving these events—a racism either endorsed by or at the very least seemingly acceptable to the right. In any case, one can see in these early immigration battles connections to what would later become the open rise of fascism in the United States.

When the US recession of 2008 hit, caused by unregulated subprime loan practices that led to bank failures and further fueled by the trillions of dollars spent annually on US military operations in Iraq and Afghanistan, it spelled big financial trouble for universities and colleges. Federal budget woes were passed down to state governments, which hacked away at education budgets to balance their books. The state of California was in dire straits, and the governor and ex-*Conan the Barbarian* actor Arnold Schwarzenegger planned to close dozens of state parks and raze the education budget. The disclosures of his plans brought thousands of students to march in the streets in protest. In 2009, UC Berkeley students held increasingly large protests after an increase in tuition of over 30 percent for the UC system was announced to make up budget shortfalls. Campus security, state police, and sheriff's deputies were called in to break up the protests, which they did violently.

When forty-three students locked themselves inside Wheeler Hall to protest tuition hikes, effectively shutting down Berkeley for a day, they were supported by thousands of students, faculty, and parents outside.[14] Those outside tried to form a barrier to protect the occupiers, but campus security and police, using batons and tear gas and firing rubber-coated bullets, violently dispersed the demonstration, sending hundreds to local hospitals, many with broken bones. The violence galvanized student opposition groups and sparked anti–police violence demonstrations in addition to more tuition-hike demonstrations on campuses across California.

The Golden State was not the only state raising the cost of education, nor was it the only one where politicians were attempting to make educational changes. In Republican-controlled states, austerity measures were seen as an opportunity. Conservative lawmakers used them to "reform" educational systems and to slash funding going toward what were perceived as the bastions of leftists and liberals. Money for tenure-track professors was moved toward hiring more cost-effective part-time lecturers, whose tenuous hold on a living made them less likely to risk their jobs for political activism or challenge administrations. And, of course, part-timers didn't legally warrant costly health-care coverage, so the net per-student cost of teacher pay was much less.

A further effect of these carefully orchestrated economic crises in Republican-controlled states that intentionally underfunded public education was that universities were faced with making economic decisions about which classes to support and which to drop. STEM classes and business classes had more financial value, so they were retained while so-called nonessential humanities courses were squeezed out of curricula. In such GOP-dominated states, university boards of governors often selected probusiness presidents and chancellors, and universities continued to fund university expansion, purchasing more and more land and selling naming rights to buildings for large donations. Increasingly operating under business models, universities bumped matriculation rates and raised tuition without keeping pace in hiring tenure-track professors, thus forcing the hiring of more exploitable nontenured teachers, all while increasing class sizes.

All this had profound effects on students and the quality of their education, but it also affected student-activism levels in those states. Disadvantaged students from underfunded, mediocre, or failing high schools had trouble scoring well enough on standardized tests to get into colleges, and had difficulty affording higher education even if they got in. On university campuses in more conservative areas of the country, such as in the South, high costs and the institutional emphasis on careerism dampened student activism, or relegated it to the realm of special-interest factions, hamstringing activists' chances of expanding their appeals and networks.

While the country would subsequently elect Barack Obama president and usher in a new era of federal liberalism (from 2009 to 2017), conservative state lawmakers would continue to consolidate their power, working to guarantee they held on to or increased legislative majorities by redrawing election maps and limiting voter rights. In the decade to come, their efforts repeatedly would be challenged by student groups and grassroots activists, but they also used the Obama presidency to cultivate conservative allies and organize donors. While waiting out two presidential terms, they planned long-term strategies for expanding legislative and judicial power on the state and national levels and cultivated their strategies through media.

In the United States in the first decade of the millennium, students were protesting in support of myriad local causes but also against what they perceived as rampant capitalism, unethical actions, and national policies—and they were doing so on a massive scale, with activism coalescing into a number of significant movements. Antiwar protests, antiracism protests, anti-sweatshop and human-rights-abuses protests, efforts against the corporatization of universities and the rising costs of education, challenges to anti-immigration laws—these causes would all receive significant student support and energy. Social media was becoming more influential than ever, and by decade's end activists were using it to generate wider support for causes, more quickly. The increase in frustration sparked violence at some protests, and experimentation began with the intentional provocation of police by students in order to garner media attention; such tactics would lead in time to highly organized anarchist intervention strategies (such as those practiced by antifa activists) often inspired by campus anarchists in Europe, that would appear at larger protests such at the Occupy demonstrations and Women's Marches.

Bush-era policies, the wars in and occupation of Afghanistan and Iraq, and unregulated corporate greed—in conjunction with widely reported domestic events such as mass shootings at schools and racially motivated police violence—revealed glimpses of the underbelly of populist conservative ideology in the United States. And already, economic imperialism, deregulation, xenophobia, and racism were fueling activism on the left. But student activism often grows out of resistance efforts. While the run-up to the election of Obama encouraged many to become politically active, his election had a paradoxical tempering effect on the rising activism levels at universities. Although institutionalized injustice continued, such as explicit racial profiling by police and clearly increased incidents of racially motivated deaths during arrests, it would be some time before it was seriously challenged through mass demonstrations. The profligacy of corporate America continued largely unabated, and although the ability to criticize wrongdoing and to call for social and economic justice seemed for many more tangible than ever during Obama's tenure, the intensity of that critique was much less than it would be under Donald Trump. Tremendous gains would indeed be made in combatting longstanding social injustice and addressing new concerns such as climate change, but with these advances came conservative countermeasures. These included political strategies for holding on to power in state legislatures in order to control laws, the arguments of right-wing intelligentsia in the popular press, the rise of populist talk-radio rants, the expansion of conservative media networks such as Fox News and, importantly, the sponsoring of conservative activist organizations by wealthy patrons such as the Koch brothers.

Resistance is always a key component of activism, and liberal student efforts flared in the coming years in the Occupy demonstrations, in the Black Lives Matter movement, in Women's Marches, in LGBTQ protests, in efforts to raise climate awareness, and in campaigns for greater gun control following campus killings. But it would not be until the 2016 election of Donald Trump to the presidency that these causes would coalesce into defining social movements as they have. Seemingly incarnating the evils that students had battled over the past decade in their causes—overt racism, xenophobia, sexism, rampant greed, income inequality, and profligacy—Trump was a climate change–denying failed businessman who boasted of having committed sexual assault in order to impress other men. He would do much for the proliferation of student activism across the United States and galvanize many of the disparate ongoing fights happening on campuses into a more unified campaign against his policies and the Republican Party that backed him.

2

WAR, THE PUSH FOR LIBERALISM, AND CONSERVATIVE BACKLASH IN THE MIDDLE EAST

In international media over the past fifty years, the Middle East has often been characterized as an endemically chaotic region of nations locked in an inextricable tangle of violent interests, many of them fanatical and with one foot in the modern world and the other in the Stone Age. The conflicts between nations and often within those nations continue to fuel outsider prejudices against the region, against the nations within it, and against its various peoples. Although historic conflicts and interests are varied and specific to their nations and even to the multiple cultures and political systems within nations, popular Western media often characterize Middle Easterners as warlike in nature, people who are all members of one religious extreme or another. If democracy didn't take hold in the region during the Arab Spring, pundits argued, it was because those societies weren't ready for it.

Such views continue to color outside perspectives on the region's nations and international relations today, fueling racism, xenophobia, and anti-Muslim sentiment, particularly in Muslim-minority countries. But in hindsight, with what has become a global epidemic of extremism, authoritarianism, chaos, nationalism, violence, corruption, and greed—even in secular nations in the West—many of those characteristics stereotypically used to describe the problems of the member nations of the Middle East just as easily apply to a significant portion of the rest of world today. In looking at some of the resistance actions going on in the region, and the authoritarian responses to them, we can see the struggles occurring within those nations as a harbinger of things to come in the next decade both within the region and outside it, especially in terms of polarizing politics, nationalism, and extremism. Yes, there was (and is) harsh authoritarianism, fanaticism, and extreme intolerance (religious, racial, ethnic, and political) in the region, and we don't want to irresponsibly mix apples and oranges, for there are tremendous differences among the various societies, governments, and belief systems in question. But in a good-faith effort toward understanding the plight of disenfranchised humans around the world, in the most general terms, we can see connections among all nations in which activists and idealist youth (of every stripe) are working for social justice, greater freedoms, and civil rights against entrenched, authoritarian power, whether those countries are organized as democracies or not, in secular countries or religious ones. To look at the specifics of the struggles of Middle Eastern countries with high levels of activism in the 2000s is to see precursors of and parallels to struggles in the region and elsewhere in the world today.

Anti–United States sentiment, predictably, ran high in Afghanistan following the US-led invasion of the country in 2001, precipitated by the September 11 attacks on the United States by al-Qaeda. US president George W. Bush blamed Osama bin Laden, who was hiding and operating in Afghanistan; the hunt for the al-Qaeda leader would occupy the rest of Bush's presidency. Afghanistan itself had been gripped by internal struggles between the Taliban (which had recently taken control of and held the capital until 2001) and the Afghan Northern Alliance forces. Hundreds of thousands of citizens had been killed in the previous decade. With US military aid (supported by Canada and the United Kingdom and eventually dozens of other countries, including all the NATO nations), the Northern Alliance forces overthrew the Taliban (which had refused to surrender bin Laden to the United States), and Hamid Karzai became the country's interim, then duly elected, president, though Afghanistan's government remained weak, propped up by international forces. Forced underground, the Taliban nevertheless continued aggressive recruiting efforts, particularly targeting the region's disaffected youth.

Although much of the country's population welcomed foreign involvement to help overthrow the Taliban, which was a fundamentalist political organization operating according to a harsh interpretation of sharia law, the extended foreign troop presence in the country was also viewed by many as Western imperialism. The majority of Afghans are not fundamentalists, but the nation is almost entirely Muslim, so it is not surprising that following a Newsweek report that interrogators at the US prison at Guantánamo had desecrated the Koran by flushing one down a toilet, thousands of Afghan students demonstrated against the United States in urban areas, burning American flags and effigies of President Bush. Local anti-American activists and political factions and religious groups joined the marches. Resentment against the US presence in the country continued to build, as did resistance to Karzai's government, which was accused of being a puppet government of the West. Government buildings were set on fire in Kabul in 2005, and protestors began throwing stones at police and security forces, which opened fire with live ammunition, wounding dozens and killing four, fueling a growing wave of anti–United States protests in cities, towns, and small villages across the country.

Many Afghans—even those opposed to the Taliban—were also opposed to occupation by US troops in their cities and the continued violence that rocked their country. They were growing tired of what they perceived as arrogant cultural and religious disrespect by US soldiers and their NATO allies. In 2006, following the Danish publication of a disrespectful cartoon of the Prophet Muhammad that received widespread media coverage, angry students and activists attacked both the Danish and the US embassies in Afghanistan in violent protests, throwing stones and Molotov cocktails and battling with security. In Bagram, thousands of demonstrators attempted to overrun the US military base and were fired upon by Afghan forces. The protests expanded. In Kabul, Kandahar, and Mihtarlam, police and security forces battled angry crowds, killing four and wounding scores of others. In the West, where freedom of the press is often viewed as sacred, the protests were seen as an overreaction to a harmless cartoon, but to many people in Muslim-majority countries, where physical, cultural, and religious struggles with Western imperialism go back centuries, the disrespect represented something else. Such growing anti-Western sentiment was further fueled in 2008 in protests in Afghanistan after a Dutch film perceived as criticizing the Koran was released internationally.

In 2007, after civilian deaths at the hands of coalition military forces in the Western province of Herat occurred, thousands of Afghans marched in urban areas, throwing stones at police and setting fires. A decade into US operations in Afghanistan, close to 150,000 foreign military personnel were in the country. Although this presence stabilized the nation in some ways, it bred intense resentment both within Afghanistan and outside it. Opposition to continued US involvement was manifest in the West as well. From the time Bush announced plans to intervene in the region until well after Obama took the reins of the US government, tens of thousands of antiwar and anti–US imperialism demonstrators took to the streets in major cities in the United States and Europe. On several occasions, crowds of close to a hundred thousand marched against the occupation in the streets of Washington.

The September 11, 2001, terrorist attack on the United States had dire implications for Iraq as well, for it gave the Bush administration (which had already been discussing the need for regime change in Iraq) a reason for invading. In 2002, Bush gave a State of the Union address in which he famously aligned Iraq as one of the countries forming an "Axis of Evil," publicly laying the foundation for the media campaign behind the coming physical assault. Saddam Hussein, Iraq's iron-fisted leader, remained defiant in the face of accusations he was building an arsenal of weapons of mass destruction (WMDs) and flouted UN resolutions passed against him. Domestically, at the start of the millennium in Iraq under Hussein, student resistance was understandably covert, for he was a brutal tyrant. Effectively using both the military and police to enforce order, he also had complete control of media and a well-developed propaganda machine at his disposal. Extrajudicial killings and the state's use of torture made protesting the government within the country extremely risky. The "Butcher of Baghdad" earned his moniker after invasions into Kuwait and Iran a decade earlier, and Hussein's genocidal operations and political murders had resulted in the deaths of near a quarter of a million people.[15] His fall at the hands of the US invasion in 2003 was hailed by many within and without the country, but the regime change and the US occupation that followed created a host of new problems.

Without a doubt, Hussein's effect on higher education had been profoundly awful. But after his fall things got worse for students. Following the US invasion, and for the rest of the decade, there is little to report as far as student demonstrations go, for although the country's universities were not themselves destroyed by bombings, they were all looted, and many of the buildings were burned by vandals. In the following decade, hundreds of professors and scientists would be assassinated outright or kidnapped and killed as fundamentalist extremist death squads targeted people who had affiliations with the universities. More than six thousand professors would flee the country, among the 40 percent of middle-class Iraqis believed to have fled the nation by 2007.[16] Iraq's educational system— on every level—remained a disaster for years afterwards due to lack of funding, corruption among officials eventually appointed to oversee it, and open violence against teachers and students. Outside of the country, tens of thousands of students worldwide protested the US invasion while it was occurring and its subsequent effects on Iraq—many of them former Iraqi citizens or members of Iraqi student groups, and many of them simply challenging expanding US imperialism in the Middle East.

Protests against the United States and Western imperialism occurred throughout the region as well. In Egypt, for example, students and angry citizens took to the streets of Cairo to demonstrate against the preparations for the US invasion of Iraq as soon as the attack was imminent. They also protested against Israel, which many Egyptians saw as egging on the United States in order to increase its own power in the region. Massive crowds led by students were prevented from reaching the Israeli embassy by security forces firing tear gas and water cannons. Frustrated, they turned their attention on any symbols of Western imperialism they happened across, resulting in, for example, the complete destruction of a Kentucky Fried Chicken (KFC) restaurant. The intensity of the protests ennobled activists in the eyes of many and frightened security forces, who suppressed them violently.

In 2003, in an effort to thwart more public demonstrations, Egyptian security forces arrested students attempting to revive the banned Muslim Brotherhood (MB). The MB continued to agitate in Egypt, though it was outlawed and actively suppressed on college campuses. Egypt's government was working closely with the United States at the time, and many perceived that cooperation, by extension, as collaborating with Israel. This made it the subject of many student protests in neighboring nations such as Iran, where hardline conservative activists, including conservative student groups, often called for the assassination of Egyptian president Hosni Mubarak.

Although the region was and remains a tangle of political, cultural, and religious interests, in terms of trends in Middle Eastern student movements, the US-led wars spurred anti-Western sentiment and galvanized widespread anti-Western sentiment. This, along with ongoing hostilities between Israel and its neighbors, gave energy to Muslim-affiliated activist organizations, many of them extremely conservative, with international networks. Compounding the volatility of this mix was the fact that while many countries in the region experienced a rise in conservative and religious activism, so too did they witness a growing desire among some youth, who were increasingly exposed to Western ideas and cultures by studying abroad and access through the internet, to liberalize their own respective cultures and laws.

As the decade wore on, advances in the reach of the internet and then social media broadcast the kinds of freedoms that many others around the world enjoyed, freedoms that an increasing number of youth in conservative cultures wanted. This was especially true on university campuses across the region, where students plugged into the rest of the world learned about what their colleagues in more culturally liberal countries enjoyed in terms of civil and political rights. They gained access to strategies for organizing resistance movements, as the leaders of revolutionary groups in Eastern Europe, such as Otpor (Serbia), Pora! (Ukraine), Unitas (Montenegro), and Mjaft! (Albania) networked and broadcast their ideas and tactics for social, cultural, and political revolution worldwide. Thus, the Eastern Europe color revolutions and uprisings of the late 1990s and early 2000s spread directly into the Middle East.

A generational push for liberalism and civil freedoms was especially visible at the beginning of the decade in Iran, and students backing liberalization suffered greatly for their efforts. In 1999, University of Tehran students protesting the banning of a reformist newspaper were attacked by four hundred members of security forces, riot police, and an armed paramilitary mob (believed to be Ansar-e Hezbollah), under orders from a local police chief. The attackers invaded the campus and raided student dormitories at 8:30 in the morning of July 9 (or 18 Tir by the Iranian calendar), setting rooms on fire, beating students with clubs and chains, and throwing them off balconies. Between three and five students were killed in the melee, and hundreds were injured. Reformist president Mohammad Khatami condemned the attack, which was subsequently known in the country as "18 Tir." Iran's government was divided, as were its views on the way to handle reform activists in the nation. The president, who had much support among the people, pushed for reforms, while the clerics and conservatives who firmly held the judiciary pushed their agenda. Presidential powers in Iran are restricted, however, while Ayatollah Ali Khamenei enjoyed unlimited powers. The ayatollah himself initially condemned the violence and called for peace, but he also condemned the continued demonstrations.

Six days of student demonstrations following the 18 Tir police crackdown brought tens of thousands of students and youth into the streets of Tehran and other major cities in protests that ended in violence and riots. Security forces hit demonstrators with tear gas, rubber-coated bullets, and clubs and, sometimes, shot them with live ammunition. Students accused pro-conservative organizations of sending members who pretended to join the demonstrations in order to foster violence, dressing like students, burning vehicles, and vandalizing stores in an effort to discredit the movement and to bring the wrath of police violence down upon the real protestors. Faced with growing unrest that threatened to become a widespread uprising, increased chaos in the streets, and hardliners agitating for forceful suppression, Khatami called for an end to all demonstrations and put the capital in a state of emergency. The protests nonetheless continued, and after one group made an attempt to take over the Ministry of Interior, the police cracked down on all the demonstrations with extreme force.

Alarmed at the intensity of the protests and fearfully monitoring the success of youth-generated protests in Eastern Europe, conservative mullahs and the Organization for Islamic Propagation went on the offensive. They sounded a call for national, patriotic, pro-Iranian, anti-American counterdemonstrations, and hundreds of thousands of people marched, chanting patriotic slogans and "Death to America." These massive groups dwarfed the student demonstrations and effectively changed the media focus on the nation, both internationally and within Iran. Iranian security and police were not idle, however, for during the students' demonstrations and afterwards (while the country's attention was on opposition to Western imperialism), hundreds of the student activists were arrested, with many of the leaders facing serious charges, some carrying the death penalty. Charged with "antirevolutionary" crimes, they were forced to make public "confessions" that were televised. Thus, activists who had been pushing for greater social and political reforms found themselves on trial for treason. More common than these spectacles, however, were reports of student activists having simply "disappeared."[17] Recognizing connections to the proliferation of similar pushes for freedoms and reforms against tyranny by youth across the globe, from Serbia to Bolivia to Guinea to China, in international media the initial protests in Iran were referred to as "Iran's Tiananmen Square." Unfortunately for the activists, like the Tiananmen protests, Iran's student uprising was violently suppressed by the state.

In 2002, though, committed students again risked protesting on the streets following the announced death sentence for an outspoken reformist lecturer, Hashem Aghhajari, condemned for apostasy. Students marched on and off the University of Tehran campus and, to the surprise of the country's leadership, were joined by thousands in support of wider government and cultural reforms. Police attacked the demonstrators, firing tear gas and rubber-coated bullets, but the demonstrations persisted for two weeks. After Ayatollah Khamenei condemned them as the work of the enemies of Iran, they were repeatedly attacked by large mobs of armed hardliners, and the country faced a growing culture war that became more intense over the ensuing months.

Although the government could and, during times of unrest, did shut down internet and cell-phone usage, generally it was getting harder and harder for the conservative clerics to control access to international media, which was bringing more and more open views of what constituted human rights to a country where a married woman could lawfully still be stoned to death for having an affair and the taking of thirteen-year-old brides was not uncommon. Students continued to protest publicly in demonstrations, in remarkable acts of bravery considering the recent history of violent repression. The cultural divide was exacerbated by the fact that even as the aging clerics continued to legislate their stranglehold on the nation, by 2003, 70 percent of the population was below the age of thirty. In 2005, the conservative populist Mahmoud Ahmadinejad was elected president, and students continued to demonstrate, though to do so always meant facing off with armed police willing to use violence. The students were learning, though, absorbing strategies and tactics promulgated by activists and organizations based in Eastern Europe, modifying them and changing them to fit their own needs and situation. They came to marches wearing homemade armor and gas masks, and they organized leaderless protests through social media networks.

While they were demonstrating over many concerns specific to Iran, the Iranian students were part of a much larger trend throughout the world in authoritarian countries with governments that restricted civil liberties and suppressed prodemocracy movements. In these countries, progressive ideas spread through the internet and social media, and students connected through international networks. Those in freer countries encouraged those under the yoke of suppression, and they offered aid. Over the next few years, students at the University of Tehran continued to agitate for liberal reforms and against ongoing arrests and the torturing of students by police, but the suppression of students continued. Ahmadinejad took a hard line and encouraged the use of force in breaking up demonstrations, and appointed a cleric to head the university itself, which led to the dismissal of liberal professors and students. In 2007, former Iranian president Mohammad Khatami viewed the ongoing changes by the current government as bad enough that he was moved to deliver a lecture to thousands of students at the university, criticizing the current president's restrictive policies—an extremely bold move, and one that encouraged students to be more politically active.

In June 2009, Ahmadinejad won reelection, but the results were highly contested. Hundreds of thousands of students and supporters of his opponent, Mir Hussein Moussavi, demonstrated in Tehran and in cities throughout the country. The reward for doing so was that many of them were dismissed by their universities and arrested by security forces at the demonstrations or afterwards. A number of those arrested died in police custody.

The protests were extremely loud, but they remained largely peaceful—at least during the day. At night, though, progovernment mobs violently attacked protestors occupying city squares and did so without fear of police reprisal. This wasn't specific to Iran. It was a tactic increasingly adopted by repressive regimes throughout the world: to use security forces to contain protests but to stand down when sponsored armed mobs supporting the government arrived to beat protestors.

As the decade wore on, the role of social media in organizing protests in the region grew, as it did in the rest of the world, and both activists and authoritarian governments became increasingly aware of its use in spreading a movement or sowing chaos around it. Security forces learned how to disrupt social media and internet service on a moment's notice. For their part, students intentionally began provoking police (witness the rise of anarchist groups across the globe that would join larger protests) in order to get an overreaction that could be caught on film, disseminated through social or news media, and used to widen support for their causes. Governments responded by turning intelligence agencies on their own citizens and infiltrating their networks, making preemptive arrests, dropping media blackouts during protests, and suppressing protests at night using third-party mobs or overwhelming security forces. Police arrested everyone they could catch and confiscated the phones, cameras, and media devices of those they arrested.

Even in a country like Iran, images of violence could galvanize massive popular support, as occurred with the video of twenty-seven-year-old Neda Agha-Soltan. On June 20, 2009, Agha-Soltan was shot in the chest and died on film while other protestors tried to save her. The video went viral on YouTube and became a rallying call for Iranian activists. The protests expanded to the point that security began simply killing demonstrators, eventually leaving some hundred people dead in the streets. A clampdown on anything that could serve as an excuse to demonstrate followed, as did a slew of restrictive decrees. Public funerals for slain activists were forbidden; families instructed to mourn in silence. When news broke that three of those arrested at recent demonstrations had been sentenced to death by hanging, angry protests again broke out in the capital, and condemnation of the government by international human-rights watchdog groups followed. Ahmadinejad, however, continued to solidify his power, using security and intelligence forces in conjunction with police to identify, surveil, and arrest activists. He used the legislature to tighten security laws and the judiciary to harshly sentence those accused of activism-related crimes.

Over the coming decade, from 2010 to 2020, the Iranian government would with few exceptions effectively suppress public displays of opposition. Although student unrest in Iran was high during much of the decade, the government was ultimately able to suppress it using a combination of technology, new laws, preemptive arrests, rapid and harsh police responses to demonstrations, jailings, and a hard-line judiciary. At the same time the government turned a blind eye to the violence perpetrated by mobs of conservative thugs attacking the protests, mobs that somehow knew beforehand when and where demonstrations would occur and what numbers would be needed to attack them.

Although diametrically opposed to Iran's government and society in so many ways, Israel too saw struggles between authorities entrenched in power and its youth. Student unrest and demonstrations repeatedly flared within the nation, though the concerns of students were much different than in neighboring states and territories. Israel has long had well-developed student organizations, and many of them actively demonstrate regarding human rights, education reform, pro-Israeli concerns, and international political issues. With service in the military traditionally mandated for almost all citizens (exceptions are made for Arabs and those whose religion forbids it) and with the country for decades suffering under constant missile or bombing attacks by hostile groups based just beyond its borders, the political and cultural climate on campuses in Israel is unique in terms of activist power politics. With minority demographics constituting twenty percent of the population, most of them Muslims, the nation and its schools mirror the complications and diversity of its national politics. But undergirding much of the political discussion, whether liberal or conservative, is a strong sense of identity and patriotism.

So even when government policies were decried in many student demonstrations in the first decade of the millennium, the protests tended to focus on the policies themselves more so than critiques of the government that created them. This would change over time, especially in the next decade under the increasingly divisive leadership of Benjamin Netanyahu. But in the early 2000s, most Israelis saw it their duty to serve the state, and students pushing for reforms often saw those reforms as opportunities for bettering and strengthening Israel. For its part, rather than suppressing student-led reform movements, the government of Israel has often absorbed them as a tactic to build and strengthen the nation.

That said, there were many large demonstrations in the country at this time, particularly around the definition of the nation's identity, its governance, its borders, and the treatment of Palestinians both within and outside those borders. In 2001, hundreds of thousands gathered in Jerusalem in a massive demonstration against a US peace plan that would divide sovereignty over the city. Many of the participants were students from Jewish religious schools, and a large percentage of these protests were sponsored by conservative organizations and political activists. This didn't necessarily undercut the commitment of the protestors, for nationalism runs high in the country. Over the next few years, students would repeatedly protest against the giving up of occupied lands and settlements whenever rumors to those effects would begin to circulate. In 2007, about three thousand students protested in Jerusalem alongside active-duty military personnel for the release of kidnapped and missing Israeli soldiers. Hamas militants had for years captured lone troops, in one case tunneling under the border to conduct a raid in which they killed two soldiers and wounded and kidnapped a third, Gilad Shalit, whom they dragged back to a hideout in the Gaza Strip where he was held for five years. Student groups worked in 2007 to coordinate worldwide demonstrations demanding Hamas release kidnapped Israelis, demonstrations that occurred in more than seventy cities worldwide, bringing international attention to the issue and pressure on Israel's allies to support Israel's fight against Hamas and Hezbollah, organizations Israel identified as "terrorist."

The focus of demonstrations connected to Israel, both within the country and internationally, would begin to shift, though. By the end of the decade, there would be increasing numbers of international pro-Palestinian demonstrations against the Israeli occupation of and settlement expansions into Palestinian-claimed territories. In international media there would also be much ado made about the violence of Israeli's military at its borders as the military stepped up operations to root out Hamas in Gaza and Hezbollah in Lebanon. Small rockets continued to be fired daily from Palestinian territories toward Israel, against which Israel's air force would respond by launching far more powerful rockets of its own, often into urban areas. Those launching the missiles from Palestine sometimes hid near schools and hospitals, hoping their proximity would forestall Israeli attacks. It didn't. Israel argued that it was defending itself and it was up to the Palestinian Authority to stop the rockets originating from the territories. The problem for Israel, though, was the images coming out of those regions. Sometimes Israeli air strikes inflicted heavy collateral damage on civilian targets and resulted in noncombatant deaths, including those of women and children. Pro-Palestinian activists began using news and social media to spread images of dead children killed by the air strikes, and as images and reports continued to surface, international attitudes began to change toward Israel's indiscriminate use of force, and toward those upon whom Israel unleashed it.

In Palestine, protests against the Israeli occupation were constant, as was the suppression of protests whenever they came too close to Jewish settlements or were judged to challenge Israeli security. In 1999, students and youth in Bethlehem demonstrated against Israeli security checkpoints near the northern entrance to the city that segregated Palestinians from Israelis and tourists. Protests intensified, and when a Palestinian was killed by security, demonstrations expanded and erupted into street battles that went on for days. Israeli security forces guarding nearby Rachel's Tomb were pelted by stones thrown by angry protestors trying to drive them off. The burial site of the Biblical wife of Jacob is venerated by Jews, Muslims, and Christians, and like other Muslim holy sites was often a place of demonstrations, but the Palestinian civilians angry at the recent killing were no match for the troops deployed to control them. Protected by full body armor and advancing behind shields, the soldiers hit the protesting crowds with tear gas, fired rubber-coated metal bullets at them, and then cleared the streets with baton charges.

Before the rise of cell phones and video technology and the pervasiveness of social media, such brutal tactics came with little international consequence. This would change as activists put the new technology to work to disseminate what was happening in the occupied territories, and over the coming decade documentary evidence would radically change both how the protests occurred and how security would respond. But at the start of the decade, for their part, Palestinian activists were still figuring this stuff out, and Israel could act with impunity. In 2000, for example, fifteen students marching in Jerusalem from Al-Ummah College in the Al-Barid neighborhood ran into a squad of Israeli security forces who shot them with rubber-coated bullets. Such violence at demonstrations and marches had become so routine that just prior to marches, Palestinian protestors and their supporters donated blood in quickly set up medical areas as part of demonstration preparations, because they knew some of them would soon need it. By the end of the decade, though, preparations for marches would include identifying locations with the best angles for recording police violence and deploying people there with cell-phone cameras. They would also include strategies for immediately uploading cell-phone images and video to international servers for live-feed media distribution. For their part, security would begin formally training troops in restraint as part of larger suppression tactics, but also how to use force and violence more discreetly.

For Palestine, things became more complicated after the US invasion of Afghanistan, when Osama bin Laden made a televised speech in which he connected Afghanistan's struggles with those of Palestine—connections Yasser Arafat, president of the Palestinian Authority and chairman of the Palestine Liberation Organization (PLO), was trying to downplay. When students demonstrating against the invasion of Afghanistan marched, Arafat shocked the world and his own people by having Palestinian security forces suppress those marches, killing two activists in the process. While Palestinians backed the end of the occupation, political divisions within the region opened up and absorbed a lot of the population's political attention.

By 2004, the climate of Palestine had changed enough that the Student Youth Movement's Martyr Yasser Arafat Bloc—which was connected to the Al-Aqsa Martyrs Brigade of the Fatah movement (responsible for numerous kidnappings and bombing attacks)—won An-Najah National University's student-council elections. Various student groups and activist organizations in Palestine continued to conduct anti-Israel and anti–United States demonstrations, but they were increasingly factional, and violence between groups blossomed. For example, student activist Ali Shamali of the Fatah Youth Movement, a member of the student council at Al-Aqsa University, was assassinated while he sat outside his house by members of the Executive Force and Izz-ad-Din al-Qassam Brigades, the militant faction of Hamas.[18] Youth groups were more and more absorbed by both the Israeli occupation and the internal conflicts among their own political rivals. In 2006, Hamas won a majority in general elections, but its disputes with Fatah led to the creation of two separate authorities (Hamas over Gaza and Fatah over the West Bank). Hamas and Fatah would battle one another for control over Palestine for the next thirteen years, briefly negotiating for unification several times but without success.

Just as activism levels, strategies, and reforms sought by demonstrators in different nations in the Middle East varied greatly, so too did the ways in which the various authorities handled protests;

not every nation used the brutality of Iran or Israel in suppressing opposition. In the first decade of the millennium, the government of Jordan controlled public protests effectively, due in great part to established laws requiring permits for demonstrations. In order to get authorization, students had to declare the subject, location, and attendance size of the proposed activities. The process often involved negotiations between organizers and officials that served to take the edge off some protests (and, of course, applying for protest permits alerted security forces that they'd be happening, and in what numbers). On the rare occasions when protests were unauthorized or challenged security or the government, security was deployed in such force that there could be no physical contest. Jordan saw many properly permitted anti-Israel and pro-Palestine protests, as well as demonstrations for educational, political, and economic reforms, but in the 2000s the country did not see a major rise in student movements paralleling those in neighboring nations.

In Jordan, as a rule, student protests were limited to campuses, and students had further hoops to jump through with their own school administrations. Sometimes they marched in numbers, but even when they did, they often showed restraint and did not riot or vandalize. For example, on May 15, 2001, students at the University of Jordan marched on the annual anniversary of Al-Nakba ("the catastrophe"), the day in 1948 that the Jewish state came into being (which to the Palestinians marked the forced displacement of seven hundred thousand people and the killing of thirteen thousand in the process). Students called for an end to the occupation of Palestinian territories, chanting "Allahu akbar" and anti-Israel and anti-US slogans. Some came dressed in white, in solidarity with Hezbollah fighters. The mostly women demonstrators burned US and Israeli flags. When they headed for the main gates leading off campus, they found Jordanian police waiting for them, but instead of escalating their protest, they stopped and remained on campus. While clearly upset, they nevertheless showed a restraint characteristic of Jordanian student protests at the time. The intensity and widespread violence characteristic of Jordan's 2012 and 2013 demonstrations were still a ways off.

Such restraint on the part of activists was not practiced everywhere in the region. In Lebanon in 2005, former prime minister Rafik Hariri was assassinated in a car bombing, setting off demonstrations that would lead to the Independence Intifada (or as it was known in the West, the Cedar Revolution). A wave of peaceful demonstrations against the ongoing Syrian occupation of Lebanon occurred in Beirut, and these also brought opposition protests.

One relatively small pro-Syrian demonstration in the capital in turn had the unintentional effect of sparking massive demonstrations against the Syrian occupation that swelled into the hundreds of thousands. Angry Lebanese citizens choked the streets of Beirut and paralyzed traffic and commerce in other cities, calling for the immediate withdrawal of Syrian troops from Lebanon and an end to the pro-Syrian government. Student participation in the peaceful revolution was only a part of the larger uprising, but it was a significant part. Students pushed for liberal, democratic reforms, and the protests, combined with international pressure from the West and from other Arab countries, forced Syria's withdrawal and a reconfiguration of Lebanon's government. The nation instituted reforms and installed a pro-West prime minister, but the new arrangement was short lived, and the rest of the decade would be marked by power struggles, political turmoil, demonstrations, and violence. Following the end of the term of President Émile Lahoud in 2007, Lebanon's presidential elections were stalled by the opposition in parliament, which was demanding more power sharing in the government. Massive anti-government rallies roiled Beirut, and in 2008, armed oppositional forces, including Hezbollah, captured part of the capital. With sympathetic members of the government the insurgents forced the configuration of a national unity government, which would itself collapse in 2011, to be once again fought over and reconfigured.

On the other side of the region, Pakistan started the decade with a military coup that installed the military chief Pervez Musharraf as the leader of the country. He would be subsequently officially elected president, and the country would soon see massive uprisings. In 2001, Musharraf allied with the United States in the War on Terror, but riots numbering in the tens of thousands overwhelmed the country's major cities after the US invasion of Afghanistan, with rioters destroying and burning businesses that had any recognizable connection to the West or to America (including movie theaters, banks, and hotels). Police were deployed to protect assets and foreigners, who barricaded themselves in hotels, embassies, and international NGO headquarters. Approximately 97 percent of Pakistan identifies as Muslim, and many of the demonstrators saw the invasion of Afghanistan in terms of Western religious imperialism. In 2001, to preclude future riots, Musharraf unilaterally banned public rallies and demonstrations.

Pakistan's acceptance of cultural changes fostered by the increasing connectivity of the world and the exposure of its citizens to Western values through social media and the internet was rocky at best. Students spearheaded many liberalization efforts in the nation, and none better characterizes the cultural and legal challenges for progressive policy than the struggle waged for women's rights and freedoms. Plugged into Western media, young women activists wanted changes to everything from sexist laws to discrimination in the workplace, from more access to voting to better representation in government, from access to education to the ability to dress as they wished in public. Sexual harassment was commonplace.

In a country in which honor killings of married women for conducting extramarital affairs occurred with frequency, where acid attacks on women were common, and where rape within marriage was not a crime until 2007 (and afterwards the law was not enforced), women bravely protested for civil rights and for cultural changes. And they did so in larger and larger numbers, even though in doing so they risked being beaten. Under pressure, Musharraf paid lip service to expanding women's rights in the country. He agreed to moderate legal reforms, but with stipulations that made them hard to enforce; for example, the stipulation that victims of rape had to produce four male witnesses to the crime to substantiate that it had occurred. And so he continued to be heavily criticized by liberal student and activist groups, who openly defied him through rallies and demonstrations, especially after Musharraf publicly stated in an interview that he thought women claiming to be victims of rape exploited the attention they received to make money and to seek asylum in foreign countries.[19] Outraged young women marched in the streets, supported by their mothers and their grandmothers. Musharraf denied he had made the remarks and quickly increased female representation in the government. But such deeply ingrained cultural perspectives on women were hard to change, and the institutionalized sexism in the government and in conservative communities guaranteed strong opposition to real reform.

At the same time that progressive students at universities were pushing for the liberalization of their culture and the modernization of Pakistan's laws, culturally conservative students in religious schools (madrassas) agitated for more restrictions and against what they saw as the moral corruption of the nation by the West. These quickly radicalizing student activists were often pawns for conservative religious groups wielding power in the country, and progressives voiced concerns that the madrassas in Pakistan were being used by extremist militants for recruitment.

In March 2007, women students at the Jamia Hafsa madrassa next to Lal Masjid, a mosque in the capital city of Islamabad, began a program of kidnapping women in modern dress whom they accused of prostitution, torturing them to force them to give public confessions of their sins—confessions which they taped and aired via social media. Images in international news media of fully veiled women behind barricades sticks and chanting anti-government slogans embarrassed the government. The students then began taking foreign nationals hostage. But it was only after they captured Pakistani police officers, in July, that the government laid siege to Lal Masjid (where the militants had barricaded themselves), ringing the complex in barbed wire and setting up sandbag bunkers along the perimeter. That the government was hesitant to attack the madrassa speaks to the power of conservative religious leaders in the country at the time, and to Musharraf's reluctance to stand up to them. Only after an extended operation did the military eventually attempt to storm the mosque, using surveillance drones and Special Forces troops to do so. Heavily armed religious students and militants threw Molotov cocktails at the charging troops and shot at them with rifles and shoulder-fired grenade launchers, and they briefly held their own before finally being overrun.

In 2007, Musharraf ran for reelection and won the majority of votes, but while the Supreme Court of Pakistan delayed endorsing the election results because it was debating whether it was constitutional for the president to also be the head of the military, Musharraf called a national state of emergency, imposed a curfew, and suspended the chief justice of the judiciary. Musharraf's actions brought widespread protests on university campuses and calls for him to step down. The growing student demonstrations were one more problem for the besieged president, adding to pressure over the inept handling of the mosque siege, an ongoing international nuclear proliferation scandal, and the starting of impeachment proceedings against him that were supported by military officials. With conviction, a coup, or a national uprising—and maybe all three—looming on the horizon, Musharraf stepped down in 2008. During the decade, student resistance groups had been all the while becoming more and more divided, and although in many ways Pakistan became more liberal and more democratic in this period, it also saw an increase in the conservative forces resisting those changes—a split that would lead to much violence in the coming decade.

The Middle East saw extensive social turmoil in the 2000s, ranging from wars and occupations to uprisings to more moderate cultural changes, but the depiction of chaos as characteristic of the Middle East in international media, somehow endemic to the region's nations and tied to its religions (particularly ascribed in the West as a characteristic of Islam), does a disservice to the separate struggles within many of those countries between forces of conservativism and forces of liberalization. There were unique political power struggles consuming many of these nations, and many of them struggled with one another. But the struggles being waged within those countries—especially those that were seen as the most volatile—were often conflicts waged by youth and student activists seeking social justice and progressive change in the face of oppressive governments and conservative cultures. Technology and access to the internet and international media increasingly exposed many to freedoms enjoyed elsewhere in the world, and uprisings in Eastern Europe inspired Middle Eastern youth to struggle for greater independence and rights in their own countries. Those same technologies that helped revolutionaries in Eastern Europe globally disseminate successful organizational strategies and tactics were being adopted in the Middle East as well.

In many ways the kind of chaos the international community associated with the social and political battles fought in the region in the first decade of the millennium would in the next decade envelop other regions of the world, including the so-called highly developed nations in the West. The rest of the world would soon witness a rise in conservative extremism, nationalism, racism, violence, and authoritarianism, to be opposed by activists promoting democracy, tolerance, progressivism, and the expansion of human and civil rights.

3

EDUCATIONAL REFORMS, VIRTUAL ACTIVISM, ANTICAPITALISM, AND THE GROWTH OF INTERNATIONAL NETWORKS IN EUROPE

In Europe, many important student activist efforts happened in the first decade of the millennium. Many of these events were concerned with national domestic issues—educational reforms, economic policies, political struggles—but students also launched massive international antiwar demonstrations against US and coalition-supported military actions in the Middle East. Then there were the international 2008–2009 financial meltdowns, which fueled anticorruption, anticapitalist, and anticorporation demonstrations and movements. We'll discuss these in detail in the following chapter, but things that are noticeable too are the beginnings of trends, issues, and forces that would play out in major ways in the 2010s. These include the rise and growing legitimation of fascist groups and nationalist organizations in many European nations, overt economic and military imperialism in the Middle East and Africa, an increase in xenophobia and anti-immigrant sentiment, and fears and instabilities caused by the expansion of the European Union. There was also the proliferation of ever larger international corporations able to evade regulation and move money globally, and the continued exploitation of the poor and of resources in developing nations. At the same time that activists sought media attention for many of these issues, they were promoting other issues, most notably climate awareness.

Technological advances in Europe in the 2000s were driving changes in resistance strategies in ways that would lead the world in the next decade. European students, at the cutting edge in terms of applying new technologies, refined media networking to organize protests and spread information. They formed new international networks, linked them virtually, and disseminated information, data, and strategies for resistance throughout the world. European nations provided a sanctuary for many activists and groups fleeing violent suppression in their home countries, and many would set up shop in Europe and continue to organize and agitate, providing support and aid to those still fighting against authoritarians under the repressive regimes they had left.

During the 2000s, international hacktivist groups increasingly waged cyberattacks on corporations and governments (the number of attacks per week peaking in 2011, before dropping off as governments around the world with vastly greater resources and new cyberterrorism laws to enforce began suppressing them more effectively). Europe, more than any other region during the decade, witnessed the shift that was soon to come to much of the rest of the world in terms of the expansion of technology-driven activism and new tactics. The continent was the first to see the move to computer-based organizing strategies and networking, which in the 2000s seemed lightning fast compared to those of the nineties but which by the end of the decade had given way to social media and cell-phone networking, live-stream video recording, instantaneous data dissemination, and rapid tactics of demonstrating such as flash mobbing.

Initially caught off guard, however, European security quickly caught up, ramping up surveillance and cybernetic infiltration abilities. In European nations, the legalities of counterresistance technologies and tactics would be debated and fought over in the public realm. Unlike a decade later, when across the region antiterrorist laws were widely enacted and enforced against even peaceful protests, European activists during the 2000s for the most part remained relatively protected by civil rights laws. Unfortunately, the advances of counterresistance technologies and strategies developed in Europe at this time would be adopted and employed by more authoritarian countries in the next decade, used in many nondemocratic states to infiltrate activist groups, identify and surveil opposition activists, and allow for preemptive arrests. But for a while at least, European authorities were bound by legal restraints. By the end of the subsequent decade, as the West descended into the geopolitical chaos already engulfing the rest of the world, when paranoia and xenophobia reached feverish pitch, even the most democratic of nations would fall prey to fearmongering politicians. Technologies of surveillance and social control would in short order be employed increasingly by governments against their own citizens. Such blows to civil rights would be compounded by the enactment of vague antiterrorism laws imposing harsh sentences, under which even those protesting peacefully for social justice could be arrested and charged. But in 2000, such things were as yet beyond the visible horizon.

One of the issues facing European nations at the turn of the new millennium had to do with linking, systematizing, and regulating universities across the region. In Austria, the 2000s was a decade in which tens of thousands of students marched in protest of changes to the educational system that brought it into alignment with the standards and practices of the European Union. This adoption of EU educational reforms was called the Bologna Process. For Austria, this largely meant shortening time-to-degree limits, without corresponding changes to the required curriculum. Students were also protesting the charging of tuition, which began in 2001. Angry youth held sit-ins and marched by the thousands in Vienna and other cities, with some protests raising fifty thousand participants. They circulated petitions and decried the fact that they had to shoulder the economic troubles caused by what they perceived as irresponsible government policy. They were joined in solidarity by worker unions and other citizens. Inspired by similar protests in Germany that were effective in blocking reforms, the Austrian students nevertheless were unable to effect meaningful changes with their protests. They did, however, forge large networks and alliances.

Other significant protests in Austria in which students participated included thousands marching in Vienna, in the early 2000s, against the inclusion of the far right in the nation's coalition government and a series of rallies against US president Bush in Vienna in 2006, marches that drew thousands. Many Americans—used to Bush's "War on Terror rhetoric prevalent in US media—were surprised to see international media coverage of students carrying banners reading things like, "Bush = World's #1 Terrorist" or "Against War and Capitalism."[20] In 2007, five thousand marched in Vienna against their own government's anti-immigration policies, which were in the news for splitting families apart and deporting individual family members (a practice that would be repeated and protested elsewhere in the West in the next decade). The driver for the largest Austrian rallies was a video shown in the media of a fifteen-year-old girl, alone and in hiding somewhere in Austria, who was threatening suicide after her father and sisters (Kosovar Albanians) had been deported.[21] Although occurring at a different time and concerning a different group of displaced immigrants, the demonstrations presaged the immigration policy protests that would rock much of Europe a decade later.

The anti–Bologna Process movement was active across Europe, not just in central European nations. It was especially prominent in the newer EU nations. In Croatia, students in Zagreb and other cities protested the regional implementation of the Bologna Process as their country struggled to change higher education as part of its transition toward European values and systems. Throughout the entire decade, Croatia underwent a long process of entering the European Union, which it officially did in 2013. The integration of EU higher-education standards did not go smoothly, nor were they consistently applied, and many students resisted the neoliberalism and capitalism that came with the transition. Corruption was also a problem in higher education, making international news when, in 2008, police raids on a number of university professors' offices resulted in "bribery for grades" corruption charges. In 2009, faced with tuition increases as social-program budgets were cut due to a struggling economy, University of Zagreb students occupied their university, taking over the Faculty of Humanities and Social Sciences buildings for over a month; hosting their own classes, workshops, and lectures; and showing films critical of neoliberalism and capitalism. The occupations spread to other universities throughout the country and resulted in the government guaranteeing free tuition for full-time undergraduates and masters students in good standing.

European youth protested against things other than educational reform, war, or politics too. Protests held by youth and students against municipal authority were occurring in Denmark, both on and off campuses, in demonstrations that would captivate youth across Europe. Riots broke out in the city of Copenhagen after the city moved to evict squatting youth from the internationally famous Ungdomshuset (Youth House), a brick building in a working-class neighborhood where city officials had given punkers and counter-culture youth permission to live since the 1980s. It had become a center for creative but decidedly leftist activities—not only for Danes but for many in the entire region. Covered in graffiti and art, Ungdomshuset was known as the countercultural hub of the city. In 2001, a Christian organization bought the building and began an eviction process, which police tried to enforce in 2007, resulting in nights of riots and battles with the occupants, millions of dollars of damage to surrounding businesses and property, scores of injuries, and about 650 arrests. Squatting is a tradition in Denmark, and the city had offered a local empty school to Ungdomshuset residents in exchange to avoid the coming confrontation, but the youth argued the building itself was a historic symbol to Danish youth and culture and flatly refused.

Prior to the eviction deadline, an international call was put out through internet networks and social media to rally support for the Ungdomshuset eviction resistance. Supporters of the resistance were bolstered by activists protesting neoliberalism, capitalism, and the conservative right, and young people poured into the city from all over Europe. When it broke out, the fighting between activists and police was intense, though with the size of the force Copenhagen threw at the resistance, the activists' suppression was foreordained. Following the eviction and the eventual suppression of the rioters, the continued arrests of activists, and the deportation of any foreign youth arrested, the city demolished the building. This ended the fight for the building, but students and activists in Denmark remained more committed than ever to fight for counterculture and for civil liberties.

More culturally mainstream protests were occurring in Copenhagen as well. In 2006, Danish masonry students made headlines by bricking in the entrance to the Ministry of Education in order to teach education minister Bertel Haarder how difficult it was for people to enter the labor market in Denmark. The protest came on the heels of other demonstrations held by students with vocational training who were having trouble finding jobs and were asking the government for help. On another front at this time, student free-speech activists would enter the fray, stirred up by the Middle Eastern protests against the publication of cartoons in a Danish newspaper that were considered insulting to the Prophet Muhammad. Denmark would see similar brouhahas flare every couple of years over depictions of Muhammad in Danish media, and demonstrators on both sides of the issue would repeatedly face off, with Muslim students protesting against the depictions and liberal students holding demonstrations in support of freedom of speech. In 2009, Copenhagen would also see tens of thousands of marchers peacefully protesting for climate-change awareness and against rampant neoliberalism.

In Finland, students and youth activists protested a range of issues in the first decade of the millennium, holding massive anti–

United States rallies against the wars in Iraq and Afghanistan and protesting against cuts to education funding, the corporatization of Finnish universities, and neoliberalism generally. A lot of Finnish activist students were globally engaged, demonstrating against international corporate greed, a rise in nationalism in the West, and the political shift to the right in neighboring European nations.

Significantly, Finnish activists began calling for climate-change action, and they did so early. As average temperatures across the globe continued to rise during the decade, the reality of the situation was being witnessed firsthand in the country, fueling a growing movement to raise climate awareness, to stop environmental destruction, and to curb CO_2 emissions. These protests, which included the famous "melting snowmen" demonstrations, were important initial actions in the global battles between climate-change environmentalists and corporate polluters. Finnish activists called out their own government and politicians who were helping environmentally destructive industries. Through internationally covered demonstrations and the pressure they brought to bear on their government, which slowly began to react to the evidence, the Finnish climate activists spread their message throughout the region. Working in tandem with activists in neighboring northern European countries, they pressured all EU governments to adopt responsible energy and industry policies.

The 2000s were a transition decade for much of the European Union in terms of activism, and although activism surged in some areas, in other areas it lagged. Not everyone was as fired up as Finnish climate activists. A certain level of prosperity for many EU nations in the early part of the decade enabled a large portion of the students in more insular nations to remain unengaged or more generally concerned with domestic issues. France was, for a time, one of those nations. The nation has always had a healthy student-activist scene, and half a century after the '68 student revolts there remains tremendous cultural cachet in being a student activist in France. But it took a significant shock in the 2000s before many students realized that like it or not, they were connected to political and social changes that had been going on in the country for some time. That shock came when the ultraright populist and National Front (FN) leader, Jean-Marie Le Pen (father of future presidential candidate Marine Le Pen), stunned the country and Europe by qualifying for a 2002 runoff election against conservative incumbent Jacques Chirac, leader of the Gaullist, center-right Rally for the Republic (RPR) party. The center-left candidate came in third.

Le Pen managed to capitalize on rising social fears, and a lot of France's trendy young bourgeois bohemians who voted far left, or not at all, had taken for granted an expected runoff between the left and the right candidates. The success of Le Pen's populist, often racist and xenophobic campaign took everyone by surprise, but the leftists rallied in vast numbers to stop him, even though many actively disliked his rival, Chirac.[22] On May Day, one million people protested across the nation, waving French flags and carrying placards that read things like, "Stop Fascism!" and "Vote Crook, Not Nazi!" Meanwhile, at a Le Pen rally in Paris, ten thousand supporters gathered to cheer their candidate. They were guarded by paramilitary security who were ominously dressed all in black. But the Le Pen rally was soon dwarfed by four hundred thousand anti–Le Pen protestors marching in the capital and the more than six hundred thousand marching against the extremist in other cities throughout the nation.[23] Chirac won the election handily and, importantly for France's youth—including the many who were not Chirac supporters—they were taught a lesson in the need both for vigilance against the rise of fascism and for civic engagement. A spirit of youth activism was renewed in the country.

Many of those young people connected through nascent social media and activist networks, and they continued those connections after the election was settled. They subsequently stepped up efforts against Chirac's proposed policies, which included changes to pension plans, privatization of social services, and education reforms. They also joined protests against the privileging of corporations, efforts at deregulation, and genetically modified crops.

And like their leftist student activist forebears, the new generation of French youth activists forged alliances with labor. In 2003, public-service unions fearing proposed changes to pensions called for a general strike, bringing transportation across the country to a grinding halt. French student organizations threw their support behind the workers, as did many other unions and citizens, and more than a million people joined in demonstrations across the nation. Three months later, two hundred thousand gathered in the south of France at Larzac to organize, educate, strategize, and agitate against the right-wing government, though Chirac's government dismissed them all as marginal leftists, political opponents, students, and disaffected youth. Interpreting his electoral win as a mandate rather than an antifascist vote, Chirac pushed conservative legislation, including a ban on the hijab in schools, packaged as part of an "anti–religious symbol," prosecularism bill. (The ban also included such items as the Jewish *kippah* and large crosses.) These actions fueled more student demonstrations against him.

In 2006, the government forced through labor legislation that included a provision allowing any worker to be fired without reason in the first two years of employment at any position (a *contrat de première embauche*, or CPE for short). This outraged students who would be entering the workforce, and it infuriated trade unions, the leaders of whom argued companies would start issuing contracts shorter than two years. Vulnerable short-term employees, many of whom were students, protested. Women's-rights groups argued the new labor rules would enable and promote sexual harassment. The backlash against the reforms was immediate, and nationally it was estimated by the end of two months of demonstrations that between 1.6 and 3 million people had demonstrated against them, with up to 800,000 marching in massive protests in Paris alone.[24]

Angry students occupied universities, erecting barricades around them. Students manning barricades recalled the '68 uprisings, gave interviews to excited news media, and garnered a great deal of attention. The demonstrators also realized that in addition to employing these traditional, physical tactics, they had a lot of new ones available to them. They used social media, blogs, and websites to promote their issues. And in what would become an important resistance tactic globally, they began using social media and cell phones to move student defenders around Paris, shifting reinforcements when needed to face off against police, matching security movements with their own. After one such call went out, riot police trying to dislodge students manning steel barricades they'd erected around the Sorbonne were physically repelled, overwhelmed by arriving reinforcements. The police were driven back and retreated until their own heavily armed reinforcements could arrive.

Labor unions called for general strikes, suspending transportation and public services across the nation. Chirac's administration was frightened by the specter of students and labor unions uniting in massive protests that harkened back to the '68 protests that drove De Gaulle from Paris. And indeed, on the tail end of some of the marches violence began to erupt, as small groups of extremist protestors and opportunistic anarchists threw cobblestones through store windows or Molotov cocktails at buildings, vehicles, and police. The rhetoric and violence escalated as images of police attacking protestors were captured on video and circulated through social media. News media continuously played images of police brutality. On the other side, extremist youth wearing hoodies and bandanas over their faces began to run along the margins of the larger demonstrations wreaking havoc and roamed the streets at night, attacking police.[25] Their fervor was initially applauded by many of the marchers, but soon anarchists and criminal opportunists began causing unwanted mayhem, attacking and robbing marchers as well, smashing storefronts and looting stores. These developments were then used by the government to discredit the demonstrations and justify harsher police suppression.

The demonstrations in Paris and other cities were quickly getting out of hand. Police regularly began hitting demonstrations with tear gas, rubber-coated bullets, and baton charges, and the Left Bank was soon filled with security troops, its narrow streets physically blocked by police buses jammed across the narrow avenues to prevent mob movement. Over several weeks, riots continued to

break out, and police-guarded civil workers began pulling up cobblestones at popular demonstration sites so they couldn't be used by
the protestors as missiles.

Students and activists nevertheless continued to engage in
pitched battles across Paris with police who used everything from
tear gas to water cannons to dislodge them from squares and parks.
On the technology front, while police were using radios and traditional communication networks, students were using social media.
Chirac took to the media as well, publicly addressing the nation and
suggesting that the trial period for new employees be lessened to
one year from two. His concession had no effect on the demonstrations, which were by then too large to suppress, and the government
was forced to strike the CPE provision from the bill entirely.

In 2007, Nicolas Sarkozy won the presidential election. He inherited and faced continuing problems with leftist students, who held
strikes at a third of France's universities against reforms to education, especially ones that facilitated aggressive corporatization. He
was also opposed by labor unions, which successfully held strikes
against proposed pension reforms. Riots in suburbs increased,
tied both to general issues such as growing economic desperation
among workers and students and to antipolice sentiment as images
of police brutality circulated on social media. When a police vehicle
in one suburb, for example, ran over two youths on a scooter, a local
protest-turned-riot ensued in which angry youth shot at arriving
police with guns and a homemade bazooka.[26] In the last few years
of the decade, students would continue to strike against Sarközy's
government, educational reforms, the struggling economy, and
right-wing, probusiness policies. Following the 2008 recession and
the loss of support from a populace growing tired of the riots, the
numbers and the frequency of the protests would slowly die down
and then, as the decade drew to a close, fizzle out altogether.

Activism in Germany began the millennium at high levels and
remained there throughout the decade. There was in Germany
in 2000 a foreshadowing of the nationalist shifts to the right that
would occur in several European nations over the next twenty

years. Members of the extreme far-right National Democratic Party of Germany (NPD) and unaffiliated neo-Nazis were emboldened enough by increasingly extreme views voiced in popular right-wing media to apply for and receive a permit to demonstrate against a planned Holocaust memorial in Berlin. Realizing its folly too late, the city administration subsequently tried to ban the demonstration, but a court ruled in favor of free speech over social taboo and allowed the protest to proceed. Shouting neo-Nazi slogans and singing traditional Nazi songs, the group marched through Brandenburg Gate, mimicking the iconic films of Hitler's Third Reich parades from the thirties. Images of neo-Nazis proudly stomping through the icon caused an international uproar and a PR nightmare for the government, which was afterwards caught in a free-speech-versus-fascist-government-overreach debate for years to come.

Students launched an antifascist movement and held antifascist demonstrations. Energized by the public response, the NDP extremists applied for a permit for a second far-right march at the end of the year. They were denied by the city, but challenged the refusal in court and saw it overturned. The court ruled the protest should be allowed but upheld a ban on the use of drums, SS uniforms, and Nazi flags during the march. The court stipulated the demonstrators could march to Brandenburg Gate but not pass through it. Both of these demonstrations (which drew huge numbers of skinheads, like flies to carrion) were heavily escorted by police, who struggled to keep the demonstrators separate from students and activists who launched giant antifascist counterdemonstrations. Violence nevertheless broke out whenever the opposing forces brushed up against one another.

In the next decade, Germany would at all levels of government repeatedly and unsuccessfully attempt to ban the NPD and similar groups, which quickly realized they could shield themselves against suppression and promote agendas of racism and xenophobia by using free-speech laws. The legal tactic of using free-speech laws to give cover for hate developed in Germany by far-right extremists would be employed in the United States in the next decade, as fascism increased there as well. To counter the far-right organizations, students used their own mastery of social media and cybernetworks to organize and raise counterdemonstrations whenever the far right held these types of rallies, and police troops—not particularly welcomed by either group—struggled to keep the opposing sides from erupting into violence.

It turns out it is not that difficult to find large numbers of people willing to protest neo-Nazis singing and marching publicly, and although it kept many of Germany's students busy during the 2000s, it was but one of many concerns occupying the attention of activists. In the country that gave rise to the *Burshenchaften*, students were well organized and tackling myriad issues in this period, organizing and launching demonstrations on a whole host of issues. In 2001, German students and activists protesting the nation's use of nuclear energy tried to stop trains carrying spent nuclear material as they made a 350-mile journey across the country from power plants to so-called temporary safe storage in a defunct salt mine in Gorleben. Following the September 11 terrorist attacks in the United States, security was a real issue for German citizens, who monitored the trains' progress closely through the media. The slow journey of these transports under intense media scrutiny was a PR boon for antinuclear activists, who planned measures to stop them all along their path.

The train and the depots along the way were heavily guarded by thousands of security troops, but activists chained themselves to tracks between the stops, set up flash barricades, and—after hiding in branches while waiting until advance guards had passed below—rappelled down onto tracks from overhanging trees to force the trains to stop. One Hamburg law student and activist summed up the issue of security nicely for journalists, saying "Gorleben is about as safe as a potato shed."[27] The students were often publicly condemned for their antics, but their efforts revealed just how vulnerable the trains were and drew attention to the dangers of nuclear refinement. Similar protests against the transportation of spent nuclear fuel would be staged in 2008 and 2009, as the movement against nuclear power morphed into a movement for safe and renewable energy. These demonstrations would seem prescient after Japan's Fukushima power plant accident in 2011, and following the accident, the protests in Germany would again grow in size and intensity.

Of course, US imperialism in the Middle East also fueled demonstrations by students in Germany in the 2000s. Approximately fifty thousand students, for example, protested the opening of the US-led war in Iraq by marching from Berlin's Alexanderplatz to the front of the US embassy, and then on through Brandenburg Gate. Anti–Iraq War sentiment was widespread in Germany, with unions, student organizations, churches, and various activist groups swelling protests, the largest of which in Berlin alone drew four hundred thousand protestors.

The most consistently staged student demonstrations during the decade, though, had to do with education reforms. Like many EU nations, Germany struggled to implement changes to bring the nation's universities into alignment with the Bologna Process, a process that called for drastic changes to Germany's institutions. As in Austria, programs that had taken students five to six years to complete would have to be compressed into a much shorter span. The changes were taking place while Germany struggled economically, so while more was demanded of students academically, concurrent budget cuts to education pared down course offerings, provided fewer teachers for courses, and gutted student financial support. Chancellor Gerhard Schröder's government began introducing the idea of perhaps charging tuition fees. Although the proposed costs were low compared to, say, what people in the United States paid, charging tuition at all was against the tradition and expectation of free education in Germany. While the government allowed some German states to start charging tuition in 2005, student reaction was intense. They repeatedly demonstrated and called strikes, engaging in a battle over the issue with state and federal governments that would be waged for years.

Students in Germany protested a whole array of reforms

throughout the decade, not the least of which were the education reforms and tuition proposals, fielding increasingly large numbers against them from 2006 to 2008 and culminating in demonstrations in 2009 in which more than one hundred thousand students participated. One march in Hamburg alone brought ten thousand students onto the streets. Students connected through social media, circulated petitions, staged sit-ins, and held marches in which they waved antigovernment, anti–European Union, and antireform signs and decried the charging of tuition, claiming free education in Germany was an inherent right of all citizens. The government backed off some of the reforms in 2009, such as the increased workload on students that the time-to-degree compressions precipitated, but admission numbers were by then regulated, and state governments began experiments in charging modest tuition at select schools. The reform issues and the demonstrations against them continued into the next decade, with the government finally scrapping the attempt to charge tuition in 2014 due to massive student resistance.

There were other changes afoot on the activism scene in Germany as well, changes that would spread across the globe, in addition to tactical changes due to social-media technology. In 2007, Germany hosted the thirty-third annual G8 summit at the Grand Hotel Heiligendamm, the country's oldest seaside resort on the Baltic, which was blockaded by protestors who gathered outside its gates. Attending heads of state had to be helicoptered in. In the nearby town of Rostock, tens of thousands of protestors showed up, including some two thousand who were dressed entirely in black—a soon-to-be international anarchist presence at many large rallies.

The protestors wore what would become signature black hoodie uniforms, with their faces covered, and homemade riot gear. They had precursors in West Germany in the black bloc protests of the 1980s (and even earlier), and they had appeared elsewhere in the late eighties and nineties, such as in San Francisco and Seattle, but their resurgence and strong showing at the G8 would bring them international attention and imitators around the world. Black-clad demonstrators smashed windows, set cars on fire, and provoked police, inciting riots during the G8 protests. They waved anarchy flags, destroyed property, and fought pitched battles with security. In the coming decade, black blocs would appear to play provocateur at all kinds of large demonstrations, from protests in Greece in 2011 to the Women's March on Washington in 2017 to the Hong Kong protests of 2019. Those donning the black hoodie and mask subscribed to a wide range of philosophies, organizations, and methods. They were anarchists, anticapitalists, antifascists, and more, united, though, by their opposition to authority.

German student activism levels were high during the decade, but other countries were witnessing student activism as well. Although meant to create uniformity across the educational systems in the European Union, the Bologna Process was perhaps more successful at unifying students in opposition against it. In some places the demonstrations it sparked were particularly intense. In Greece, for example, education reforms that tightened restrictions on university admissions in an already chronically underfunded education system ignited protests from students that turned particularly violent, as extremists on the fringes of the marches and demonstrations vandalized property and provoked fights with police.

In 1999, thousands of students across Greece marched against educational reforms and against the European Union generally. Anarchists in several of these demonstrations threw petrol bombs at police and, in one instance that was caught on video, set an officer on fire in Syntagma Square in Athens. Although such violence was publicly condemned in the media, student demonstrations continued as economic prospects for young people remained grim. But these extreme incidents did not turn public opinion against the students, for incidents of police brutality during demonstrations were common and made the news regularly. Besides, student activists held a respected place in much of Greek society, especially due to their role in the overthrow of the military dictatorship in 1973. Greek universities tend to be political institutions, so the public expected students to be up in arms over even moderate government reforms. At the time—this was before the cybersecurity, cyberinfiltration, and antiterrorism laws to come—there was a sense of security for activist students because there was a constitutional ban on police stepping foot on campuses. In 2007, the underfunded education system was still struggling to implement reforms, and the job outlook was worse than ever for university graduates, who took to calling themselves the "700-euro generation," referring to the monthly amount they expected to earn upon graduation.

In December 2008, two Greek police officers shot and killed a fifteen-year-old student, Alexandros Grigoropoulos, in the Athens neighborhoood of Exarchia, setting off three weeks of riots that would spread across seventy cities in Greece. Students turned their frustration with the government into an anti–police brutality and antigovernment movement. They used their campuses as sanctuaries both for peaceful protestors and as bases from which anarchists, who had begun more and more to don the black uniform, could operate. At the National Technical University of Athens (also known as Athens Polytechnic), for example, black-clad students began openly stockpiling Molotov cocktails just within the boundaries of the university.

Already under international pressure politically and financially, the government publicly urged restraint on the local police, fearing another incident would ignite violent, large-scale unrest. But this emboldened anarchists, who marched in the thousands in Athens and Thessaloniki, battling police with petrol bombs and stones. During the student protests, which were compounded by unions and laborers deciding to hold strikes over the country's economic woes, security troops exhausted the nation's entire stockpile of tear-gas grenades, some five thousand canisters, forcing the government to ask foreign allies for more.

In cities, the state of things devolved. Opportunist youthful arsonists began firebombing European businesses and schools, international banks, and a police academy. Teachers held strikes, and while most of the demonstrations remained peaceful, there were also pitched battles between police and anarchists, images of which spread daily across the internet and through social media. Using flash-mob text-stringing tactics and websites like indymedia.com to call young people to demonstration locations or move so-called resistance fighters around the city as needed, students and anarchists were conducting their own independent guerrilla wars in the streets of Greece's cities. Airlines cancelled flights coming into the nation. Tourists avoided the country and, fearing the nation was on the brink of collapse, international companies pulled investments. The economy plummeted.

In many places, anarchists freely roamed urban streets at night, setting fires and battling police. They fought groups of shopkeepers who banded together and started fighting back against the rioters. Provoked by black-bloc participants at student demonstrations, police would charge and begin beating people indiscriminately—many of them not wearing black. The subsequent violence was then recorded and disseminated through social media. In dozens of countries around the world, students held demonstrations and marches against police brutality in solidarity with the Greek students.

The massive annual Christmas tree in Syntagma Square was set on fire while demonstrators ringed it and sang carols. Exhausted by the social disruption, the financial cost, and the increasingly open violence on the part of the anarchists, public favor eventually turned, and the majority of Greeks wearied of the riots, though it took weeks for the protests to finally burn out. Police and military security, fearful that anarchists would connect with terrorist organizations—or that terrorist groups would take advantage of the unrest to gain a foothold in the country—clamped down on the protestors, hunting them down and arresting them on a battery of charges.

Greece gained international attention for the intensity of its riots and for the violence of the clashes with police, but in terms of sustained and widespread student protest, other EU countries surpassed it. Since the turn of the millennium, Ireland has been one of the busier places for youth activism in Europe. In 2000, students protested on campuses for more government support after EU education reports revealed the country was at the bottom of EU nations in supplying individual education grants. But government resources available to the educational system were the source of much discontent at every level. In 2001, the Association of Secondary Teachers, Ireland (ASTI) began a series of strikes, asking for up to a 30 percent increase in pay for then-unpaid time spent supervising students. The strikes closed schools across Ireland, angering working parents and eventually students, who, with time on their hands and access to social media, launched massive counterstrikes of their own, gathering in the tens of thousands outside Dáil Éireann (Ireland's lower parliament house) and in parks in major urban areas. The protests were nonviolent, but a lot of eggs were thrown at government buildings. The strikes put pressure on the government and ASTI to negotiate, which they did, though chronically underfunded unionized teachers would continue to strike throughout the decade.

In 2002 and 2003, university students in Dublin, Limerick, and Galway held strikes and sit-ins over increased registration fees and the lack of medical benefits. They marched for more support grants and affordable accommodations. As the decade progressed, the costs associated with attending colleges and universities continued to increase at the same time that government funds for education were axed. Protests against Ireland's prime minister were common.

There were anti–Iraq War protests and anti-Bush protests, along with protests against neoliberalism and Western imperialism in the Middle East. There were a number of demonstrations and actions particular to Ireland. In 2005, People for the Ethical Treatment of Animals and anti–animal cruelty activists began anti-KFC campaigns across the nation after a PETA investigative video surfaced of KFC employees beating and stomping live pullets in one of its plants. Outside KFCs and secondary schools in Dublin, activists handed out "bloody KFC buckets" stuffed with "dead" rubber chickens and carried signs scorning the company. News media covered the demonstrations and played scenes of the protestors alongside clips from the plant video. KFC responded with press releases about the spread of corporate terrorism by promotors of vegetarianism and a media blitz of pro-KFC commercials. The demonstrations and the company's bizarre response proved a PR nightmare for the restaurant chain.

Spectacles aside, Irish university students continued during the decade to protest against the economic burdens they faced. In 2007, the Union of Students in Ireland (USI) began a "Sleep Outside in the Cold" campaign to highlight the lack of accommodations and affordable housing for students, inviting politicians to pitch a tent and join Dublin students sleeping in parks. The education budget crises continued, though, with the education department cutting support for programs for students with autism, a move greeted outside the Dáil with demonstrations and the release of thousands of black balloons—one for each student who would be affected. Primary and secondary teachers and classroom assistants continued demonstrations and repeatedly called strikes throughout the year, and university students continued to demonstrate against ever-increasing fees.

Officials refused to listen to the protests, though, and in 2008, registration fees for universities were almost doubled, bringing out fresh rounds of protests. Ten thousand students marched in Dublin, three thousand marched in Sligo, and more participated in protests around the country. In Cork in 2009, the leader of a massive anti–fee increase protest rang the personal phone of Minister for Education Batt O'Keeffe from center stage to discuss the matter, encouraging those in attendance to do the same, overwhelming the minister's phone account. In 2009, fifteen thousand students marched against registration fees, beating drums outside the Dáil and putting the government on notice that the anti–fee hike campaign had already registered tens of thousands of voters ahead of upcoming elections and would register more.

For all the agitation and anger voiced by students, violence at their protests was relatively rare and was condemned by both sides when it occurred. At one "Free Education for Everyone" protest in Galway in 2009, for example, a police officer was investigated after it was reported to authorities he had been too rough in his handling of a student demonstrator. In the decade to follow, however, as black-clad provocateurs increasingly appeared at protests across the European Union, violence would become more common, as mass demonstrations turned into unmanageable riots, and police would respond with increasing force.

In contrast to, say, Ireland's steady, high levels of largely nonviolent activism, Italy saw tremendous spikes and dips in terms of activism, with many demonstrations turning violent. In 2001, antiglobalization and anti-G8 demonstrations in Genoa resulted in full-scale riots that local police were simply unable to quell once they began beating students, protestors, and anarchists, many of whom had travelled internationally to attend the demonstrations. Video of police throwing students down dormitory stairwells, kicking and punching protestors already on the ground, and shooting tear gas and live ammunition into crowds spread through social media and international news agencies.[28] International condemnation by European nations such as Germany and France, and by international human rights groups and multinational student organizations, of the excessive police violence followed. This did not affect the status of those arrested by police, however, including the foreign students, who were prosecuted or deported. Media tycoon and prime minister Silvio Berlusconi supported the police actions and condemned the demonstrators and anarchists, blaming outsiders for fanning the flames of unrest.

The travel destination for many vacationers throughout Europe, Italy is also a destination for international activists. In 2002, more than four hundred thousand activists and students from all over the world descended on Florence for a week of protests, workshops, and meetings regarding a range of concerns. There were antiglobalists, anticapitalists, anti-GMO demonstrators, and anti–Iraq War protestors. Florentine security adopted a different tactic than the police did in Genoa; the demonstrations and gatherings were monitored but not attacked by police troops, and the protests remained largely peaceful, though there was graffiti vandalism throughout the city. But knowing the activists were coming, the city spent weeks preparing for the demonstrations, walling off historical monuments with scaffolding, covering building windows with plywood (which protestors with spray paint found made particularly good canvasses for demonstration slogans), and draping sculpture in plastic. In the years that followed, more anti–Iraq War demonstrations and antiglobalism demonstrations would occur, though, keeping pace with the rise of extremism and Berlusconi's authoritarianism, they would not remain so peaceful.[29]

In 2008, Italy would see demonstrations against globalism and the global recession, but university students were protesting domestic issues as well. At Sapienza University of Rome, secular and science students held demonstrations against a planned university speech by Pope Benedict XVI, who had once given a speech defending the Catholic Church's persecution of Galileo. The demonstrations were large enough that the Vatican called off the event, a move that activists claimed as a victory for the separation of church and state. But 2008 was a disastrous year for education in Italy, as the government planned a ten-billion-dollar cut to the federal budget for education and the liquidation of close to ninety thousand teaching positions. Part of the state's answer to its own financial mess was to raid the education budget and pass the problem on to its youth. Students and teachers responded with massive demonstrations, fielding tens of thousands of marchers in urban areas throughout the country. The protests went on for months and included marches, sit-ins, and open-air teach-ins in public parks and squares. The government struggled over the next two years to legislate and implement education austerity reforms as the economy worsened, finally passing reforms with the close of the decade. But students and teachers continued to demonstrate and call strikes.

Spain mirrored Italy's range of international demonstrations, with anti–Iraq War protests, anticapitalism protests, and antineoliberalism demonstrations in the early 2000s. And it also mirrored the violence that often attended them. Students protested a range of domestic issues as well, including national educational reform efforts to tighten entrance exams into universities. And like Italy, Spain's government stumbled in handling its response to demonstrations, with police overreacting to demonstrators in the presence of cameras.

In 2003, antiglobalization protests were suppressed on the touristy Las Ramblas, in Barcelona, and the excessive violence on the part of police sparked riots and running street battles as demonstrators fought back against them with bottles and bricks. Antiglobalist students joined antiwar activists in large marches in Madrid, Barcelona, and other cities that drew tens of thousands of protestors. Thousands gathered outside the gates to the joint US-Spain Naval Station (NAVSTA) in Rota, shouting anti–United States and anti-imperialist slogans, condemning Spain's support of US military operations in the Middle East. (The base was a primary US jumping-off point for Middle East operations.) Police were in these cases kept restrained to avoid escalating unrest, because students had massive popular support. The US war in Iraq was vastly unpopular among the majority of Spain's citizens, even though Prime Minister José Maria Aznar was an outspoken supporter of US president Bush's invasion.

After a 2004 terrorist train bombing in Madrid killed 191 and injured more than 1,000 people, millions marched in the streets of Madrid to demonstrate in nationally organized commemoration marches for victims, in spontaneous antiterrorism demonstrations, and in anti-Aznar protests by those blaming the prime minister for opening up Spain to attacks by Al-Qaeda because of the country's close alliance with the United States. Many more marched in protests held across the nation, with total estimates exceeding ten million participants. In the media, the demonstrators repeatedly attacked government policies as the reason for the deaths.

With an election looming in just three days, the government called for three days of mourning and in its own media campaign blamed the bombings on the Euskadi Ta Askatasuna (ETA), a separatist Basque liberation organization it asserted had encouraged street fighting, trying to counter the argument that ruling-party policies supporting an unpopular war had brought international violence to Spain.[30] Opposition candidate and member of the Spanish Socialist

Workers' Party (which had allied itself with the students) José Luis Rodríguez Zapatero won the election and became prime minister, afterwards fulfilling a campaign promise to withdraw Spanish troops from Iraq.[31] A group of Islamic ideologues were later convicted of the bombings, with three of them (a Spaniard and two Moroccans) sentenced to thousands of years in prison.

The new socialist administration of Spain, however, would in 2005 face student protestors sponsored by conservative organizations, after it legalized same-sex marriage and tried to implement educational reforms limiting the role of religion in schools. The large activist movements in the country that had shepherded in a change of government subsequently splintered apart, though demonstrations continued to proliferate on a smaller scale. In 2009, the annual Día de la Hispanidad, the national day of Spain, which is celebrated across the nation with fireworks and military parades, saw a demonstration of thousands of students and other antiglobalization and anti-imperialism activists at the Christopher Columbus memorial in Barcelona, where protestors climbed the tower and draped banners on it with antineoimperialism slogans. Black-clad anarchists roamed the fringes. The statue would continue to be the site of large annual demonstrations, though none approached the size of those following the train bombings. A decade later, as right-wing extremism rose in Spain and other EU countries, the Barcelona site would become a common site for far-right demonstrations, including anti-immigration protests sponsored by the right-wing political party Vox.

Although Sweden had impressive student activism levels, unlike many of the other EU nations, its government responses to protests were typically tolerant, even discreet, as long as protests remained nonviolent. From the beginning of the decade's EU educational reform efforts, Sweden saw protests against the Bologna Process. Restructuring efforts were continually demonstrated against, with notably large protests occurring in 2006, when Swedish students held demonstrations against their government's cutting of support for doctoral students.

But even Sweden fell prey to the rising violence of demonstrations in the region. When Sweden hosted an EU summit in Gothenburg, the meeting drew antiglobalization, anticorporation, proenvironment protests and marches, which the government expected and prepared for. Freedom of expression, government transparency, liberalism, and tolerance—all have long been part of the country's international image, and that has traditionally extended to its handling of student demonstrations. The 2001 EU summit protests were attended by twenty thousand, including a large contingent of anarchists, and the demonstrations unexpectedly erupted into violence. A faction of the marchers began smashing windows, burning café furniture, and throwing rocks and bottles at police, some of whom were dragged from their horses and beaten. The government and many of the Swedish organizers blamed the violence on foreigners who travelled for the event from other EU nations and on anarchists, and their assertion seemed to be borne out in that for most of the rest of the decade, subsequent demonstrations would remain peaceful. That relative peace, however, would not last.

In 2008, following the youth riots in Greece and France, riots would also occur in Sweden. Disaffected second-generation immigrant youth, joined by leftist students, battled police in the port city of Malmö during protests against the closing of an Islamic cultural center. That year and the next, other demonstrations over immigrant- and ethnicity-related issues turned violent. As the decade drew to a close, more and more violence at protests would occur as demonstrations became increasingly unruly and police began using more force in suppressing them. Particularly violent riots would break out in 2010 and repeatedly from then on, as political battles over Sweden's immigration policies began driving national politics.

The increasing violence at demonstrations and the changing nature of public activism that occurred over the decade in Sweden revealed a number of forces at work. Like other EU nations, Sweden would see a polarization and political divide between the left and the right. Facilitated by the porousness of EU borders, masses of humans would continue to migrate northward, escaping conflicts in the Middle East. In addition to putting economic pressure on host nations, the increasing numbers of immigrants heightened racism and xenophobia in the European Union. The changes in the Swedish protests also revealed how provocative responses to police presence at protests caught on as social media homogenized representations of authority and gave attention to black-bloc actions. Just as the economies, politics, and governments of the EU nations became increasingly entangled, so too did some of the organizations and tactics used against EU governments.

In the United Kingdom, students were active in the first decade of the millennium, and many of their efforts were focused on domestic issues, such as proposed education reforms in 1999 that would raise the cost of higher education in Scotland. As part of the protests, students from seventeen institutions marched from Glasgow to Scotland's parliament in Edinburgh to attract media attention and galvanize support. Similar to other members of the European Union, students in the United Kingdom paid nominal fees to attend university, and like students in neighboring countries that were instituting educational reforms to raise tuition and privatize education, they were unhappy with the prospect of shouldering the bill for what they generally considered a citizen's right to affordable education. Although Bologna Process reforms forced different changes for the various regions of the United Kingdom, the changes were universally disliked. From Glasgow to London, separate student groups argued that not only would raising fees make attending university that much harder for most people, tuition hikes would force the poorest out of the educational system entirely and thus cement their futures as members of the underprivileged classes. The Scottish students were successful in getting plans to increase tuition in Scotland scrapped, but students in England were not successful and faced continuing tuition increases.

In 2000, inspired by the success of the antireform campaign in Scotland, twelve thousand English students from various schools and organizations, such as the National Union of Students (NUS) and Save Free Education, peacefully marched in London's West End from the University of London on Malet Street to Kensington Gardens while a breakaway group occupied Whitehall. Further plans to raise tuition by a staggering amount brought twenty thousand protestors to the streets of London in 2002. NUS led the largest student march London had seen in decades, with angry students chanting antireform slogans and carrying unflattering effigies of Prime Minister Tony Blair. They would be joined by Scottish students who feared that if England successfully raised fees, Scotland would soon follow suit. The massive protests were for the most part peaceful, though there was a scuffle with police when a group of students held a sit-down protest in the middle of Waterloo Bridge. NUS would organize a number of anti–educational reform marches and demonstrations against raising tuition over the next decade, with a 2005 march in London surpassing the 2002 protest in size.

But like in neighboring EU nations, many of the student protests in the United Kingdom were over international issues as well. In 1999, a fourteen-year-old girl, Nejla Kanteper, set herself on fire in London in a Kurdish nationalist protest after the arrest of Abdullah Ocalan, who was the leader of the Kurdistan Workers' Party (PKK) and an icon for millions of Kurds struggling for an independent Kurdish state. Expecting to die in the act of self-immolation (she survived), the flaming Kanteper ran through the demonstration, her arms raised in victory signs. Televised video of her burning horrified the British public, but it brought an awareness of the plight of Kurds into the living rooms of many who otherwise would not have paid attention. Kanteper also reminded citizens of the United Kingdom the measures to which the extremely ideologically driven would go to promote their causes.

Over the next year, UK students repeatedly launched campaigns against imperialism in the Middle East and other antimilitary demonstrations. In 2001, a thousand students and activists, including a Labour Party MP (minister of parliament) and a Scottish Socialist Party MP, attempted to block the entrance of Faslane, the British naval base in west Scotland, home to four Trident nuclear-missile submarines. Led by Trident Ploughshares and the Scottish Campaign for Nuclear Disarmament, the protests were joined by three dozen students from the Republic of Ireland, including the president of the Union of Students in Ireland. The protest was violently broken up by police, who arrested 340 individuals. The action received a boost in media coverage after demonstrators were publicly supported by ex-James Bond actor Sir Sean Connery.

Those antiwar demonstrations soon included protests against the US occupations in Iraq and Afghanistan. In 2003, thousands of students turned out all across the United Kingdom in opposition to the US and British invasion of Iraq. These ranged from massive demonstrations against the war and Tony Blair to marches, sit-ins, occupations, and internet campaigns. As the decade progressed, UK students, like their EU compeers, became more and more media savvy, increasingly using the internet and social media to organize and disseminate information. Students also adopted provocative tactics meant explicitly to attract media attention, such as the Masturbate for Peace movement, which had slogans such as "Whack your sack, not Iraq." It lacked gravitas, but Masturbate for Peace membership increased in short order to 9,500 members, from more than eighty different countries.[32] Other media-grabbing student protests were tried as well, such as a die-in of students covered in blood-red paint at the base of the Victoria Monument.

On a less dramatic front, students pressured their universities to pull investments that went to corporations dealing arms or that resulted in environmental destruction, such as in ExxonMobil, or those that supported human-rights violations through unregulated factory work. Students at the University of St. Andrews, the oldest university in Scotland, held a series of demonstrations and sit-ins in 2005 to protest the university's support of unethical corporations. The ethical investment campaigners settled in to a prolonged battle with the administration and successfully pressured the school to change its investment policy in 2007.

Students were successful at demonstrating in the United Kingdom on several fronts, and those successes encouraged more activism. For example, in 2007, when HSBC bank announced new overdraft charges that would cost students dearly, angry students started a Facebook campaign. Students volunteered for flash queues at all bank branches, where they would join service and cashier lines and, as each student's turn in line came, each would ask for specific and complicated details on how the proposed charges would affect students. The protest's goal was to bring in-person bank transactions throughout the country to a grinding halt, thus paralyzing the bank and all its subsidiaries. After thousands signed up and pledged to join in the protests, alarmed HSBC leaders (who were monitoring the numbers) did the math, scrapped the overdraft plans, and publicly thanked their customers for drawing attention to issues important to them.

By 2007, the level of student activism in the United Kingdom was extremely high. Antiwar demonstrations brought two million protestors into the streets of the nation during this time, and thousands of students were battling tooth and nail to stop more tuition hikes. But while UK students were energetic in protesting in the first decade of the millennium on a variety of issues, and participated in big numbers, they lost the larger, politically based battles. This resulted by the end of the decade not so much in apathy (as some argued) but in a pragmatic awareness of where to put, for the time being, their own daily political efforts.

The defeats on the larger political scale came at the same time as young people realized they could make personal political choices that were informed to a great extent by increased consumer power. They became less committed to street protest and joined causes for ethical investment and ethical consumerism that, while criticized by the more ideologically extreme as less engaged, had profound effect in shaping corporate practices. So although UK students were aware and activist, by the end of 2007 they had begun a clear shift toward personal action rather than sustained mass action.

That's not to say large demonstrations didn't occur, and they would be fully back in fashion a decade later. Following the financial meltdowns of 2008 and 2009, thousands of protestors gathered in the Square Mile, the heart of London's financial district. In 2009 again, some ten thousand activists against global capitalism, greed, and corruption marched peacefully in London and were not initially attacked despite the heavy police presence, security having showed up in riot gear but been ordered to show restraint. Politicians did not want a media scandal caused by police brutality. But when a group of anarchists rioted outside of a Royal Bank of Scotland branch and smashed the windows of what they identified as the national symbol of greed, police responded. A faction of the protestors rampaged through the building, destroying property and attempting to set the place on fire. Police suppressed the riot. One man was killed in the melee, and dozens more were injured; hundreds were arrested. This late-decade example in UK protest, and in the violence that came with it, was unusual for the country, but it would foreshadow what would soon come in the decade of chaos to follow.

Like the other countries in Europe, Switzerland, Iceland, Greenland, and Portugal saw antiwar and anti–United States demonstrations in 2003. They also witnessed—relative to their respective populations—large antiglobalization and anticorporatization demonstrations following the 2008 and 2009 international economic crises. In 2009, Iceland saw the largest demonstrations in its history, with angry protestors occupying the square outside the Althing (parliament) in Reykjavik, banging pots and pans to disrupt legislative meetings taking place inside. Their protests thus earned their name in the media—the Pots and Pans Revolution. This series of demonstrations repeatedly ended in violence, because security repeatedly attacked the demonstrators. On their part, the demonstrators would scatter when faced with troops, dispersing into nearby streets and then, using social media to communicate, regrouping blocks away and launching a counterattack, throwing smoke bombs, rocks, and snowballs. Facing growing unpopularity, an economy in ruins, and strong opposition that was only increasing in strength, the prime minister of the right-wing government resigned, and the subsequent elections ushered in a leftist coalition government for Iceland.

As a whole, the 2000s were an extremely active time for student resistance actions across the European Union, with major issues uniting student protests into trends that included demonstrations against US wars in Iraq and Afghanistan, against neoliberalism and the spread of multinational corporations, and against nation-specific education "reforms" demanded by the Bologna Process. In terms of tactics and strategies, European students were exploiting the use of media coverage in widening their struggles, and they began exploring advantages offered by the internet in networking and disseminating information. Toward the end of the decade, they shifted to social media and developed tactics that quickly conjured large numbers at rallies. The new technology allowed them to rapidly redeploy protestors when attacked by police and to disseminate information quickly to other activists and news media, including images of police brutality.

On their part, EU governments began developing technological countermeasures that included cyberinfiltration to identify and target protest members and to discover plans and the numbers of attendees expected to demonstrate at actions. Although it took some hard lessons when police overreacted in the presence of media, governments began to see the value in tactical restraint when news media was present. In the next decade, tactics would again change as technology allowed activists to organize through social media and draw crowds to protests ever faster. They would be able to record police violence via cell-phone cameras and communicate through encrypted channels, while on the side of authority surveillance would dramatically increase as intelligence agencies infiltrated and monitored those same cell-phone networks. And authorities would pass new antiterrorist laws that would allow for activists to be surveilled and preemptively arrested, identified through facial recognition when they did protest, and be charged afterward.

Pulled into the United States–Middle East conflicts, increasingly joined through the spread of neoliberalism and efforts to make member nations economically and socially more intertwined, the

European Union also witnessed a dramatic rise in domestic terrorist attacks in the 2000s, which brought with them widespread
fear regarding national security, exacerbated by a certain level
of hysteria in the media. In hindsight, the 2000s, for the region,
seem different in kind from the decade to follow, but many of the
sociopolitical characteristics associated with the next decade were
already clearly developing in the 2000s—characteristics only rein-
forced by the anxiety of the economic crashes of 2008 and 2009.
The widespread, slow but steady rise in nationalism and fascism
throughout the European Union was already well underway, as was
an increasingly polarizing political division between the left and the
right in member nations. Anti-immigration sentiment rose, and so
too did xenophobia, racism, and hate crimes. These elements would
all come to the fore in the 2010s, as populist politicians engaged
in fearmongering, but all were clearly germinating throughout the
region in the 2000s.

4

PRODEMOCRACY REVOLUTIONS, THE COLOR REVOLUTIONS, AND THE CHANGING TACTICS OF ACTIVISM IN EASTERN EUROPE AND RUSSIA

Eastern Europe saw a vast number of student movements and demonstrations in the first decade of the new millennium. Some resulted in social and political change, even revolutions. Others were suppressed before they could germinate or grow into anything larger. The range of actions, responses, and outcomes was considerable, largely due to the rapid spread of new technology and social media. Particularly notable is how much the actions, successes, and failures in a given country inspired student groups and movements in others. The conditions were right for the ignition of protests, and aided by technology and media coverage, multiple flash points flamed into large-scale youth-led social movements.

Resistance groups seemed to flare up spontaneously everywhere, though most were in fact carefully organized. In Serbia there was Otpor, in Kosovo, KAN (Kosovo Action Network). Croatia saw the rise of Gong, and Georgia, Kmara. Macedonia had Loja, and Albania had Mjaft! Ukraine had Pora! Montenegro had Unitas, and Belarus, Zubr. And these are only the more famous groups. Many countries saw dozens of youth groups fighting for social justice and freedoms. The decade is particularly important because of the extent to which these and other groups were willing to help one another, and because of how effectively activists adopted and employed new networking strategies and technology to do so. The networking, influence, and international support among these groups rapidly grew as the decade progressed. Amid a wide range of governments, social contexts, and cultures, this period of resistance in Eastern European nations saw tremendous experimentation with new technology and strategies that effectively yielded many of the modern forms of protest and tactics that were used globally in the 2010s. Following the lead of many of this region's countries, movements and revolutions would flare in Asia, the Middle East, Africa, and South America.

Serbia's resistance movement was arguably the most internationally influential movement of the 2000s. To understand it, we'll begin with a discussion of the nation just prior to the new millennium. In Serbia under the brutal regime of Yugoslavian president Slobodan Milošević, students, activists, and citizens who had gathered in the tens of thousands in Belgrade over 1996–97 election fraud continued to protest on a much smaller scale against corruption and police violence and for civil rights for the rest of the decade. The government routinely suppressed these actions with police attacks, arrests, and draconian laws against protesting. By the end of the decade, activist youth were in hiding, as people apprehended for troublemaking in the streets were automatically conscripted into military service. Milošević had clamped down hard on dissent, using intelligence and security agents to infiltrate groups and arrest organizers and dispersing protests whenever they occurred. This did not keep university students from analyzing the mistakes they'd made in prior years, though, nor did it stop them from organizing. In 1998, Otpor ("Resistance") was formed to challenge a new law restricting the autonomy of the University of Belgrade, and once it formed its members decided to go all in and directly challenge Milošević's rule instead.

The prodemocracy group employed nonviolent, often humorous tactics to challenge the government at the same time as it used new computer-networking technology to reach large numbers of activists. For example, protestors staged a massive public birthday party for the president in 1999, at which everyone signed a card and noted what they really wished for Milošević (the suggestions were not pretty). They held multimedia demonstrations, including live music happenings, such as a "Blow on the Head Against Violence and Fear" rally in Novi Sad, attended by more than ten thousand people, mostly students.[33] Their efforts gave common Serbians confidence to speak out, and they began calling forth peaceful demonstrations across the country, many of which were hit hard by riot police.

Other groups, such as Alliance for Change, joined the fight and began demonstrating as well. Encouraged by growing support despite the violent suppression they knew was coming, Otpor released its "Declaration for the Future of Serbia," which demanded Milošević step down and the country hold free elections—a document distributed widely and signed onto by increasingly large numbers of NGOs, members of opposition political parties, and worker unions. Their writings and call for action were widely available on the internet, both nationally and internationally, and they began a massive street graffiti campaign to show resistance was everywhere in the country. By the end of 1999, the Otpor symbol—a clenched fist—had been spray-painted on sidewalks, buildings, and bridges across the country. Many students were arrested for stenciling the image. Young people were randomly stopped and frisked, arrested if caught with cans of spray paint on them. Information about the harsh treatment doled out upon them was disseminated widely by Otpor, which further infuriated and energized the opposition to Milošević. When they gathered, students and activists in the thousands raised their fists in solidarity at rallies, and when police violently attacked them with baton charges, more and more people came out to protest.

Thousands marched in Belgrade, Novi Sad, Niš, Kragujevac, and other major cities. Milošević's government blamed the unrest on efforts by NATO and the United States but did not launch a convincing counternarrative in the media. Building up to the 2000 election, Otpor managed to bring together the two main opposition parties, for many individual members from both groups already belonged to Otpor. Together they launched a single campaign against the president, in the process marshalling the recruitment networks and financial support of both opposition parties. They formed the Democratic Opposition of Serbia (DOS) and agreed to put forth a single candidate for president.

Although members were willing to risk taking a beating and face arrest for speaking out, Otpor ultimately wanted a peaceful transfer of power and sought to make individuals feel they could change Serbia's future by speaking out and voting. They launched a well-organized ad campaign, including placing their clenched-fist symbol on the front page of tabloid newspapers, distributing hundreds of thousands of leaflets and flyers, and plastering "Resistance, Because I Love Serbia" posters everywhere.

Taking a page from a French Situationist tactic of the 1960s called *détournement*, they printed more than a million "He's finished!" stickers that members slapped on top of the ubiquitous "Elect Milošević" campaign signs littering Serbia. Opposition voter turnout for the election was overwhelming, but Milošević refused to concede defeat. He called for an election runoff, which brought more widespread demonstrations in the streets and public charges of voter fraud. Hundreds of thousands of people poured into Belgrade, surrounding and then pressing their way into government buildings. Their sheer numbers precluded police suppression, and Milošević was forced to resign.

One of Otpor's founders, Milja Jovanovic, would later reveal that up to 85 percent of the organization's funds had come from the United States, through organizations such as the National Endowment for Democracy, the International Republican Institute, the National Democratic Institute, and USAID, as well as private donations.[34] Other funds came from organizations in the European Union. Milosevic and his authoritarian allies, of course, saw the revolt as Western capitalist imperialism and specifically as an incursion by the United States into Eastern Europe and yet another step in NATO's expansion efforts. From Otpor's perspective, the NGOs were a way to fund the country's prodemocracy movement to secure free elections. Otpor's success inspired prodemocracy activists around the world, many of whom would seek to imitate its organizational structures, strategies, and tactics either directly or by modifying them to the specifics of their own societies. After the revolution, Otpor members travelled to meet prodemocracy activists throughout the world, holding workshops and training sessions.

With activists in other countries appealing to Otpor for help after the revolution, Srdja Popović, another of the group's founders, decided to share his activist knowledge, network, and organizational abilities with the world by starting the Center for Applied Nonviolent Action and Strategies (CANVAS), an international organization to foster nonviolent prodemocracy reforms. It would become active in more than four dozen countries. In 2015, searching to reach more people, he published *Blueprint for Revolution: How to Use Rice Pudding, Lego Men, and Other Nonviolent Techniques to Galvanize Communities, Overthrow Dictators, or Simply Change the World*.[35] CANVAS would allow free downloads of the book in the thousands to would-be revolutionaries around the world.

It is worth noting that post revolution, in 2008, Serbian students came out on both sides of Kosovo's struggle for independence from Serbia, playing out a national ambivalence regarding both self-determination and greater Serbian nationalism. Following the revolution and quick embrace by the European Union, there was a slow backwards drifting of Serbia's politics and popular culture away from the West and toward authoritarianism and the East, a drift that would increase over the next decade and would be repeatedly challenged by students.

In Albania, students and activists began a four-month campaign in 2003 that would evolve into the Mjaft! (Enough!) movement. The idea was to tackle apathy and increase civic engagement by addressing a new social theme or issue each week, rotating through them while growing the larger movement through social networking and demonstrations. The group promoted a revolutionary spirit along the lines of the Otpor movement, but instead of aiming that spirit toward overthrowing a government (since there was no longer a dictator in Albania to kick out), Mjaft! combined the spirit of resistance with civic responsibility and social engagement. The group tried to stop ongoing violence at EU borders, created campaigns for cleaning up waste dumps, drew attention to the improprieties of elected officials (who were repeatedly videotaped doing things like running red lights), and challenged government policies. They promoted ecological concerns, labor issues, and progressive cultural issues. Under the symbol of a red handprint, Mjaft! became Albania's best known civic organization and, in 2004, received the United Nations' Vienna Civil Society Award.

Much of the group's success hinged on its ability to field massive, nonviolent demonstrations. Its inventive protests were disarming but pointed, such as an anticorruption flag-washing protest—a sit-in to which everyone brought Albanian flags and bowls of soap and water to clean them in. With hundreds of thousands of dollars' worth of support from Western embassies, the group began a snappy television ad campaign for social engagement. Mjaft! would also bring pressure on the government to address violence on the border with Greece, and draw attention to the plight of suffering refugees.

In 2007, Mjaft! effectively held a massive free-speech demonstration in Tirana, after Prime Minister Sali Berisha attempted to curb the rights of journalists. The group continued to grow, and by 2008, it boasted thirty full-time employees and ten thousand members who could be mobilized on a moment's notice via text messaging on cell phones. Demonstrating its popularity and how much the movement had become a mainstream player in Albania (and as a sign of the force it wielded on politicians), Mjaft!'s founder and leader until 2007, Erion Veliaj, would be appointed minister of social welfare and youth in 2013. This was no small post, for the cabinet position controlled 30 percent of the government's annual budget.

Like Otpor members, activists for Mjaft! would go on to work with activists in other countries, including those organizing the Orange Revolution in Ukraine.

Ukraine had been an independent nation since 1991 and formally adopted its constitution in 1996. In 2000, tape recordings of President Leonid Kuchma ordering the kidnapping of journalist Georgiy Gongadze were leaked to the media in what became known as the Cassette Scandal. The murdered journalist's body was later found.[36] Protests against Kuchma started on Maidan Nezalezhnosti (Independence Square) in Kiev, with students setting up a tent city. Demonstrations continued into 2001 but did not spark a larger uprising, and were finally subdued when military shock troops crushed the remaining protestors in March. But the scandal, and the hardline approach from Kuchma, was credited with shifting public preference away from a Russian style of leadership, toward the West, and setting the stage for the Orange Revolution that would follow.

In 2004, the Ukrainian youth organization Pora! (It's Time) was formed, with members travelling to Serbia to be directly trained by Otpor activists. They began nonviolent demonstrations and actions with an eye toward peaceful revolution in coming presidential elections.[37] Activist teens and college students staged sit-ins, blocked roads, distributed flyers, pasted antigovernment posters, and marched. They began internet-based campaigns and networked through social media. Police came down on them hard, ransacking Pora!'s offices, taking computers, and confiscating what they claimed was a large cache of explosives. The government called the group a terrorist organization, and police began a campaign of arresting members, infiltrating and using the internet networks of the students to identify and locate targets. Thousands of students protested against police corruption outside the Ministry of the Interior in Kiev, demanding justice for arrested Pora! members. When prosecutors signaled they would begin criminal proceedings, group members who were not yet jailed called for nationwide student strikes and demonstrations, arguing that the government was beginning its own terror campaign in advance of the elections.[38] The state was publicly embarrassed when one of the MPs present at the Pora! office raid confessed that police had planted the explosives, a charge the government continued to deny. It did, however, quietly release the detained Pora! members.

Pora! and its members rallied behind the opposition candidate running in the 2004 presidential election. The nail-biter election resulted in a runoff race between prodemocracy leader Viktor Yushchenko (of the opposition party Nasha Ukrayina or "Our Ukraine") and Prime Minister Viktor Yanukovych (Kuchma's man). The runoff resulted in an official win for the prime minister, though the elections were clearly fraught with widespread fraud. Exit polling results differed enormously from state-published numbers, so Pora! orchestrated massive protests in Kiev, the largest of them drawing close to a million citizens. Pro-Yanukovych rallies were held in eastern Ukraine, and he ignored the charges of fraud that the official Elections Commission certified had taken place. But the anti-Yanukovych demonstrations continued, and under the threat of a massive uprising, parliament held a no-confidence vote. Ukraine's highest court annulled the election results, calling for a new election to be overseen by international observers, an election that Yushchenko decisively won.

Known as the Orange Revolution (the official color of Yushchenko's campaign), Ukraine's transition to a democracy occurred relatively peacefully, though it would come out that intelligence officials in the government leaked information to protesting activists to alert them when a crackdown was coming so they could disband and reform elsewhere. Military leaders also held back troops when large demonstrations occurred to prevent accidental violence.[39] Yushchenko, who advocated for democracy, government transparency, and joining with NATO, would eventually lose support and fall victim to widespread dissatisfaction. Ironically, he would lose to former rival Yanukovych in the 2010 presidential elections.

The social unrest and societal changes happening in Serbia, Albania, and Ukraine—especially early on in the decade—had profound effects throughout Eastern Europe in the 2000s and helped fuel a growing fever for democratic social revolution. Students and many first-time activists around the world saw that committed activism could push their societies to change.

The path to independence for Kosovo in the new millennium began a year earlier, in 1999, when tensions escalated between Serbs and Albanians in Kosovo, then an autonomous territory of Serbia (which, with Montenegro, formed the Federal Republic of Yugoslavia, or FRY). The watershed moment in the push for independence came after forty-five people in the village of Račak were executed by Serbian security forces. The Yugoslavians claimed those killed had all been members of the Kosovo Liberation Army (KLA), a paramilitary guerilla force fighting for Kosovar independence. International inspectors visiting the site reported that these were in reality crimes against humanity, and that many of the victims, villagers of all ages, had been shot in the head. International human rights groups and the United Nations denounced the killings.

NATO began a bombing campaign against Yugoslavia to stop the aggression and maintain peace. Following the FRY's military withdrawal from Kosovo in 1999 and the establishment of a UN Interim Administration (UNIA), students and activists demonstrated against the administration consistently for years. Protests included marches, throwing eggs at UNIA headquarters, leaflet campaigns, and internet and graffiti campaigns. The Kosovo Action Network was active in agitating for independence and for bringing perpetrators of the 1999 Račak village massacre to justice, and the group constantly demonstrated against UNIA. By 2005, it had morphed into the Self-Determination Movement, stepping up its independence efforts. Supported and financially aided by the European Union in the West, proindependence students protested for Kosovar sovereignty in larger numbers. In Moscow, the Russian state sponsored student protests for Serbian control of Kosovo.

Following the International Court of Justice's decision that Kosovo's declaration of independence was indeed legal, the European Union brokered negotiations between Serbia and Kosovo, resulting in a 2013 accord signed in Brussels and paving the way for the transition from governance by UNIA to full independence. Throughout the decade, international student networks continued to keep the issue present on social media and thus on international political agendas.

Just as in Kosovo, citizens in Montenegro were harshly divided in the 2000s over support for Serbia and control by the Federal Republic of Yugoslavia or Montenegrin independence and alliance with the West. In 2000, thousands marched in Podgorica against the NATO bombings of Yugoslavia. Students marched in force against the Montenegrin prime minister, Milo Đukanović, and held spontaneous protests for independence and democracy. In 2003, with Serbia facing its own internal governance challenges, the two regions negotiated the Belgrade Agreement, resulting in a decentralization of government that established respective authorities in both regions. Students continued to agitate for self-determination, however, and in 2006, a referendum on independence was held in Montenegro, which ended with those favoring independence narrowly winning. The country claimed independence and would by 2017 join NATO.

Montenegrin students protested on both sides of the independence issue, but the social turmoil they raised in doing so helped energize the population and pushed the country toward independence. In 2008, Montenegro recognized Kosovo's independence from Serbia, setting off more protests against Đukanović by pro-Serbia Montenegrins, who waved Serbian flags and shouted anti-Đukanović slogans. A number of riots broke out, with demonstrators battling police in front of the parliament building.

Activists in other countries in the region were trying to start prodemocracy movements of their own but couldn't replicate the successes of Serbia, Albania, or Ukraine. In Azerbaijan, after President Heydar Aliyev died in 2003, his son, Ilham Aliyev, ran for the presidency and won. The election results were vehemently contested. In October 2003, thousands of students and youth joined the opposition party in peaceful protests, calling for an end to government corruption. Police troops rolled up with water cannons and blasted the crowds, even firing upon children, and masked security forces in body armor indiscriminately clubbed demonstrators. A number of activists were killed outright in the attacks, and hundreds were injured. Some three thousand students amassed outside Baku State University to protest the violence, but security and intelligence operatives identified attendees, and they were arrested in the following weeks. Although a democracy in name, the country, which had been an authoritarian regime under the father, became more restrictive over the following decade under the son, with journalists and those critical of authority facing arrest, torture, and imprisonment.

Despite the crackdown, a number of prodemocracy Azeri student and youth organizations, inspired by the successes in other countries, formed and began networking and holding peaceful public demonstrations. In 2005, Yox! (No!) protested and engaged in creative actions such as prodemocracy "leaflet rains," in which they threw hundreds of leaflets out of upper-story building windows. The organization quickly grew in size. In a move to connect internationally, representatives from Yox! attended a 2005 international student and youth organization regional summit and signed a pact to work for democracy through peaceful means and to aid all signatory prodemocracy groups in their struggles for freedom.

The 2005 regional summit was remarkable for a number of reasons, not least the coordination and support it afforded attendees in tactical education and networking opportunities, which included international funding streams. Its attendance reveals the extent of youth engagement in social unrest throughout the area and how activist groups were influencing one another; also signing the pact were representatives of Gong (Croatia), KAN (Kosovo), Kmara (Georgia), Loja (Macedonia), Mjaft! (Albania), Otpor and the Youth Initiative for Human Rights (Serbia), Pora! (Ukraine), Unitas (Montenegro), Youth Human Rights Movement (Russia), and Zubr (Belarus).

In Azerbaijan, such links to outside organizations fueled government fears locally, and rumors spread among government supporters and through media that Ukraine's Pora! had been training Azeris in revolutionary camps in preparation for an armed revolt. Pora!'s leader, Yevhen Zolotarev, vehemently denied the accusations, but he did afterwards offer, if given official permission, to help peacefully grow the prodemocracy network in Azerbaijan. However, the government's disinformation campaign and the role of media in spreading fear to drum up popular support for conservative power were decisive in countering the rise of a prodemocracy movement. Casting the liberalization of government as a conspiracy of extremists wanting culture-threatening change and stoking xenophobia proved to be effective countermeasures. Populist authoritarians across the globe would use these tactics repeatedly in the coming decade.

Student and youth demonstrations nevertheless continued to occur in the country on a range of issues and in many different forms. The Dalga (Wave) movement was started by students in 2005 and rapidly picked up numbers and momentum as it began protesting against corruption in universities, against US involvement in Afghanistan and Iraq, and against the Interior Ministry in 2007 following the government's decision to deport to Iran activist Hadi Musavi, who was working for the national liberation movement of ethnic Azerbaijanis there but had left Iran under threat of arrest. The government ramped up efforts against the myriad opposition groups that formed, surveilling them, infiltrating their ranks, and making arrests. Its reach extended into university administrations and forced activists out of schools. In 2006, the chairman of the Yeni Fikir (New Thought) organization, Ruslan Basirli, was charged with trying to organize a coup and tax evasion, and that same year the high-profile student leaders Turan Aliyev (of People's Front of Azerbaijan) and Namiq Feyziyev (of Yeni Fikir) were expelled from their schools. In protest, they went on a hunger strike with fellow supporters, but they had to do so off campus.

Such efforts could not stop the wave of activism sweeping the country, though. In 2007, members of the National Awakening

Movement of South Azerbaijan (NAMSA) and Dalga held a rally against Iranian policies outside the Iranian embassy in Baku. They were attacked by Baku police, but this did not stop future protests. By 2009, though, the government of President Ilham Aliyev had had enough of the seemingly endless number of protest groups and actions. The government redoubled its antiopposition efforts, brutally crushing demonstrations, arresting bloggers and journalists critical of the regime, infiltrating phone and computer networks to identify people for arrest, and prosecuting leaders of prodemocracy groups whenever caught. There would be no prodemocracy revolution in the country. Aliyev had the constitution changed to end presidential term limits so he could continue to rule the country, and although he would be reelected in a landslide with over 70 percent of the votes cast in 2013, election officials mistakenly released the official results of the election in a phone app *prior to the opening of the polls.*

While Serbia and Albania were torches of inspiration for prodemocracy activists in the region, the various authoritarians had their own models of effective dictatorship. In Belarus, President Alexander Lukashenko had a well-established program of eliminating opposition through the use of police death squads who simply "vanished" opposition leaders; high-profile kidnapped opponents included former government officials. His urban shock troops mercilessly attacked peaceful protests.

There had been a momentary flare-up of activism in Belarus in 1999, when activists holding a freedom march fought back against security, but this rebellion had been crushed, for Belarussian riot troops were well trained in tactics of urban savagery. The peace march was met by troops carrying aluminum shields, advancing as a wall like some medieval army. When the two groups collided and the police began clubbing marchers, demonstrators pushed back, hitting police with volleys of bricks and stones. The troops contracted their lines into a circle and stacked their shields for protection until reinforcements arrived. When the other troops arrived, they did so in such numbers that they overwhelmed the marchers.

Those caught or lying wounded on the streets were severely beaten for fighting against the police. The clubbing went on for some time. Skulls were cracked and bones broken.

A harsh crackdown on demonstrations followed, though as in neighboring nations, the fever for social-reform activism was spreading. In 2004, the government issued court orders to ban scores of individual nongovernmental youth and opposition organizations. Over the next few years, the list would grow to hundreds of forbidden groups. Associations that were not banned outright were warned not to engage in political protests or to engage in activities that could be construed as critical of the government, and although small demonstrations and actions continued, fear of Lukashenko's police kept public demonstrations in check.

Lukashenko would be reelected in 2001, 2006, 2010, and 2015 in rigged elections. These results were all met with demonstrations by students and opposition activists, but such demonstrations came at great cost. The protests were viciously attacked by security forces, and activists who were caught or identified by surveillance photos were arrested, beaten, and sentenced to lengthy prison terms. Many simply disappeared, in what were likely kidnappings and extrajudicial executions.

Members of youth and activist organizations routinely had their offices and homes ransacked by security forces and the Belarusian KGB, who confiscated materials, leaflets, posters, books, red-and-white nationalist flags, and computers. Those coming under heavy suppression included the Zubr movement (named after the wild bison that live in Belarus), the Young Belarus Coalition, the United Civic Party's youth wing, the Young Front (an opposition youth movement), and the Seventh Facet (an NGO). Students were routinely expelled on the slightest evidence of activist efforts, and protestors were imprisoned for everything from demonstrating to distributing leaflets. Student organizations were infiltrated, and many activists found themselves arrested after discussing the idea of planning or attending demonstrations.

Although activists continued to gather, they did so at great risk. They were arrested, sentenced to prison, and heavily fined. In 2005, a hundred people gathered on October Square in Minsk to publicly protest the government, and they were predictably crushed by security troops. Police sealed the offices of opposition groups, such as Young Front, but such actions had the opposite effect from the one the government intended, for instead of eliminating opposition, it galvanized it.

In the face of growing resistance, President Lukashenko publicly vowed violent suppression should Belarusian activists attempt an uprising along the lines of the Orange Revolution in Ukraine or the Rose Revolution in Georgia. By 2005, intelligence and KGB operatives had effectively infiltrated the larger youth and student groups, and so opposition was forced into separate, smaller groups, linked together by webs of limited social networks. To counter the new social-networking strategies, government security conducted cyberwarfare against the seemingly endless number of groups sprouting up, shutting down networks and webpages as soon as they appeared. Prior to city visits by the president, security forces, well informed as to who would lead demonstrations locally, would sweep through the area, arresting activists and detaining them until after Lukashenko departed.

In one demonstration in September 2005, after authorities seized the banned red-and-white nationalist flags used by the opposition, one youth leader with nothing else at hand raised his denim shirt and proclaimed it the new flag, inadvertently giving the civil uprising its new moniker, the "Denim Revolution." It seemed that no matter how much the government beat down the resistance, the prodemocracy movement could not be completely stamped out. The group Jeans for Freedom was subsequently formed, and the title of the revolt caught on, as it appealed to young activists through its immediate connection to democratic Western youth culture. The Denim Revolution was also called the Cornflower Revolt, as denim blue is locally known as "cornflower blue," and thus it was associated with the other "color revolutions" sweeping Eastern Europe. To Lukashenko's chagrin, like the Orange Revolution, it spread like wildfire among disgruntled youth.

In 2007, the government began employing a new tactic against student activists. In addition to having them expelled from their universities, it began drafting them into military service when arrested. Its campaign of harassing and detaining activists on charges of hooliganism, petty vandalism, and obscene language increased. Thwarted at home, activists networked internationally and spread a call for help, disseminating reports of the human rights abuses taking place. Under pressure of economic sanction from the European Union and the United States, the government released a number of imprisoned activists in 2008, though it continued its harassment of opposition groups, stepping up its use of military conscription as deterrent. Nevertheless, small protests of anywhere from two to a hundred activists continued to occur, though they were inevitably violently dispersed by police.

In 2009, activists staged a number of demonstrations against joint military maneuvers with Russia, and in an effort to get Belarus ultimately accepted into the European Union, formed a new coalition called the Belarusian Pro-Independence Bloc. But there would be no democratic revolution in Belarus. As would happen in Russia in the 2000s, vicious suppression of opposition groups by the state forced activists to go underground and turn to more guerilla-style tactics, using social media to conduct virtual campaigns in which they would stage provocative actions of short duration that could be filmed for dissemination later.

In Bulgaria in the first half of the decade, students protested for improved educational measures, for environmental concerns, and against government corruption. They also marched for membership in the European Union (which Bulgaria joined in 2007) and in solidarity with youth in Greece. In 2008, they protested in large numbers in the capital of Sofia for better security and against rampant crime. These protests, which would make international news, started after locals beat a student to death in a nightclub located in an area built in the eighties to house and cater to university students called Studenski Grad. What had begun as a contemporary housing project where students could reside, ideally for next to nothing, quickly turned into a massive student ghetto with close to fifty thousand residents. Due to corrupt government officials that granted building and business permits with little or no oversight, Studenski Grad became a magnet for crime, gangs, and illegal activities of every stripe, making it by 2000 easily the most dangerous area in the capital.

Soon, many of the people residing in the Studenski Grad area were not in fact students, and ramshackle buildings were illegally wedged into every space that could be built upon, including former parks and playgrounds. Sidewalks were used for parking, provided they were not already covered with garbage. Prostitutes, drug dealers, and packs of feral dogs roamed trash-packed streets that were never cleaned. The beating death of the student, though, was a tipping point, and approximately a thousand students marched through Studenski Grad in a demonstration against the condition of the area, the death of the student, and the dire need for better security.[40] Other protests followed, and the pressure on the government forced the removal of officials overseeing the area, who were eventually charged with corruption, and the rehabilitation of the area.

In the Czech Republic, student protest levels were moderately low during the 2000s. There were numerous limited student demonstrations on myriad issues, but it was the announcement of new unified end-of-school exams for secondary schools in 2009 that brought students out to protest in force. Some seven thousand students, for example, marched through the center of Prague, snarling traffic and closing businesses. The students protesting in the city and elsewhere in the nation called for the suspension of the tests, which could well determine their futures. Police monitored the marches, but did not engage, and the students registered their complaints with chants and signs. There was no reported violence and, other than a few students throwing tomatoes, no real vandalism. In the decade to follow, student activism would again increase in the Czech Republic, mirroring levels of student activism throughout Europe and Eastern Europe, but for the time being, the republic was a relative center of calm in the region.

In Georgia, by contrast, many prodemocracy student groups organized in opposition to the government and began agitating loudly. Members of Serbia's Otpor, which had effectively and peacefully led the Serbian revolution, travelled to the country in 2003 to help organize and train activists in resistance strategies. Taking cues from the Azerbaijani government's use of xenophobia to inspire fear of its growing prodemocracy movement, the government of Georgia sought to discredit the rapidly growing Kmara (Enough!) movement in the country by fanning ethnic tensions, suggesting the group was an Armenian plot. (The mother of the leader of the opposition party, United Democrats, happened to be Armenian.) Vakhtang Rcheulishvili, one of President Eduard Shevardnadze's representatives, called on patriots to start an "authentic Georgian" movement (confusingly, also called "Enough!") to counter what he called the Armenian extremists.

In parliamentary elections, the leader of the United National Movement party, Mikheil Saakashvili, claimed to have won the majority of votes after independent counting of election exit polls suggested the win, but the government disputed the claim. Saakashvili cried foul and called on all Georgians to rise up against President Shevardnadze and his government, and massive antigovernment protests broke out in Tbilisi. These were followed by demonstrations in every major city in the nation. For twenty days, protests rocked the country. During a parliamentary meeting attended by President Shevardnadze, Saakashvili and supporters stormed into the meeting carrying roses, and thus the Rose Revolution got its name. Shevardnadze fled the chambers and attempted to deploy the military, but when his own elite troops refused to secure his residence, he decided it prudent to meet with opposition leaders. Without military backing, he was forced to negotiate his resignation, and Saakashvili became the president of Georgia.

This did not stop demonstrations from happening, though, as students now realized the power they wielded. Demonstrations were held in the following years complaining about widespread administrative corruption in university admissions; many of the lecturers previously administering the admissions tests took bribes to let students in, ranging from the equivalent of fifty US dollars each for public schools to tens of thousands of dollars for prestigious schools. Saakashvili responded by imposing end-of-the-year tests that would be impartially graded along EU standards by people not administering the admissions tests and who had no contact with the students. The results were mass failures in the next rounds of exams and increased competition for slots in universities, for the government reforms implemented raised accreditation standards.

Improvements to the nation's education system also included the stopping of bribes paid by private schools to the education ministry and the closing of more than a hundred diploma mills. A lot of angry students marched in public demonstrations, but their protests were widely viewed as purely self-interested, so they gained little support. Ultimately, the corrupt university system was reformed, and the value of a degree in Georgia significantly increased.

Georgia saw other student unrest as well. In 2006, in the breakaway region of Abkhazia, a pro-Kremlin youth movement called Proryv (Breakthrough) demonstrated in Sukhumi on the fourteenth anniversary of the start of the Abkhaz war, with protestors publicly burning Georgian flags. The demonstration was reported as having been attended by a Russian official, and the demonstration was widely viewed as Russian financed. Just as NGOs based in the United States and the European Union were funding prodemocracy activists in Serbia, so too was Russia providing support to pro-Russian groups throughout Eastern Europe, especially in countries that bordered it. Countering local efforts by pro-Russian groups, Abkhazian students protested against Russian meddling and the continued threat to to the region's independence posed by the superpower.

In 2007, students in Tbilisi demonstrated against Russia outside the Russian embassy and outside the UN office. In 2008, claiming they had been provoked by Georgian aggression, Russian troops crossed Georgia's territorial borders with separatist South Ossetia and Abkhazia, starting the Russo-Georgian War. Russian troops supported by aircraft, tanks, and a naval blockade forced hundreds of thousands to flee the border regions and captured a number of cities before international pressure eventually forced the Russians to withdraw, after which Russia recognized the separatist regions as allied independent states.

By the end of the decade, even in Eastern European countries that saw moderate to low protest levels, violence on the part of protestors was becoming more and more common when activists found themselves frustrated. Such acts may have in part been a side effect of an increase in images of violent student protests appearing in the international media. In Latvia in 2009, for example, thousands of protestors against the government called for early elections following a national economic crisis and tremendous unemployment that resulted in the government's asking for a 7.5-billion-dollar rescue from the International Monetary Fund (IMF) and the European Union. The massive but peaceful protest marched on Latvia's parliament building in Riga, but the demonstrators found their path blocked by heavily armored riot police. Instead of peacefully demonstrating, many of the younger marchers went on a rampage through Riga's Old City, prying up cobblestones, throwing them through store windows, and smashing parked police vehicles. The riot was suppressed by police after reinforcements arrived, but not before more than a hundred people were injured. The riots and the damage done to private property, however, lessened public support, and for some time undercut sympathy for student causes.

Other late-decade flare-ups of violent protest over contested elections in the region also met with violent suppression. In 2009 in Moldova, after elections saw the ruling Communist party under President Vladimir Voronin retain control, violent protests broke out. Ten thousand people marched on the parliament building in Chişinău, organized by youth and students on Facebook and the wider internet and through Twitter (hence its moniker, the "Twitter Revolution"). An armored police barricade formed a shield wall to stop them, but the protestors, who were agitating for more freedom and independence, attacked the troops with stones and drove them back. Police used water cannons and fire hoses on them, but the security forces were overwhelmed by students who commandeered the water trucks, turning the water cannons on police before getting in and driving the vehicles away. The police retreated as students sacked the parliament building and the presidential office, throwing desks through the windows and setting fires. Seven thousand people protested in the city of Bălți, and smaller numbers marched in other cities, though there were also progovernment demonstrations as well. Students were immediately threatened by their institutions for participating in protests. The diminishing crowds in the streets were set upon by riot police, who beat protestors both before and after taking them into custody.

Even Eastern European countries that were relatively stable and fully democratic in the 2000s saw high levels of activism, and as the decade wore on, protests became increasingly violent as anarchists and black-bloc participants incited riots. In Poland in 2000 and 2001, many of the protests that made international news were solidarity protests with students in other countries. Students gathered outside the Iranian, Belarusian, Russian, and other embassies to draw attention to the plight of students protesting in those countries. In 2001, a government plan to raise rail-service fees was protested by more than a thousand students in Warsaw, bringing enough pressure on the government to force negotiations. In 2005, students joined railway workers to shut down railway lines at the largest freight terminal in Poland, Tarnowskie Gory. They demonstrated against layoffs, low wages, and a plan to move a railway school. Combinations of worker and student alliances have often been extremely effective in forcing reforms when they occur, and in this instance in Poland the strategy brought negotiations.

Student demonstrations took place over educational reform, the high cost of living, politics, and civil rights, but they also increasingly decried growing nationalist, homophobic, and xenophobic sentiment in Poland as well. In 2008, for example, participants in the annual March for Tolerance parade in Krakow found their route blocked by a large counterrally, sponsored by the National Renewal of

Poland movement. International media captured the standoff taking place before the Basilica of Saint Mary: rainbow flags fluttered above one crowd, while above the other waved scrawled placards reading "No Faggoting." The pro–civil rights chants were shouted down by a nationalist chorus of "Get the fuck out!"[41] And while tatted-up skinheads abounded in the nationalist camp, there were also many hoodie-wearing high schoolers alongside them, the next generation of Polish nationalists in the making. In the coming decade, Poland would continue to see a populist shift to the right supported by hard-right government attempts to limit individual freedoms. Images of nationalist rallies would spread in the media, aided by a government that encouraged intolerance, and in a climate of prejudice, chauvinism, and xenophobia, those rallies would grow.

While much of Eastern Europe was in chaos in the 2000s, activism in Russia remained at a fairly low level. Vladimir Putin won the presidential election by a wide margin in 2000, and reelection in 2004. The economy grew for the duration of his first tenure. Constitutionally dictated term limits at the time kept him from running for a consecutive third term, but he had a solution for that, installing a short-term puppet who would let him continue to rule. Nonetheless, hopes for greater freedoms in the country would be sparked middecade, though they would not last. Inspired by Ukraine's Orange Revolution in 2004, activism began to stir once more in Russia.

Changes to benefits and pensions, a reduced infrastructure budget, higher transportation costs, and a high cost of living made life difficult for many in Russia. Adding to this, high gasoline prices and the cutting of social program funds encouraged discontent with the Putin administration. In 2005, the elderly and transportation workers began demonstrating in numerous but localized marches. When an official let slip the government was considering ending draft deferments for college students, students joined them. Some of these marches reached more than a thousand participants. Individually, the protests were not large, but added together the number of participants was in the hundreds of thousands. Student opposition groups formed and agitated, such as Walking Without Putin. (They took their name in response to the state-sponsored pro-Putin youth organization, Walking Together.) In April, four thousand students marched before the Government House in Moscow demanding the armed-services deferments be kept in place and that government grants for students be increased. An intimidating number of police were present, but they were held in check and did not attack the demonstration.

Putin had his own ideas for student activism groups that did not include prodemocracy agitation. In 2000, the state had formed the youth group Nashi (Ours), ostensibly to fight the proliferation of "capitalist fascism" and other threats to the nation. Following the successes of oppositional groups in Ukraine, Georgia, and Serbia, Russian authorities decided to absorb youth discontent and to constructively channel the dissatisfaction of young people. The professed goals of the group from the outset were that through demonstrations and activities they could cultivate leadership, civic responsibility, and an end to "oligarchic capitalism." They would patriotically strengthen the sovereignty of the state. Their program was articulated in terms of the people's freedom to choose the direction Russia would take in the future, including rejecting American-style capitalism, democracy, and hegemony.

Nashi members held rallies, did charity work, maintained war memorials, worked with orphanages, built housing, held debates on ideology and the future of Russia, and attended mass summer encampments. (Ironically, rewards at Nashi camps were often meals from McDonald's.) Government officials, including President Putin, would sometimes attend the retreats. Among outsiders, the organization elicited parallels to Komsomol or Hitler Youth, but for half a decade Nashi grew in popularity and size.

When it was sufficiently large, the state made it into an arm of government suppression. Permits to demonstrate were rubber-stamped for Nashi, while opposition groups' rallies went unauthorized, and by middecade unauthorized demonstrations held by opposition groups, such as the Drugaya Rossiya (Other Russia) coalition, were met by mobs of Nashi members blocking their path, wearing red and waving red-and-white Nashi flags. Opposition groups were being monitored by Russian intelligence, and Nashi was fed the location of planned demonstrations. In 2005 and 2006, after a series of ethnically motivated beatings and killings took place in Russia, with several foreign students among the murdered, demonstrations against the killings were held in Saint Petersburg and Moscow. They were met by Nashi counterprotests, one side shouting to end the fascism of the Kremlin and the other shouting to end the fascism of capitalism being imported from the West.

More than a few international journalists have pointed out Nashi's ultraconservative wing was, from all outward appearances by then, populated by skinheads and delinquents—the very group of people Nashi was supposedly originally formed to counter. Along with paramilitary conservatives, Nashi members' social aggression was increasingly empowered by Putin's government, and the group embarked on a public harassment campaign aimed at opposition group members. They also began overtly targeting minorities— Armenians, Azeris, Circassians, Chechens, Georgians, and Jews.[42] By 2006, Nashi had more than a hundred thousand members aged eighteen to twenty-five and was fielding crowds as large as seventy thousand in massive nationalistic demonstrations. Leaders were apprised by Russian security of when and where opposition groups would protest, and in what numbers, and they would show up at those demonstrations in greater numbers. Violence was common, and police would watch or participate.

Unlike Nashi members, opposition activists in Russia during the decade were arrested at their demonstrations or beaten by police. Their groups were surveilled and actively infiltrated by security. Following arrest, opposition activists were interrogated and often imprisoned. In 2006, at the G8 summit in Saint Petersburg, for example, approximately three hundred antiglobalism activists wearing bandanas to hide their faces defied a ban on protests and briefly marched in the streets before being crushed by armed riot troops. Even the foreign students participating who were caught were imprisoned. But even with the suppression and violence, oppositional protests against the government continued for the rest of the decade. In 2009, the Strategy-31 group would begin protests on the thirty-first of each month, shouting antigovernment slogans in front of government offices, dressed in red or black T-shirts emblazoned with the number 31 in a circle on the front. The symbol represented Article 31 of Russia's constitution, which grants the freedom of assembly.

With violence and imprisonment awaiting those undertaking traditional marches and street protests, many Russian activists chose not to, and went underground. They experimented with and refined technology-based hit-and-run actions. In 2007, a tight-knit group of former and current university students, performance artists, and radical leftists began to operate as the guerrilla art group Voina, led by Oleg Vorotnikov, a philosophy major from Moscow State University. The group began a series of politically charged artistic happenings, which they would record and later disseminate over the internet and through social media. Among their first actions was the invasion of a Moscow McDonald's on May Day, the international workers' day, in which they hurled live cats at employees across the counter while shouting, "Death to fast food!" They were arrested by plainclothes officers who happened to be nearby.[43] This did not, however, stop the group from conducting further protests.

The following year, Voina released a video online of the group having an orgy in the Timiryazev State Biological Museum, after Putin's anointed presidential candidate and puppet Dmitry Medvedev called on Russians to increase their birth rate. Similar provocative actions would continue be videotaped and disseminated online with the hope that they would go viral. There were mock hangings of foreigners and homosexuals in department stores. There was a video critiquing corruption among police and church officials of a Voina member boldly walking out of a grocery store pushing a cartload of food without paying, while wearing a mishmash costume made of a police-officer uniform and priest's robes. Other, similarly acerbic actions followed. Voina couldn't field large numbers or stage prolonged demonstrations and not be arrested, so they recorded guerrilla-style protest actions and dispersed them through the internet.

The immense popularity of Voina's videos was due to their audaciousness, their willingness to break rules, and their cutting satire. "Survival tactics for living under the regime" included a DIY instructional video on "how to steal a chicken" in which one member of the group inserted an entire raw chicken into her vagina in a supermarket aisle and then walked out (the action's joke hinges on the fact that the Russian verb "to steal" is also slang for "vagina").[44] The group's youth followers grew in number, swelled by artistic activists and students drawn to edgy street actions. In 2008, Voina members broke into the building across from Russia's White House and projected a twelve-story-high image of a glowing green skull and crossbones on the building while others reenacted (and filmed) a scene from Sergei Eisenstein's *October* by scaling the building's gates. The government was not amused and hunted Voina members relentlessly. In the next decade, under increased suppression, the group would radicalize, splinter, and go in different directions, staging increasingly provocative and ever more risky actions.

Russia maintained its tight grip on student organizing and public demonstrations in no small part because Eastern Europe was consumed by student activism in the 2000s. Young people throughout the region challenged authoritarians, formed pro-democracy movements, agitated for social reforms, and fought for social justice. Advances in computer-driven networking and the proliferation of social-media platforms allowed students to organize and communicate both domestically and internationally, and many activist groups quickly invented new tactics and strategies for protest. Successful, relatively peaceful revolutions occurred in places such as Serbia, Ukraine, and Albania. These in turn inspired students and young people across the region and the world to push their own governments and societies for reforms. Concern for others beyond their nation's borders led many of the leaders in the more successful movements to form international networks to help others launch antiauthoritarian movements in their own countries.

At the same time, despots such as Lukashenko and Putin were busy stamping out opposition whenever it flared, no matter the cost in human suffering. On the technological front, a war of strategies was already well underway, with resistance groups using networking and social media to communicate quickly with one another, to disseminate images and reports of violence, or to protest virtually. Authoritarian governments responded by using internet and cellphone blackouts to shut down opposition communications, and government advances in surveillance and cybersecurity allowed them to infiltrate opposition groups, identify individual members, and facilitate preemptive arrests. In the next decade, the foundation laid here for modern technological warfare would lead to global hashtag movements (that often came with international support) and highly sophisticated hacking attacks on computers, servers, and networks by both authoritarians and resistance fighters.

By 2016, especially with the election of President Donald Trump in the United States, it was clear to both the rulers and the ruled throughout the world the extent to which social media could be weaponized. Social-media platforms allowed for flash mobbing, and advances in encryption would be vital to social-media organizers. Surveillance technology would (on the side of protestors) allow monitoring of police troop movements by hackers, even outside of a given country, that could be relayed to demonstrators on the streets. On the side of authoritarians, facial-recognition technology would allow for individuals among massive crowds to be individually identified and targeted for later arrest. In Eastern Europe, the beginnings of this technological evolution in the struggle for social power, particularly with prodemocracy movements fighting authoritarianism, spread quickly and early. In Asia and across the Middle East, it happened a little more slowly during the decade. In Africa, which saw a lot of student resistance actions but was the last large area to see a wider technological transition, it happened more slowly still. But the fact that so many prodemocracy generational revolts were occurring in Eastern Europe in the early 2000s, some meeting with great success, fueled a fever of demonstrations and protests across the entire globe.

5

TECHNOLOGICAL EXPLOSIONS, REVOLUTIONS, AND GENDER JUSTICE MOVEMENTS IN ASIA AND AUSTRALIA

Asia during the first decade of the millennium was, like Eastern Europe, a hotbed of student resistance, and student protest actions took just about every conceivable form. The region's wide variety of cultures, societies, religions, and governments, which had often historically defined themselves in contrast to their neighbors, also influenced one another through an ever-increasing economic globalism, the proliferation of more affordable technology, and the constantly expanding reach of social media. For nations like Australia that had strong ties to the West, students' issues often mirrored those in Europe or the United States. But even in authoritarian nations, the transmission of Western media and culture spread by new technology and networks encouraged the growth of prodemocracy and civil rights movements. Adding to these cultural influences, the prodemocracy revolutions in Eastern Europe inspired hope in many seeking to overthrow their own authoritarian regimes. Such influences were offset or directly countered by robust dictatorial countermeasures. As China's government consolidated power domestically, its influence spread across the region in aggressive territorial and economic imperialism and through its internet and social-media platforms.

Student resistance has long played a major role in the histories
of the region's nations, and student-led reforms have changed the
courses of the area's nations, from China to Japan, from South
Korea to India. But in this first decade of the millennium, the
technological advances and social interconnectivity spreading
throughout the region began to radically transform student resistance in unprecedented ways. Technology changed the nature of
how demonstrations occurred and what they were about, for access
to global media expanded the reach of Western ideas, exposing relatively isolated areas to contemporary views on civil rights, ideas
of social justice, and, of course, fashion. Globally influential popular culture—from pop singers to movie stars, from hairstyles to
clothes—fueled the desires and attitudes of a younger generation
often willing to challenge their conservative elders, religious codes,
and governments in many of the area's cultures and societies.

That said, while interconnectivity and globalism aid increased
activism levels, and a number of resistance efforts in the region's
countries sought to engage on international issues, most of the
resistance struggles in the region remained localized and coun-
try-specific. They mostly had to do with specific nations' struggles
over their own citizens' identities, ideas of self-determination, and
rights. South Korean students, for example, would protest in giant
numbers against Japan's school-curriculum reforms, but what they
were demonstrating against was the national and personally felt
slight in Japan's whitewashing of the crimes its soldiers committed
during their early-twentieth-century invasions of Korea. Because
the region's many societies are so different from one another, and
the relations among them so complex, it's hard to summarize the
various student actions beyond saying that a lot was going on and
that the nature and efficacy of the protests were changed by rapidly
evolving technology. How quickly those changes swept through the
various countries of the region depended on the extent of civilian
access to modern technology.

In this chapter, the number and range of actions are at times
mind-boggling, due to the sheer number of different political sys-

tems and forms of governments under which they occurred. But one way of understanding the region during the 2000s is to think of it as a place in which almost every permutation of governmental authority, from absolute tyranny to liberal democracy—and everything in between—battled to control or stop internal forces of social change that were fueled by the technological innovations of the internet and social media. One can track by relative activism levels which countries enjoyed the proliferation of affordable new technologies and when. Unlike in Eastern Europe, except for in the countries that produced technology for capitalist markets, such as Japan, the spread of affordable personal technology happened at a slower pace, expanding mostly in urban environments with a rising middle class. By the end of the decade, though, access to social networks and to newly developed resistance strategies had spread across the entire region, from Australia to Malaysia and from India to the Philippines.

Governmental responses to the elevation in student activism ranged from seemingly medieval acts of violence, especially early on in the decade, to sophisticated cyber-countermeasures. When suppression failed, authority turned to co-option and absorption. For their part, activists deployed and refined their strategies and developed new tactics such as flash mobbing. They created sophisticated networking structures and added social-media platforms to their practices alongside the building of street barricades. In almost every instance, the outcomes of conflict between the forces of change and conservative control were situational, that is, tied to their unique historical and political context. But over the course of the decade, an effective combination of strategies for resistance grew out of the region's mixture of different forms of physical struggles and tactics. During the following decade, and certainly by the end of it, protestors across the region would have a sophisticated playbook of effective tactics and strategies for widespread resistance. The region thus served as a broad testing ground for new strategies of resistance. This wide range of experimentation with and development and refinement of effective protest strategies, tools, and actions would, by 2020, be combined with innovations occurring in the West to create highly effective, globally codified forms of resistance.

Counterresistance methods were similarly experimented with in the region, developed, and refined. With many nations not bound by the same civil-rights laws as nations in the West, this decade was one of experimentation for advocates of social control. As authoritarianism proliferated across the globe, some of the practices developed in the 2000s in authoritarian Asian countries would be adopted by governments around the world. The passing of anti-terrorism laws, government surveillance of citizens and groups identified as vaguely threatening to national security, preemptive arrests, draconian prison sentences, the hacking of opposition groups' networks, and national disinformation campaigns—all these strategies were developed and refined as much in Asia as in Eastern Europe and Russia. Their influence in the West was profound. In the next decade, US President Trump's comportment in office, his policies, and his corrupt exploitation of the nation's executive branch would reflect both his general admiration of dictators, such as Kim Jong-un and Vladimir Putin, and his appreciation for their ability to suppress internal opposition.

We begin this chapter with Australia, which is a unique outlier in the region because of its strong ties to the West and because of its paradoxical cultural identity as both a fiercely independent democracy and an extremely multicultural and diverse nation with a substantial immigrant population. That combination is evident in its student resistance efforts, which both kept its conservative democratic government in check and supported prodemocracy resistance movements occurring in neighboring nations in the early 2000s.

In 1999, Australia's conservative government under Prime Minister John Howard sought to disempower student unions through a carefully orchestrated campaign that included legislation and budget cuts, and although students protested the actions, they found themselves losing power. Student union membership had been compulsory, and unions charged mandatory fees that were funneled toward promoting or agitating for causes. Prior to Facebook, Twitter, and the social-media explosion to come, the unions were an important way for students to connect, inform, and mobilize. Over the next decade, legislation was repeatedly introduced to abolish mandatory membership, which the government argued was undemocratic. The conservatives feared the student unions were becoming similar to Mexico's UNAM activist organizations, through which leftist students were able to wield tremendous social power.

Underfunding education forced university administrations to raise educational fees, with some universities raising student loan fees by 25 percent. The increasingly corporate and bureaucratic climate on campuses resulted in students being prosecuted more often when they broke laws and university policies. Students rightly perceived all of this as part of an institutionalized campaign to dismantle the strong student networks and their collective bargaining power. In tandem, these moves isolated students and made their investment in their education more costly, thereby increasing the risk students took when jeopardizing their place at the university by protesting.

Students held peaceful marches and sit-ins against the reforms, but they also stormed administration meetings and barricaded themselves in university libraries. Many of the educational-reform protests during the first few years of the decade were peaceful, but at other times, such as at the University of Technology Sydney (UTS) in 2004, they erupted into violence. At UTS that year, a demonstration grew violent when four hundred angry students attempted to force their way into the vice-chancellor's office. They were attacked by police and suppressed with pepper spray.

In the 2000s, educational and national and global issues kept Australia's student activists busy, though their concerns shifted over the decade from domestic issues such as educational reforms and indigenous rights to antiwar campaigns, and then back to domestic issues. In 2000, students helped organize the Walk for Reconciliation across Sydney Harbour Bridge, a demonstration effort to unite indigenous Australians and Australians from nonindigenous backgrounds. It drew some fifty thousand people. Immediately following the US invasion of Iraq, the antiwar rallies began, and they happened often. Although they continued in various campaigns, such as the "Books Not Bombs" movement, by middecade they too had lost much of their momentum.

That's not to say that students, when protesting, were not passionate or engaged. They were. An anti–Iraq War demonstration in Brisbane in 2003, for example, fielded between fifty thousand and a hundred thousand protestors—the largest demonstration the city had ever seen, eclipsing the anti–Vietnam War rallies of the sixties. But by 2006, antioccupation demonstration numbers had dropped, often reaching only the low hundreds. Although anti–US military actions and protests against Australia's troop involvement in Iraq continued, by the end of the decade, the issue had played itself out as a protest generator.

As in the West, Australian students took full advantage of rapidly changing technology in order to build, link, and reinforce their networks. This trend was displayed in the evolution of the students' antiglobalization movement. Out of an antiglobalization blockade of the World Economic Forum in Melbourne in 2000, in which factions clashed with police, the M1 Alliance was born. "M1" stands for "May 1" or "May Day," the international workers' day celebrating the 1886 adoption of the eight-hour workday. The M1 Alliance was a collection of socialist, human rights, and environmental activist groups, M1 included, that also included the National Union of Students, the International Socialist Organization, Friends of the Earth, the Socialist Alliance, Jabiluka Action, QUEER (Queers United to Eradicate Economic Rationalism), Autonomous Web of Liberation, members of the Greens (environmentalist party), and various women's-rights organizations. The government's efforts to break up student collectives had motivated students to weld their disparate issues and forces together.

M1 would organize massive antiglobalization rallies over the coming years, and overly harsh response by authorities to their protests only swelled their ranks. In 2001, for example, ten thousand activists protested at the IMF summit in Melbourne, effectively shutting down the stock exchange and vandalizing a McDonald's (a symbol to them, as to many activists, of capitalist globalization). Brisbane police responded violently to the M1 Alliance protest there, pepper-spraying hundreds and dragging students into police wagons. When other students threw themselves in front of the vans to block them, they too were sprayed and arrested.

News of the violence and calls for support were spread through the linked networks, and sister rallies and responses occurred throughout Australia. Effigies of Prime Minister John Howard and Victoria premier Steve Bracks were burned all over Australia. But these responses did not come without backlashes of their own. In Perth, for example, officials used mounted police to smash the lines of protestors gathered before the city's stock exchange. The Australian antiglobalization efforts were significant, but the machinery of globalization had too much economic momentum and political backing to be stopped. It did provide a common foil, though, that many different Australian student groups opposed, and thus linked their networks, forging alliances that would quickly expand from being internet-based to being social media–based.

Toward the end of the decade, especially in 2009, other notable activist flare-ups occurred in Australia over protections for foreign students as incidents of violence against them increased. This was especially true for Chinese and Indian students studying in the country. One particularly large demonstration occurred in Melbourne, by Indian students enraged they had been labelled "soft targets" by Victoria police. As the numbers of foreign students had increased dramatically in Australia (due to the country's marketing of its universities to the wealthy throughout the region), those students began to feel empowered by their numbers. They demonstrated against prejudice, arguing that since foreign students pumped millions of dollars into Australia's economy, they should not be met with hate speech by locals and racist police policies.

There was a particularly notable trend in the country in the 2000s toward increasingly internationally connected universities, thereby increasing the solidarity Australian activists had with foreign students both within and outside the country. Australian students increasingly supported protests for students fighting injustice in neighboring nations from Bangladesh to Indonesia, from Tibet to Papua New Guinea.

To the east of Australia, students in Fiji began the decade in a state of turmoil. A coup was attempted in 2000 against the government of Prime Minister Mahendra Chaudhry (who was of Indian descent) by nationalist insurgents who took government officials hostage. This resulted in massive uprisings, followed by military intervention, and then sustained riots in which more than two hundred buildings were burned. Such internal divisions within the country were evident on campuses as well: at Fiji's only university, the University of the South Pacific, the year saw massive student protests after an Indo-Fijian was selected over an indigenous Fijian to head the university administration. The demonstrations included sit-in occupations and walkouts by students and teachers. Throughout much of Asia, spanning the central mainland nations and spreading across the many island nations, sustained conflict between groups of strongly self-identifying people remained a defining characteristic, especially in a context of postimperialism. While grudges and hatred are often maintained by older generations over past violence and wrongs, much of the force for tribalism in the new millennium, in the West as well as in the East, was driven by younger generations.

In contrast to historical tribalism—whether ethnic, religious, national, or political, entrenched on one or both sides of a conflict—young activists were also creating a new form of tribalism centered on efforts to change their societies, cultures, and governments. Rallying around ideas of democracy, social justice, or liberalization, they forged networks and alliances with other groups to work for joint reforms and created generationally based group identities in order to try to build numbers.

This is where new technologies available internationally in the 2000s made a huge difference in organized civil disobedience and activism, and why they globally energized youth, particularly students who were engaging with social media and taking their identities from it. The successful organizing of social revolts in Eastern Europe resulted in more than local changes, for activists were explicitly disseminating a fashion for revolt and their strategies, tactics, and technologies. Social media and pop culture mixed in the formation of international networks and distribution channels. Even where the free internet was banned or difficult to access, savvy activists found ways to get it and the revolutionary ideas and strategies it contained.

Those looking could find guidance on how to organize and protest, how to build large-scale organizations, and strategies for advancing social reforms. Organizations such as Otpor or CANVAS would disseminate step-by-step instructions on how to generate nationwide prodemocracy movements against authoritarians. But more influential was simply the exposure to contemporary fashions and the cultural materialization of ideas of self-determination, individualism, and self-empowerment. These are, after all, extensions of ideas of democracy, civil rights, and social justice, and the internet, social media, and pop culture were spreading them to young people around the world in the 2000s.

There was no country in Asia where students identified more as a powerful social bloc than in Indonesia. Just before the turn of the millennium in Indonesia, massive student protests had changed the course of history, helping forcing Suharto from power in 1999 and aiding the liberation of East Timor. But the history of Indonesian activism was marred by extreme violence. On the eve of the new decade, thousands of students and activists protesting new security measures that would give sweeping powers to the military were suppressed by police and military troops in Jakarta. The crackdown occurred over two days, eventually leaving seven dead and hundreds wounded. Three of the victims were killed by snipers. Outraged at the first day's violence, more students and workers poured into the streets. Police opened fire upon them with rubber-coated bullets and, in some cases, live ammunition. They hit protestors with tear gas and then attacked them with clubs. The second day of the violence began with a predawn raid by the military on Atma Jaya Catholic University. The resulting riots, however, forced the military to suspend its plans for security reform and greater control over citizens.

From 1999 to 2001, under president Abdurrahman Wahid, in a show of reforming the military and addressing past wrongs, twenty-four Indonesian soldiers were convicted of killing fifty-seven activists in Aceh. Eleven of the soldiers had attacked a boarding school, killing thirteen students, while thirteen other soldiers were convicted of slaughtering injured student activists, even though they claimed the murders had been carried out under orders. Student protests continued in Indonesia over a variety of issues across the nation, from students being knifed by police to government corruption, from fuel hikes to US imperialism. In 2001, spurred by corruption charges against the president and frustrated with Wahid's authoritarianism, ten thousand students demonstrated for his resignation in Jakarta.

Following these and similar demonstrations, thousands of pro-Wahid supporters held their own demonstrations, many waving machetes and bamboo truncheons. These demonstrations were sponsored by key supporters of Wahid's government, in a made-for-media tactic historically employed by authoritarian government sponsors from China to Argentina. Undeterred by the threat of violence, anti-Wahid students marched in Jakarta in larger numbers, with one student demonstration attracting twelve thousand participants. They laid siege to parliament and skirmished with police, who were desperately trying to keep them separated from pro-Wahid demonstrators marching from another direction. Increasingly besieged, Wahid dismissed cabinet members, attempted to call for martial law in Jakarta (an order refused by the chief of police), and then was impeached. Seeing the timing was opportune and that Wahid's removal would have popular support, Indonesia's military leadership moved forty thousand troops into

Jakarta and surrounded the presidential palace with tanks pointing their guns toward the building.

In 2001, the newly installed Indonesian president, Megawati Sukarnoputri, backed the US war in Afghanistan, which prompted more anti–United States protests in Jakarta. Sukarnoputri was quick to condemn the 2003 US invasion of Iraq as illegal. Following the invasion, Jakarta exploded in student-led protests against the United States. Protestors burned George W. Bush in effigy, chanted "Down with USA," and vandalized US businesses and fast-food chains. Students gathered at the gates and threw stones at the US embassy. The government called for calm, but was mostly relieved their anger was trained elsewhere.

Demonstrations were common that year, and the largest, including one that amassed a crowd of ten thousand at the US embassy, were repelled with water cannons. The intensity and size of the demonstrations made it clear that a significant portion of the population was intent on having its political voice heard and taken into account by the government. For the time being, the corrupt strongman style of authoritarianism characteristic of past governments had been effectively put in check. In 2004, in the country's first direct election of a president, Susilo Bambang Yudhoyono won, and he was reelected in 2009. Student protests continued on a variety of issues in the capital for the rest of the decade, but the momentum and common cause that had united them against authoritarianism faded.

Elsewhere in Indonesia, students battled authoritarianism locally and their own state governments while seeking social reforms or agitating over local issues. In 2006 in Papua, for example, students protesting Freeport mining operations were attacked by police, leading to riots that left three police and a member of the military dead. Paramilitary troops were unleashed by local officials to suppress the demonstrators, and the armed mobs came down hard on students, raiding campuses and skirmishing with protestors. Security forces were accused of attacking random youth with tear gas, guns, and machetes, and many of the activists fled into mountain jungles where they continued to be hunted by security and mobs. Troops that ventured too far into the jungles, however, reported sometimes coming under arrow fire. Other causes—anti–United States movements, anti-Dutch campaigns (after the 2008 anti-Muslim cartoon scandal), and opposition to fuel cost hikes due to government shortages in 2008 would draw student protests—but not on the scale they had a decade earlier.

After Suharto had resigned from power in 1998 and before Wahid's subsequent election, Vice President B. J. Habibie had taken the reins of leadership and embarked on a series of liberal reforms for the country, including offering East Timor autonomy under Indonesian sovereignty. Students began demonstrating in East Timor in large but peaceful marches, protesting that limited self-rule wasn't enough; others agitated for complete independence. These student marches grew as large as fifteen thousand participants. A long way from Jakarta, students in East Timor were often met with violent police suppression or attacked by government-backed local militias. But violence and government-sanctioned torture (which was common under Suharto) was nothing new to the students of East Timor, and though it continued, they did not relent.

Resistance leader Xanana Gusmão, who was newly freed from prison but under house arrest, called for the students of East Timor to eschew violence, counting on international pressure to work more effectively, but violence was common and more was coming. Bowing to international and internal pressure, President Habibie allowed the United Nations oversight on an independence referendum for East Timor and was surprised to find over 80 percent of the province's population voted in favor of complete separation. The following day, the Indonesian-backed militias that had been causing sporadic violence were mobilized and unleashed on the general civilian population to punish them for their honesty, and the violence was enough to provoke international intervention. An Australian-led multinational force reasserted control over the region, and in 2002 the Republic of East Timor was formed, electing Gusmão its first president.

But within months of their independence, East Timorian students were protesting that not all seemed to be benefitting from the international aid flowing into the country. Activists on the ground thus learned perennial lessons for those protesting for reforms in countries where corruption is commonplace—the struggle for social change and justice is a struggle against corruption that is structural and imbedded. Foreigners in the country had incredible wealth, and a small, well-connected segment of East Timor's citizens were funneling off aid funds while the majority of the population was suffering. Social turmoil continued. Students demonstrated in massive numbers. Vestiges of the militias that had rampaged across the country in 1998 coordinated attacks on government buildings and sparked riots throughout Dili. The prime minister's house was set on fire, and ten buildings were gutted. Police on several occasions fired into rioting crowds, killing several and wounding many. The seven hundred UN security forces troops still present since the election shielded government buildings as best they could in these uprisings, but they were vastly overmatched by the chaos and hunkered down.

As the country struggled to find its way toward more and more stability, student protests lessened in size, though individual student groups often continued to protest against government reforms they didn't like. And corruption remained a problem. In 2008, while most of the country was averaging the wage equivalent of twenty-five US cents per person per day and the country had a 46 percent unemployment rate, the government made the mistake of purchasing sixty-five luxury Toyota Land Cruisers—one for each MP. This set off large student protests against government corruption. Fueled by massive poverty and an inexperienced government often accused of corruption, demonstrations that would often end in violence would force UN peacekeeping troops to stay in the country until 2012.

In many Asian nations, a new generation of people began agitating in large numbers, straining under the yoke of authoritarianism and seeing others in the region and elsewhere try for, and in some cases achieve, large-scale social and political reforms. In Cambodia, for example, students began to demonstrate against their government in weekly marches at the turn of the twenty-first century, something that would have been unthinkable only a few years before. The last major demonstration prior in Cambodia, in 1991, had been brutally crushed by police, and all opposition newspapers had been subsequently outlawed. Although in name a democracy, the country was ruled by one political party, shot through with endemic corruption.

It was really not until 2000 that students began consistently and openly experimenting with newly legislated, limited freedoms of speech. They were in part inspired by a number of successful workers' marches that had occurred at the end of the nineties, which had tested government tolerance and activist determination. In 2000, four thousand demonstrators marched openly in the capital, demanding higher wages and a shorter work week for garment workers. Emboldened by the garment workers not being immediately crushed, students began protesting for everything from legislative reforms against corruption to Vietnamese immigration policies to stopping military landgrabs. Although the protests caused traffic jams on a weekly, sometimes daily basis, they were tolerated, a sign that Cambodia was changing. By 2010, under international and local pressure, the government would establish anticorruption laws, though it would not do much enforcing and corruption would remain among the country's worst problems. Still, students were risking speaking up about the nation's social ills, and this was impressive given the government's earned reputation for human-rights abuses, tolerance of widespread human trafficking, and police torture of those arrested for any reason.

The socialist republic of Laos has since 1975 been a one-party communist government that, although constitutionally granting civil rights, has often been accused by international human-rights organizations of imprisoning and torturing activists. Although another one-party authoritarian system, it serves as a counterpoint to Cambodia's relative permissiveness toward demonstrations in how the authoritarian government of Laos responded to demonstrations in the 2000s. To wit, demonstrations were simply not tolerated. Inspired by students agitating for political reforms in neighboring countries, in 1999, activists tried anyway and formed the Lao Students Movement for Democracy. They made posters and attempted to stage a peaceful protest for democratic reforms. Hampered by unfamiliarity with how to stage a demonstration, the leaders were arrested before they could get the march underway, and police scattered the marchers. The five organizers were convicted of treason, and each was handed a sentence of from ten to twenty years in prison. One of the activists died in prison from abuse. Two others were released in 2017, and the remaining two simply disappeared while in prison.

Bolstering its zero-tolerance policies, the government passed Article 66 of the Lao Penal Law, which assigned a one-to-five-year prison term for anyone participating in a public protest against the government. The activist spirit is hard to kill, though. In 2001, a small group of people held a demonstration marking the anniversary of the 1999 protest and called for government reforms. It was viciously attacked by government troops. Those arrested included five foreigners—a Belgian, a Russian, and three Italians.

It turned out that those arrested were members of something called the Transnational Radical Party, a nongovernmental international organization that claimed ten thousand members—many of them students—across nearly four dozen countries. TRP members agitated for democracy in China, Myanmar, and Vietnam. They protested for Tibetan independence, would back Uighurs against the Chinese, and demonstrated for Chechens and Ukrainians against Russia. The result of the Laos arrests was an international brouhaha with the countries represented by the five arrested foreigners—especially as one of the arrested was a member of the European Parliament. Individuals or small groups of people continued to challenge the government from time to time and were arrested for their efforts. But the government's overwhelmingly brutal response to protests or actions, its reputation for human-rights abuses against those it arrested, and the relative isolation and insularity of Laos forestalled the surge of student or youth movements happening elsewhere in Asia. Sporadic incidents of suppression would remind Laos citizens not to rock the boat. In 2013, for example, a prominent Lao environmental activist, Sombath Somphone, who was making waves internationally, would be abducted in the middle of the afternoon and disappeared, never to be heard from again.

The Lao government's exercise of control over unrest and demonstrations in the 2000s is an example of the level of top-down suppression and social control that most authoritarian governments dream of imposing on their own societies. It lacked the sophistication of states that in the 2010s would use physical suppression in combination with highly developed propaganda machines, such as China or North Korea, but it was crudely effective. Most members of the opposition feared to protest, and when they did protest, they did so ineffectively and were simply arrested and prosecuted under laws that guaranteed they'd disappear for some time. Most would not be heard from again.

Following the rise of international terrorism in the decade to come, every nation on earth would pass new and purposefully vague antiterrorism laws, and most of these imposed harsh penalties. Although some actual terrorists would be caught and prosecuted under the new laws, authoritarian governments would use them with impunity against opposition leaders and activists and find legal justification to suppress peaceful protests. Notably, the type of international networking done by TRP, CANVAS, or Lao activists such as Sombone that often generated outside support for causes and international awareness of human-rights abuses would often be used to justify arrests, with governments claiming activists were connected to international terrorist networks.

Although authoritarians around the world have discovered how useful in suppression the misapplication of antiterrorism laws could be in the last two decades, Malaysia's government was already well versed in the art. In Malaysia at the turn of the new millennium, students feared to protest publicly as the government suppressed public opposition via the Internal Security Act (ISA), known locally as the "white terror." Those convicted of transgressing the law included labor agitators, activists, religious leaders, and political opposition leaders. Convictions carried harsh prison terms, a lifelong criminal record that prevented employment and, in more than a few cases, the death penalty. More than ten thousand people have been prosecuted using the ISA since its adoption. For students thinking about political issues, the risk was compounded by the Universities and Colleges Act, which forbade political activity by students. The punishment was expulsion, which carried subsequent prospects of lifelong unemployment. The government continued to refine its antiactivism and social-order laws that limited freedom of speech and assembly, and some students mobilized. But fearing arrest and prosecution for speaking out, they protested silently, by wearing white armbands.

Following the US invasion of Iraq and the expansion of American military involvement in the Middle East, a number of anti–United States and anti-Israel protests were staged in Malaysia by student members of the ruling party's youth organization, the United Malays National Organization. More than ten thousand people protested, burning US and Israeli flags. As international media coverage increased in the 2000s, and with it the pressure that could be brought to bear on governments when large demonstrations occurred, there was also a growing awareness that mass uprisings and large demonstrations could be used politically by governments to support international policies. Countries like Malaysia and North Korea routinely began staging large student protests supporting domestic or foreign policy decisions that could be filmed and broadcast through their government-controlled media services.

In 2007, at great risk, students and civil-rights activists came out in force against what they saw as corrupt elections and for the furtherance of human rights. Their protests were bolstered by thousands of lawyers who publicly supported the students. But unlike the anti–United States demonstrations supported by the government, their actions were interpreted by the government as a threat to social stability, and once more, student leaders and lawyers were arrested and prosecuted. For the remained of the decade, activism in the country was dampened. Levels of activism in the country would increase some over the next ten years as social-media networking and new technologies flooded into the country, but the risks were still too high for it to really take off.

In countries like Nepal, where the government has been notoriously unstable, student resistance was extremely high. Demonstrations mirrored larger national political divisions. After the end of Nepal's brutal civil war in 2006, political wrangling and shifting coalitions continued to wrack the country and toppled one set of leaders after another. Students constantly protested against chronic social and governmental problems in the 2000s, including high fuel costs, fee hikes, and black marketeering, but these protests were strongly affiliated with political-party interests. Even so, student collectives realized the power they had and wielded it, repeatedly calling nationwide strikes and fielding demonstrations of considerable force.

In 2006, students and activists aligned with the opposition to King Gyanendra's government began massive demonstrations against the government's use of violence to quell demonstrations. Although they were attacked, they were able to overrun city streets, blockade highways, and paralyze the country. The Maoist-led oppositional challenge to the monarchy morphed into wider, massive prodemocracy demonstrations in 2007. The movement was a coalition of seven oppositional political parties, including the Maoists. The students and activists had strength and numbers enough to challenge power in the streets, and their marches were violently hit by shock troops firing tear gas and rubber-coated bullets. The government set curfews in the capital, but Maoists roamed the streets at night, attacking government forces, known supporters of the monarchy, and suspected informants. By day, government troops reasserted control, beating prodemocracy demonstrators, known Maoist supporters, and anyone else caught near the protests.

In many ways the struggle had turned into a generational battle. The wider population was by 2007 tired of years of violence and national turbulence and had lost faith in the monarchy and the king's ability to rule. Following a UN-monitored peace accord, parliament declared Nepal officially a republic, effectively deposing Gyanendra, and his palace was subsequently turned into a museum. This did not lessen student activism in the country, though, as infighting over government power sharing, corruption, the slowness of reforms, and criticism of whoever happened to be in charge at the moment incited protests. Factional fighting between rival student groups would occur at numerous universities, and tensions (and tires) burned between rival student factions for years to come.

Similarly, Bangladesh's student activism mirrored the larger battles fought over control of a perennially turbulent state. Since Bangladesh was recognized in 1972 by the United Nations as an independent and sovereign nation, its government has gone through numerous permutations, seen both free elections and coups d'état. It has had socialist and democratic governments, a military junta, and provisional governments, and was occasionally ruled under martial law. The two major parties wrestling over control were the progressive National Awami Party (NAP) and the Bangladesh Nationalist Party (BNP). The struggle for self-determination, independence, stability, and identity spilled over onto campuses, which were often rocked with protests and violence. The two main student groups in the country were student wings of the two majority national political parties, and like members of their parent organizations, they often attacked one another.

When the Bangladesh Student League, which was allied with NAP, called a university strike and marched in opposition to the BNP at the University of Dhaka in 2003, marchers were attacked by the BNP student wing, the Nationalist Student League. When the Nationalist Student League marched, the other group attacked. Clashes between the groups and injuries were commonplace, and university administrations had trouble controlling them. Unable to handle the students, the university administration relied on Dhaka police to suppress them. At a 2005 demonstration protesting the killing of a local woman, attended in force by both student leagues, a bomb went off between the groups. Each side blamed the other, and the violence resulted in attacks and counterattacks by the two groups that would go on for years and leave many students dead.

Social turmoil was a constant in Bangladesh. After national elections were called off and emergency rule imposed in 2007, students of both parties staged strikes and marches, culminating in a mass demonstration against the military-backed provisional government in August. This march was violently suppressed by baton-wielding police troops, who fired so much tear gas that the capital appeared to be burning. Tired of student protestors, police invaded the more politically active campuses, gassing residence halls to pry students out. The military occupied the University of Dhaka, and a citywide curfew restored momentary calm, but these moves also sparked larger demonstrations across Bangladesh. The government ordered curfews in six major cities, shut down cell-phone service nationwide, and set up highway checkpoints and security blockades after students began blocking traffic on roads and highways by setting cars and tires on fire.

After a week of turmoil and continuous demonstrations and riots, the government of Bangladesh had filed criminal charges against some eighty-seven thousand people. Although the government shut down cell phones and tried to block internet use, images of police brutality spread throughout the country and internationally, bringing heavy international pressure on the country to stop the violence and to hold elections. In 2008, the Awami League (AL) alliance led by Sheikh Hasina won parliamentary elections in a landslide victory. Over the course of the decade, student demonstrations continued to reflect the larger political struggles wracking the country. It was an object lesson in how do-or-die rhetoric and hardened ideologies can lead to uncontrollable violence.

In this region of the world, a number of developed nations still remained relatively isolated from much of the rest of the world in the early 2000s in terms of media coverage and international trade. This allowed authoritarians to severely punish opposition activists with impunity. Myanmar has been the site of civil war and internal struggle since gaining its independence in 1948. Unlike Bangladesh, though, it saw little in the way of student protests in the first decade of the millennium, as the military dictatorship preemptively arrested students and activists before any sizeable demonstrations could gain traction and imprisoned them in horrendous conditions. But even in these regions, changes in technology and the rise of social media would soon have tremendous influence on the efficacy of student activism. Myanmar illustrates why student resistance is a seemingly perennial driver of social evolution, one that even if stamped out for a while always returns.

Violent attacks on protests in 1988 under the military regime that ruled for almost two decades had left activists with little stomach for public demonstrations. Quietly, however, they chafed under authoritarian rule, and they were accessing and watching generational uprisings as they occurred in nations around them. In 2007, two thousand monks under the All Burma Monks' Alliance staged long-planned peaceful marches for economic and civil-rights reforms. They were joined by a new generation of activists and student groups largely without memories of the 1988 crackdowns, activists encouraged through international social media in their desire to participate in social reforms in their own country. The protests swelled in Yangon, Mandalay, and several other cities into what became known as the Saffron Revolution.

The military junta controlling Myanmar was also watching the civilian-led uprisings around the world and feared the demonstrations would lead to a national movement. It unleashed police and military troops on the marchers, and the brutality of the attacks was incredible. Troops bludgeoned civilians with truncheons and rifle stocks. Students and locals tried to protect the monks, forming human chains around them, but they too were clubbed, and a number of monks were beaten to death in the streets.

By 2007, though, widespread access to cheap technology had come to Myanmar, and reports and images of the violence spread internationally across the internet. Scrambling to counter the students and stop the rapidly expanding protests, the government attempted to shut down internet service, confined nonprotesting monks to monasteries, and emptied campuses of their students. Police confiscated all computers and cell phones they could find and arrested thousands of people. Fifteen hundred people subsequently "disappeared" into Burmese prisons, according to international human-rights groups, never to be heard from again. In 2008, fourteen arrested members of the 88 Generation Students Group were convicted of crimes against the state and were each sentenced to sixty-five years in prison.

Had the suppression occurred ten years earlier, the government would not have encountered the kind of pressures it faced following the crackdown. But due to the technological revolution, times had changed, and news and images of police violence made it out of the country. International condemnation put tremendous pressure on the government, as did economic sanctions by the West over the violence and the imprisonments. The main party of opposition was the National League for Democracy, still led by Nobel Prize winner Aung San Suu Kyi, who following the 1988 revolts remained under house arrest until 2010. In 2016 she would rise to power, but would soon face demonstrations and protests against government corruption and her role in enabling genocide.

There were many other countries in the region facing chronic problems of corruption, and one of the biggest challenges to activists in places where corruption is historically endemic is stopping it, even after old leaders are overthrown and new leaders are installed. The Philippines began the decade with the peaceful revolution and overthrow in 2001 of Joseph Estrada. A nine-year stint of economic growth followed under the administration of President Maria Gloria Macapagal Arroyo, but her presidency also became embroiled in graft and corruption controversies. Arroyo was successful at boosting economic prosperity for parts of the Philippines, but she was also seen by many as pandering to stronger nations while feathering her own nest.

Government corruption wasn't the only things students protested against, though. In 2002, when Japanese prime minister

Junichiro Koizumi visited the Philippines to strengthen economic ties and arrived at the Malacañan Presidential Palace to meet with President Arroyo, he was greeted with a demonstration. Hundreds of students, workers, women's-rights activists, and indigenous people protested Koizumi's refusal to officially acknowledge the use of Philippine women as "comfort women" for Japanese soldiers during World War Two. A group of aged women, formerly sexually enslaved by Japanese troops, tried to intercept him as he visited Luneta Park and the tomb of José Rizal, the Philippines' national hero. Police stopped them and covered them with tarps as Koizumi's limo passed. Activist students supporting the survivors condemned the police action in further protests.

While challenges to the government came with the risk of violent suppression, students in public schools in the Philippines were nevertheless active on a wide range of issues. They marched for causes ranging from social reforms to anticorruption measures. They called strikes and demonstrated after the 2004 elections were marred by accusations of ballot stuffing. But public opposition to corruption could be fatal in the Philippines, especially in more isolated areas. In 2009, in the Maguindanao province, fifty-eight people were kidnapped and killed on their way to file a candidacy certificate for a challenger to the local mayor. Thirty-two of those killed were journalists. Demonstrations in the capital ensued, with students turning out in large numbers, and President Arroyo was forced to declare a state of emergency for the region. Under pressure to seem as though it was holding the killers accountable, the government opened an investigation and had some people arrested and charged, though the trials themselves were marked with accusations of bribery, unexpected dismissals, and seemingly endless appeals.

There are countries in Asia, however, where authoritarianism is so effectively entrenched in societal and governing structures as to keep student resistance at almost nonexistent levels. While Laos served as an example of crude oppression, Singapore served as a model of another extreme. The nation by 2000 had tremendous control over its citizens. It underscores what is at stake when an authoritarian regime is fully empowered and codifies that power through laws with draconian punishments for opposition. Singapore has laws severely limiting freedom of expression and assembly and imposes harsh penalties when they are broken. The state uses the spectacle of punishment as deterrence, including mandatory caning for some thirty offenses and execution for drug trafficking. The constitution does not guarantee privacy to its citizens, and the Internal Security Act allows for indefinite detention without trial of people suspected of threatening religious or racial harmony, espionage, terrorism, or subversion. A political opponent of the government was "held" under this act in prison for thirty-two years.

A slew of other acts expanded on such government powers in the new millennium, allowing for things like keeping those *thought to be about to demonstrate* under house arrest. With police firmly in control of the general population and a zero-tolerance policy for whenever unrest threatens to occur, illegal public actions have been few and far between. Demonstrations without permits for citizens are allowed on only one corner in Singapore, a spot under heavy, constant surveillance. Despite the risk, sometimes a person will voice opposition on local and national issues, such as unfair labor practices, on that one corner, but for the most part citizens' critiques stay private and within safe bounds.

There are occasionally sanctioned demonstrations held by students for moderate cultural reforms, but attendees at these are careful not to challenge authority, and the demonstrations are rather weak. In 2003, a protest against the consumption of shark-fin soup was held in which participants dressed in shark suits walked a 10k course and then had their fins symbolically cut off by a knife-wielding chef as they crossed the finish line. That said, illegal demonstrations do sometimes occur in places other than the protest corner, but they do not happen often and they end quickly. In 2008, a group of about twenty activists peacefully protesting outside the Parliament House against the rising cost of living were arrested for their audacity, and in 2009, two activists protested outside government buildings against the deportation of Myanmar nationalists. They also were arrested.

North Korea, like Singapore, has for decades kept an iron grip on student protests. Students are allowed to demonstrate in state-sponsored actions that support the government of North Korea or in demonstrations that are politically useful to the government, but students don't demonstrate directly against the government. This stems in part from outright fear, for publicly challenging authority in this country ends in certain arrest and imprisonment, probable torture, and possible death. But the other reason one doesn't see opposition demonstrations is that many students support the government, which has everything to do with its control over all media, education, and recorded history. Students take patriotism classes in school and are taught obedience to the state from the earliest possible age. The North Korean propaganda machine is effective, promoting loyalty to the state over family.

But even were one inclined to question the state, the fear thwarting public recalcitrance is certainly understandable. Satellite surveillance has, for example, identified six massive slave-labor camps in the country holding a total of around two hundred thousand people. Into these prisons are thrown suspected dissidents, who are forced to work in state factories and are "reeducated" before being allowed to return to society. Many of those imprisoned simply disappear into the camps, never to be seen again. Amnesty International calculates around ten thousand people die in North Korean prisons each year—an incredible number of so-called "defectives" purged from the population annually. The Orwellian nature of North Korea's security includes its own form of thought crime, for the State Security Department regularly arrests and imprisons without trial suspected enemies of the state, and, for not reporting them, jails family members as well.

It's no wonder that demonstrations against authority in North Korea don't occur. Why would a citizen protest when even visiting foreigners picked up for petty vandalism are sentenced to hard labor and face horrendous physical abuse? In 2016, for example, travelling

US student Otto Warmbier was arrested for trying to peel off a propaganda poster in an airport and sentenced to fifteen years of hard labor. He was released after seventeen months, but by then he was blind, deaf, and in a persistent vegetative state with severe brain damage. Warmbier died a few days after being returned to the United States.

Widely considered as the nation that perpetrates the worst human-rights abuses on earth, North Korea has for decades been accused by the United Nations of crimes against humanity. The accusations are largely based on interviews with defectors from the country that reveal the government uses torture, starvation, rape, forced abortion, hard labor, medical experimentation, and murder to coerce and control citizens.

Luckily there are few countries as bad as North Korea in terms of institutionalized abuse. Depending on how you measure it, Vietnam has at best a mixed record on human rights. The country has made social progress on the one hand, instituting reforms such as constitutionally banning torture and guaranteeing "human rights," but on the other hand it also has characteristics specific to systems of one-party rule like those in neighboring Cambodia, Laos, and North Korea. It forbids political parties other than the Communist Party of Vietnam (CPV); outlaws communications, including email, that critique the government; and heavily regulates the internet, using technology to block banned material, words, and phrases and a robust censorship program referred to in international media as "the bamboo firewall." Vietnam does have many newspapers and journalists, though, and does allow some newspapers to be *relatively* outspoken, though not against the Communist Party or its programs.

Economically the country has been a powerhouse in the region. In the 2000s, it heavily invested in infrastructure and in higher education. By 2009, the country had more than two million students in state- and privately sponsored universities and colleges. A number of those students attended extension programs of universities based in other countries, where they were increasingly exposed to Western ideas; Harvard, for example, has a campus there.

Even so, bloggers and activists who find ways around the bamboo firewall are surveilled, monitored, and constantly harassed. Non-threatening demonstrations are allowed to occur from time to time without suppression, but if activists try to protest the government, they are arrested. And police have many legal tools for detaining suspects. In 2003, students held large demonstrations against the US invasion of Iraq, which was an act that for Vietnam carried a lot of historical baggage—but the protests were useful to the government in its own international negotiations. Notably, in 2009, ecological activists tried to stop a Chinese-backed bauxite-mining operation in the country, though they were unsuccessful. And in 2016, the country would see rare large-scale student protests against other policies dealing with China, against Taiwan-based factories, and against the United States. All these protests were significant for their size and the fact that they occurred at all, but then again, they were focused on foreign governments.

Unlike Vietnam, Thailand's various governments have had a much more difficult time dealing with unruly students. By 2000, conflict between those in power and politically oriented activists in the country had been going on for a quarter of a century and would continue well into the new millennium. So too did the viciousness of the tactics those in charge used to suppress demonstrations. The country was already notorious for how it dealt with students, especially due to the 1976 Thammasat University massacre in Bangkok, in which troops opened fire on students with M16s and blew them up with grenades. The ensuing riot was used to justify a military coup on the same day. Thailand was also famous for a 1992 demonstration in which two hundred thousand marchers in Bangkok were attacked under a military crackdown known afterwards as "Black May" or "Bloody May." The various governments and military juntas that have taken control of the country in recent decades feared the volatile, spontaneous, large demonstrations that occasionally occurred in the country, forcing regime change, and they dealt with that fear with violence.

Prodemocracy students, for example, helped push the efforts that eventually resulted in the elected populist Thaksin Shinawatra government (2001–2006). Shinawatra was eventually overthrown by a military-backed coup in 2006. Despite the danger, people came out in massive protests in Bangkok against the overthrow, though predictably they were immediately and violently suppressed. Students defied military bans against assembly. Dressed in black and carrying coffins representing the death of democracy, they marched and were arrested and imprisoned. Weakened by arrests, suffering from disorganization, and barred from holding public protests and assembly, the prodemocracy student movement of Thailand sputtered and fell apart.

It would rise again in 2009. Thaksin accused the Privy Council president and its members of corruption and, taking advantage of the internet and social media, broadcast a video call for a "people's revolution." A hundred thousand demonstrators led by the recently founded United National Front of Democracy against Dictatorship (UDD) answered the call and, wearing signature red shirts, took to the streets of Bangkok. They skirmished with police and military troops over several days, and as the conflicts escalated, the troops opened fire on protestors with both training rounds and live ammunition. Many were wounded, and several UDD activists were later found drowned in the river with their hands bound behind their back, but the government denied involvement in the deaths. Public demonstrations dropped off after the crackdown, but they would rise again early in the next decade.

In contrast to the limited, controlled protests of Vietnam or the volatility and suppression of protests in Thailand, South Korea has for decades had high levels of student activism that effectively pressed for social and governmental reforms. This had everything to do with being a stable liberal democracy with multiple political parties and rights to freedom of speech and assembly. In countries such as South Korea, activism blossoms, and people feel empowered to voice their concerns publicly, though demonstrations perceived as too unruly can be sometimes suppressed forcibly. In South Korea at the beginning of the decade, reforms were under way under newly elected president Kim Dae-jung. He was a former political prisoner who, as president, advanced human rights in South Korea and offered a stance of reconciliation with North Korea, for which he was awarded a Nobel Peace Prize in 2000. He would lead until 2007, when increased provocations from North Korea, including occasional limited attacks on vessels or islands, helped the election of a more conservative administration.

But as happens in democracies that allow free speech, South Korea's protests sometimes ended in violence. In 2000, several hundred students, labor activists, and villagers marched on a US bombing range southwest of Seoul, demanding the base be relocated. They were met by riot police blocking their path. Neither side would back down, and the standoff ended in violence, with police beating the students. It was not an uncommon response for South Korean police to use force when demonstrators refused to disperse, though police violence was increasingly publicly condemned. In a gendered effort to forestall violence at protests, which was started by demonstrators as often as by police, troops in 2000 began staging a "women's line" of defense. For example, 273 female police officers holding a neon tape line blocked a march on a Seoul train station by angry villagers and students. They were supported from behind by standard shock troops, but the reinforcements were not needed. The gendered tactic worked to the extent that violence was avoided when it was employed, but it remained more of a novelty and was not widely implemented.

The most famous South Korean protests during this time period were against the neighboring country of Japan, not the government of South Korea. In 2001, thousands of students launched protests, calling for boycotts after Japan's implementation of revisionist history textbooks in Japan's schools—books in which Japan's aggression throughout Asia was whitewashed. Like the Philippine protestors, activists were particularly upset that Japan refused to acknowledge the war crimes Japanese troops committed against South Korean women during the Second World War. Under internal public pressure as a result of the demonstrations, the Korean government withdrew its ambassador from Tokyo.

When Japan's prime minister, Junichiro Koizumi, visited Japan's war shrine in Yasukuni in 2001 to memorialize its World War Two dead, thousands of South Koreans marched against his visit in Seoul and Pusan. Students burned Koizumi in effigy and waved placards with slogans reading "Kill Koizumi" on them. The intensity of the anger was extreme, with a group of twenty young nationalists in Seoul going so far as to each cut off the tip of a pinky finger to protest.

Anti–United States sentiment was also high. In 2001, two thousand members of the radical, North Korea–supported student group Hanchongnyon (Federation of Student Councils) marched in protest of the US proposal to install a missile-defense shield in South Korea. The next year, thirty-two of its members raided the American Chamber of Commerce building, attempting but failing to hold the Am Cham secretary general hostage. Student leaders of the group were arrested and prosecuted, but this did not deter members of the group from demonstrating further. In 2003, they broke into a US military base and raised their banner and anti–United States signs above an armored vehicle, a diplomatic embarrassment for South Korea's prime minister. The US wars in the Middle East fueled long-standing sentiment against American imperialism and inspired many protests in South Korea.

In 2003, students and workers combined in a rally of a hundred thousand attendees in Seoul demanding labor reforms from the government, which responded by bringing in about ten thousand police troops from other cities to control them. More demonstrations followed. Aided by new technology and social-media platforms, student activism really heated up in the nation in 2005, with students pouring out of campuses to protest myriad issues. Thousands of students, locals, and activists from around the country, for example, formed a human chain and marched on Camp Humphreys, a US military base that the United States was planning to expand. When three hundred of the seven thousand demonstrators tried to push past the police line blocking the road to the base, a melee broke out, with the police using batons and water cannons on the marchers and the protestors fighting back with rocks and metal pipes. Approximately a hundred people were seriously injured.

Students put the internet and social media to work enthusiastically in 2005. Thousands again protested against Japan when it approved new national textbooks for its own schoolchildren that continued to whitewash the country's imperialist past and its enslavement of Korean women in sexual servitude to soldiers. In Seoul, students protested globalization, and as many as fifteen thousand students and farmers marched to protest in Pusan during the 2005 regional Asia-Pacific Economic Cooperation (APEC) summit, where US president George Bush and Asian leaders were meeting to discuss trade. In an extreme action against South Korea's agreement to import rice, two farmers proclaimed it would be quicker to die by their own hands than to starve and committed suicide, intensifying the level of anger among the protestors. The scene in Pusan turned violent, with demonstrators hurling rocks at the more than fifty thousand security troops protecting the summit, but such actions were immediately suppressed with overwhelming force.

The next year, Korean resistance levels remained high. Free trade was a sore topic among students and leftists in the nation, as were more planned US military base expansions. One anti–United States and international trade demonstration in the capital that year numbered ten thousand participants, and more demonstrations followed. After gathering in Pyeongtaek, four thousand students and activists again descended on Camp Humphreys. Thousands of police troops blocked them, but neither side attacked, and the protests stayed peaceful. In 2008, decrying a trade deal lifting a ban on importing beef from the United States, thousands of activists took to the streets of Seoul in a demonstration that expanded to more than a hundred thousand participants, with multiple marches occurring throughout the city. Despite their sizes, the massive demonstrations were mostly nonviolent, with only a few protestors skirmishing with police on the peripheries.

The leaders of the anti–beef import protests cautioned throughout the planning stages that the actions must remain issue-oriented and not turn overtly political or antigovernment. But President Lee Myung-bak's cabinet resigned under pressure from the outpouring anyway, and the US deal was eventually renegotiated. Although the demonstrations had immediate effects on the government, the beef imports were nevertheless resumed, and the demonstrations against them ultimately failed. In 2009 and 2010, there were a number of causes that sparked protests and clashes with police, including more international economic issues and accusations of government corruption. Students used social media to organize and to raise numbers quickly, but the large-scale protests were over for the decade. Having caught up with activists in terms of cybertactics, South Korean security was able to infiltrate their networks and identify when and where demonstrations would happen. They also knew in what numbers students would march, and deployed larger numbers of police to suppress the protests.

Like South Korea's, Japan's student organizations had a long history of political activism. Freedom of speech and civil rights were protected in the country, and being a member of a student group carried cultural cachet. And as in South Korea, protests were commonplace. With the proliferation of the internet and social media, the country's already high level of activism increased more. Large-scale student protests broke out across Japan in 2003, when Japan's government announced it would back the US-led attack on Iraq. Students poured off of campuses, and tens of thousands of activists took to the streets in major urban areas, rebuking Prime Minister Junichiro Koizumi for his support of the invasion. After the war began, students continued their protests on campuses and in front of US bases in Japan. In Tokyo, Osaka, Okinawa, and Nagoya, demonstrators before US installations and headquarter buildings were joined by survivors of Hiroshima and Nagasaki, some of whom also staged hunger strikes. In Hiroshima, antiwar students hoisted banners and held "die-ins for peace." These traditional tactics were combined with internet campaigns enabled by new technologies, and images of the massive demonstrations soon spread around the world. As the war continued, so did the demonstrations. In 2006, students protested in large demonstrations against North Korea after it tested a nuclear warhead.

In response to another highly politicized international issue, in 2008 the Japanese leg of the Olympic Torch relay was caught between demonstrating groups of Free Tibet student activists on one side and pro-Chinese students on the other. Both groups had taken the opportunity of international media coverage of the Olympics to promote their respective causes, and both groups were monitoring each other so they could protest where and when the other appeared. It was not long before the social-media networks of both student organizations began to be hacked and monitored by security. Both groups of demonstrators were intercepted by police in force whenever they converged on the relay. Although vocal and provocative, the students were kept from interfering with the torch's journey. Order was maintained, and violence was avoided. Probably most importantly to authority, the embarrassment of having a violent clash over Tibet air on international news media was averted.

Although student activism in Japan was high in the 2000s and focused on a great many different issues, unlike in previous decades, the demonstrations were controlled but not suppressed. The police monitored them, arrived at demonstration locations with overwhelming numbers, and fenced off certain sites to prevent demonstrations from occurring, and the protests remained relatively violence free. Japan was shifting its tactics in light of new technological advances, relying on increased surveillance and the monitoring of social media and computer networks. Police were taking preemptive actions to avert conflict that could be captured on phones and used to expand support for protests. And they increasingly used restraint so as to not hand students damaging images.

So Japan, like other liberal democracies around the world, countered activism though infiltration strategies and by monitoring networks to thwart protests in their early stages. Realizing cameras were everywhere, police visibly showed restraint or conducted physical suppression out of the public eye. In liberal Asian democracies in the 2010s, such tactics would increasingly be used, which also explains the subsequent rise in provocative actions at demonstrations—black-bloc tactics explicitly meant to goad police into recordable acts of violence.

Taiwan is a unique place in terms of social protest. It is one of the Asian countries that have a governing system based on partial political freedom, thus politically straddling the East and the West. The region is semiautonomous, though it is officially under Chinese authority. Managing a fairly young democracy that to a limited extent is self-governing, the nation's administration has walked a political tightrope that both allows and closely monitors dissent. This is because China has threatened military action should Taiwan claim full independence or should an uprising occur that it cannot control.

There have been two main political coalitions in Taiwan: the Pan-Blue coalition, led by the Guomindang (KMT), who are nationalists supporting eventual unification with China; and the Pan-Green coalition, a political alliance led by the Democratic Progressive Party (DPP), which seeks independence, though not in the short term. In 2000, the DPP candidate won the presidency and was reelected in 2004 for another term. In 2008, the KMT candidate won, and the KMT also held a majority in the legislature. Not surprisingly, student protests in the 2000s often followed the larger political divisions in the country and called for party-line reforms and agitated against the constant, aggressive posturing by China. There were demonstrations on local issues, as well, such as against the 2005 demolition of the Losheng Sanatorium, a leproseum for aged sufferers of the dreaded disease. The institution was in the path of a new Taipei subway, and the protests had three thousand students demonstrating against the patients' evictions.

Toward the end of the decade, however, activists turned their attention increasingly on China as the giant nation ramped up the expansion of its global influence. In 2008, a Chinese delegation arrived in Taiwan, a landmark event heavily protested against by prodemocracy students. Some of the demonstrators began throwing rocks and bottles at police, and the larger demonstrations were roughly suppressed by security forces. The police actions only inflamed prodemocracy students, who saw the government as pandering to Beijing. The battles escalated, producing still further protests, most notably a large, peaceful sit-in in Liberty Square. Participating students took the moniker "wild strawberries," in an appropriation of a derogatory term often used by critics for Taiwanese youth (as in "pretty but quick to rot"). They wanted police leaders removed and called for right-to-assembly reforms that would do away with the need to have permits to demonstrate. They also wanted the end of the regulations limiting demonstrations to specific areas. Three large cages were hung in Liberty Square, and in them students sat holding antigovernment signs. A coffin was hoisted in a somber funeral for human rights.

Taiwan's citizens were largely sympathetic to the students, and in one a case a resident set himself on fire in support of the students and to protest the police violence. The incident had five thousand students and prodemocracy activists marching on the presidential palace. Taiwan's security, though, like that of Japan, was heavily surveilling and monitoring activist networks and was not caught off guard. Security forces intercepted the protest, and police detained activists and bused them out of the city. Many of the students arrested later reported that out of the view of cameras, they were beaten.

Like Taiwan, Hong Kong had special status as a partially autonomous state in the 2000s. It had been returned to Chinese control in 1997, after 156 years of British colonial governance, and immediately after the handover, all further democratic reforms were stopped. A period of apprehension fell over the area as citizens waited to see how Chinese rule would change their daily lives. Hong Kong had become a "special administrative sector" of China; the catchphrase used by authorities for saying, "one country, two systems." Compared to many cities in China, Hong Kong was an economic powerhouse, with incredible international networks and influence. Financially it was a boon to China, explaining much of the Chinese government's reluctance to meddle with Hong Kong's administration.

That said, the handover had immediate effects on Hong Kong's sense of independence and prosperity. In 2000, on the anniversary of the handover, a massive prodemocracy demonstration with a large student contingent marched in Hong Kong carrying prodemocracy signs and "democracy coffins." The demonstration has taken place annually since. Economic troubles and increasing incremental restrictions on freedom of speech and press by the administrative government of Hong Kong brought more and more people to join the marches every year. In 2003, spurred by the local government's move to adopt a law recharacterizing the terms on which one could be accused of sedition and limiting political organizing, the annual prodemocracy march drew five hundred thousand protestors.

Over the next six years, the yearly marches, which focused on opposing collusion and advocating for universal suffrage, drew crowds of 150,000. As China's prosperity and power grew in the 2000s, though, the "special status" consideration given to Hong Kong by China would diminish, and the country would increasingly encroach on local authority. The numbers of protestors would again spike in 2012, with some estimates in excess of four hundred thousand. By the end of the decade, after Hong Kong authorities tried to pass an extradition bill that would allow dissidents to be handed over to Chinese authorities, the city would erupt in massive protests, many of them violent. The largest of these would be attended by well over a million people.

This brings us to the discussion of student activism in mainland China, which has grown the most sophisticated large-scale program of population subjugation on earth today. China's imperialism continues unabated, and the state has refined a process of social and cultural domination of minority populations and land acquisition that is as comprehensive as it is brutal. Those coming directly under Beijing's heel resist and protest—but they do not do so for long. China's modern, programmatic suppression became fully operational in the first decade of the millennium. The efficacy of the suppression of the prodemocracy movement following Tiananmen Square, combined with the radical redevelopment of Tibet, led directly to the establishment of the concentration camps for the Uighurs and the systematic destruction of their culture by 2020.

While in Taiwan and Hong Kong in the 2000s activists had the freedom to challenge the state, demonstrating in mainland China was a completely different matter, and central China's control of resistance actions grew increasingly sophisticated and subtle. The government developed a multipronged plan of domination. Underskirting everything was, of course, sheer military force and a willingness to use it. But since the government controlled the television news media and newspaper publishing, and even exerted censorship over the content of books published in China, it also was able to launch effective propaganda and education machinery. China's complete control of communications and of the Chinese internet let the government censor and surveil its citizens. It monitored activists, letting networks grow to a limited extent and then sweeping in to make preemptive arrests before demonstrations. Aiding this surveillance was the country's explosive economic growth that resulted in an almost 30 percent rise in the middle-class population. Students and youth were clearly financially rewarded if willing to work within the confines of the system. At the same time, however, in outlying provinces, on the front lines of the nation's imperialist program, where poverty was extreme and minority-led resistance to authority flared, Chinese troops violently suppressed resistance and successfully kept most of that suppression hidden from the rest of the world.

Since the infamous Tiananmen Square crackdown, in which as many as ten thousand people were massacred (the number has been confirmed by leaked Chinese military reports), China has kept firm control on prodemocracy activism in its major cities. The prodemocracy movement remains a taboo topic, banned from public speech, illegal to commemorate, and scrubbed from official historical and popular accounts. The government has confiscated and destroyed tens of millions of books, photographs, journals, and videos documenting or mentioning the event and heavily censored all references to the Tiananmen massacre on China's internet. In addition to physically suppressing references to the demonstration, China has also employed sophisticated software to seek out and eradicate the prodemocracy movement throughout Chinese-accessible cyberspace. To those unwilling to forget, the shadow of the event continues to cast a pall over prodemocracy efforts such as they are. But China's scrubbing of history has also effectively kept the event from the consciousness of most of its citizens born after 1985. What the Chinese government learned it could do and get away with at Tiananmen would inform its treatment of dissent for the next thirty years. For if it could, with a systematic approach, murder thousands of its own citizens on the most famous square in its capital while the rest of the world watched, keep most of China in the dark about it, and afterwards make that event disappear from history, well, it could do just about anything.

The massacre itself was brutal, with tanks and troops ringing in the more than one hundred thousand prodemocracy demonstrators, citizens, and workers attending. The majority of the violence took place in the streets surrounding the square, which was filled primarily with workers, the students having gathered in a central spot on the square around a giant "goddess of democracy" sculpture they erected. Once the word was given to engage the protestors, troops violently began to press in toward the square from all sides; armored vehicles were used to simply run over opponents, a process referred to in one military memo as "making pie."[45] Troops used automatic weapons and live ammunition and set up machine-gun nests around the square, into which panicked demonstrators packed once slaughter on the perimeter began. The middle-class students huddled beneath "the Goddess" were the last to go, the military consciously avoiding attacking them while it mopped up the remaining workers on the square. Opening up an avenue of retreat for them, troops encouraged students' retreat by firing a barrage into the goddess above them with automatic weapons. After the square was cleared, human remains and protest detritus were removed by bulldozer.

International condemnation and harsh economic sanctions against China followed the massacre, but China stood firm in its characterization of the students and the workers as dissidents having threatened the security and stability of the state. Leaders of the prodemocracy movement that remained alive were arrested. Those who had international fame and who continued to draw media attention were tried, sentenced to prison terms, and then later deported under medical parole. Those without fame were tried and given harsh prison terms in the provinces. In a strategic move, the Chinese government attempted to address concerns of the demonstrators, and tolerated subsequent suggestions for reforms as long as activists didn't self-identify as prodemocracy or against the state.

The government did, however, begin a program of arresting and charging leaders of organizations it saw as potentially threatening before they could gain momentum or size, in a process likened by officials in China to cutting the head off a snake before it grows. Many in the West wrongly viewed China's response to the demonstrations as anachronistic, something akin to, say, a nineteenth-century Russian Cossack style of suppression of activism. But overwhelming force was only a part of the Chinese government's strategy, and that force was used systematically and in a highly controlled fashion. China then used sophisticated cybersurveillance, arrests, and the judicial system to eliminate those suspected of resistance. Finally, it scrubbed the event from the internet and the country's collective public consciousness. Unlike its smaller authoritarian neighbors, China's approach is subtle. Chinese citizens do not have choices, but the government wants its citizens to do more than comply—it wants their willing, enthusiastic support.

With what can and can't be said in China clearly defined, students did hold numerous demonstrations, and they knew how far they could go in publicly speaking about issues or criticizing specific policies. Prodemocracy protests were forbidden, but demonstrations on other issues were allowed, encouraged, or sponsored. In 1999, after a US/NATO missile accidentally took out the Chinese embassy in Belgrade, killing four, tens of thousands of students held anti–United States rallies in major cities across China, all heavily covered by state media: ten thousand marchers reported in Beijing, fifteen thousand in Shanghai, twenty thousand in Anhui Province, thirty thousand in Shaanxi, and thousands more in other cities. While these were demonstrations, they weren't protests against China's government but demonstrations aided by government support and state-run media. China would use the protest as a form of international power currency when dealing with the United States.

The Chinese government would similarly use student demonstrations as political currency with other countries. In 2001, when Japanese prime minister Koizumi went to visit the Yasukuni War Shrine for Japanese soldiers, a rash of student demonstrations were held in China, again covered by state-controlled media. More were to follow as Japan, in 2005, revised its state-sanctioned history books for secondary education, sanitizing its history when describing Japanese expansion in the 1930s and 1940s. Ignoring its own whitewashing of history, China's government exploited the student protests to support aggressive policies toward Japan. With territorial disputes erupting as Japan extended its search for gas and oil reserves in the East China Sea, China's government would again stir up students, couching the actions as Japan's continued legacy of imperialism. In Shanghai, the Japanese embassy was attacked by protestors, and rioters destroyed Japanese businesses and beat Japanese students while police looked on. Protests were particularly intense in Shenzhen and in Nanjing, the site of Japan's 1937 invasion during the Second Sino-Japanese War.

Tensions between the countries escalated in 2001, with the government of China clearly whipping up nationalist fervor with anti–United States and anti-Japan sentiment, which also had the benefit of keeping student unrest directed internationally. When the appropriate moment to ease diplomatic relations and reassert security came around, so-called criminal or anarchist elements of otherwise lawful, peaceful protests were arrested and charged, and further anti-Japanese demonstrations were banned. The activists arrested happened to be people the government had identified as potential social threats. In 2006, students staged quieter anti-Japan protests, such as passing out "flowers of shame" leaflets at fashionable cherry blossom festivals, in locations where Japanese soldiers had planted the trees in the thirties and forties to remind them of home.

But China is a large country, and the government's ability to thwart or control unrest was uneven during the decade as it experimented with its techniques. In Hunan Province in 2006, about ten thousand people demonstrated after a city staffer beat a student. The protest turned into a riot that was eventually quelled by police force. And that same year, in Nanchang and Guangzhou, thousands of students protesting new Ministry of Education restrictions and tighter scrutiny on private university qualifications burned cars and smashed windows before being suppressed by riot police. Such uprisings could not be tolerated, and by 2006, China had perfected a response to these kinds of demonstrations.

The government developed a rapid-response strategy to physically stop protests whenever they happened, hitting them with overwhelming force. Police confiscated all cameras and media technology present at protests and arrested activists, particularly leaders. Interrogations followed, to identify others in activist networks, and they too were arrested and their computers confiscated. China also used cybersurveillance and street-level infiltration to identify organizers, who were monitored as they planned demonstrations. They and others in their circles would be allowed to communicate until as many members as possible were identified, and then they would be preemptively arrested before actual marches. Police would then mobilize troops in areas likely to see further demonstrations. Meanwhile, state-controlled media would broadcast that future demonstrations in an area were forbidden.

In the case of the Ministry of Education reforms, protests nevertheless broke out in cities other than Nanchang and Guangzhou as students realized their diplomas from private universities might be rendered useless, but these too were quickly suppressed. And because the protestors at many of these demonstrations were challenging the government in their slogans and signs, coverage of the protests and the police suppression of them was kept out of Chinese media.

China could not, however, keep all of its authoritarian violence hidden from the rest of the world. In 2008, regional resentment over Chinese settlements in Tibet boiled over in a series of escalating exchanges between police and students who had come out in support of demonstrating Tibetan monks in Lhasa and other cities in the region. When the plight of Tibetans gained international media attention and reports, and smuggled-out images of security forces beating activists began to spread in international media, China ejected tourists and journalists from the region and mobilized the troops and tanks. After a hard deadline to end demonstrations expired (a deadline marked by peaceful and quiet candlelight vigils by students in universities across China who, despite the risks, had networked to organize these silent protests), troops in Tibet were given the order to suppress the protests with force. They did so brutally, killing students, activists, and monks. International anger over the aggression was further stoked when the rumor spread that troops had orders to shoot on sight monks seen in public after the deadline to end the protests expired. Even where allowed in China, international broadcast media such as CNN and the BBC were blocked and went black when reporting on the crackdown in Lhasa. The coverage of the region was replaced by a state-sponsored media campaign of disinformation reporting that a dozen or so civilians had been killed following a riot orchestrated by the Dalai Lama.

If one is asked today about China's brutality toward its minority citizens, one is likely to think of the plight of Uighurs and the recent establishment of internment camps aimed at "reeducation." But the current suppression of Uighurs has a history leading back directly to the suppression of student and worker demonstrations throughout China in the last decade and in prior decades, and the story is one of the government continually refining its program of stamping out dissent, even if the government's current goal with regard to the Uighurs actually centers on land and mineral acquisitions.

While these suppression strategies were developed across China, they were also historically tied to the region as well. Ethnic tensions between Uighurs and Han Chinese citizens (92 percent of China's total population is Han) increased in the area as more and more Han were moved into the territory through state-sponsored migration programs meant to displace the indigenous Uighurs and establish a Han majority. Han Chinese also packed the local administrative government of the province. In Ürümqi, the capital of Xinjiang Uighur Autonomous Region in northwestern China, a 2009 protest in People's Park turned into an ethnic riot in which Muslim Uighur protestors destroyed businesses and vehicles, attacked a police station, and began indiscriminately beating and stabbing Han Chinese caught on the streets. Chinese media broadcasts indicated that more than 1,500 civilians had been wounded in the chaos, and the Han witnesses interviewed claimed most of the victims were Han. The Uighur riot was brutally suppressed by the Chinese military and local riot police, leaving some 175 dead, though the Chinese government did not officially release exact numbers or the ethnicities of those killed.

Although the government media narrative began with the riots, the story goes back further, as the original Uighur protest in the park was against an incident in which a group of Uighurs had been beaten by a mob in a factory in southeastern China, after a rumor circulated that Uighurs had raped Han women there. This protest was violently suppressed by police, who attacked the protestors, including children, with clubs. Some of the victims reported to international journalists that police opened fire with live ammunition as well.

This sparked the subsequent Uighur riot that was reported in state-controlled media. Following the ethnic rioting in Ürümqi, which garnered international news attention that depicted the brutality of local police as much as the ethnic violence by the Uighurs, the Chinese military clamped down on the entire area with force. Journalists were ejected, and Chinese media scrubbed of references to anything other than Uighur ethnic rioting. The international attention had embarrassed China's government, and that set into motion a long-term plan to eradicate the Uighur problem for good. Chinese media pounded on Uighur separatists, blaming them for the uprising, and stirred up anti-Uighur sentiment to the point that tens of thousands of Han Chinese residents surrounded Ürümqi's government buildings calling for arrests, with many voicing anti-Islamic sentiments and calling for harsh punishments for Uighurs. This began what became a trend of nationalist Islamophobia, and gave rise to a systematic displacement program and landgrab that would end in the massive internment camps a decade later.

On the opposite end of the activist spectrum from China is India, a democratic nation in which engaged students constantly meet to discuss politics and protest loudly against a government that deals with them in unsystematic ways. While China's government used the decade to systematize suppression, consolidate power, plan long-term international influence campaigns, and refine its control of its domestic population, the control of India's coalition-based government shifted back and forth between political parties, consumed with alternating political reforms, and as a result always reacting rather than responding coherently to historical events. What was constant was a high level of violence in the country and chronic corruption. And students protested a lot. Unlike in China, students in India often challenge the authority of the state, and they persistently protest for social justice, civil rights, and social reforms. Myriad student organizations regularly demonstrated for reforms in the 2000s, such as the Students' Federation of India (SFI), the Democratic Youth Federation of India (DYFI), the Revolutionary Students Front (RSF), and the All India Students' Federation (AISF). India is so crowded with so many different religions, ethnicities, political affiliations, and traditions that making generalizations, or deciding what to include in a history such as this one, is difficult.

The nation is full of paradoxes—an economic powerhouse with rampant poverty, it is also a democracy liberated from foreign occupation that is often accused of imperialism, a secularly governed nation where violent acts of religious intolerance are not uncommon. Freedoms of the press and assembly are constitutionally guaranteed, though demonstrators are often suppressed by police attacking in *lathi* (baton) charges. Western media is popular and widespread, but hugging and kissing in public remain taboo. Although in 1999 Sonia Gandhi became the first female leader of the opposition in parliament, and in 2007 Pratibha Patil became India's first female president, women still suffer from systemic cultural, legal, and social inequality. Violence against women today remains commonplace, though in the second decade of the twenty-first century the women's movement in India radically expanded following international coverage of horrifying acts of sexual violence.

In the first decade of the millennium there were literally tens of thousands of demonstrations and protests in India. Unlike in China, where security policies and counterresistance strategies and tactics were developed and systematically implemented across the nation, the governmental responses to activism in India lacked coherence and remained piecemeal, with much of the country mired in corruption, which meant local authorities pursued their own interests in terms of suppression. Although internet and social-media use boomed in India the 2000s, and these tools were embraced by activists for their usefulness in networking and spreading information, twentieth-century tactics of suppression of demonstrations dominated, resulting in a lot of unregulated police and mob violence. By the end of the decade, students were adept at using images of police brutality to draw media attention, widen their own support, and bring state and national attention to their issues, which ranged from educational reform to intercultural strife, government corruption, and women's rights.

In 2000 in Tamil Nadu, for example, after All India Anna Dravidian Progress Federation general secretary Jayaram Jayalalitha was prosecuted for corruption, party members began road blockades outside Chennai, with mobs sometimes going berserk and stoning approaching cars and buses. These types of political displays were not uncommon, but one particularly violent group set a bus of women college students from Tamil Nadu Agricultural University on fire and burned three to death. Demanding justice and fearing the incident would be swept under the carpet by local authorities, students surrounded the bus and refused to release the bodies of the dead until they were guaranteed an investigation would take place. They quickly formed the Anaithu Kalloori Maanavar Kootamaippu, a federation of students, student organizations, and volunteers that pressed for the arrest and prosecution of the perpetrators.

Large demonstrations soon followed, as did battles with police, who used tear gas and *lathi* charges to disperse the students, acts which further inflamed the demonstrators. But while the local authorities relied on brute suppression, the students were availing themselves of new technology. They used social networks to disseminate news and images about the violence and draw more people to the streets in ever larger protests. These demonstrations soon gained national media attention, spotlighting the original deaths, the subsequent police brutality, and the students' concerns that local corruption would undermine the investigation. They raised the profile of the issue to the point where the federal government took control over the local investigation, an action that ultimately resulted in arrests.

Police brutality itself, however, remained the most common tactic by local authorities in breaking up even peaceful protests. In 2005, students from Chennai were again on the streets, this time protesting for a local company to accept graduates. Demonstrators blocked a highway in an often-used tactic called a *raasta roko* (road blocking), but they didn't threaten anyone. They were simply sitting quietly in the road when they were violently set upon by police, who began indiscriminately beating them with sticks. Unlike in the event of the previous student murders and police violence, though, the group was ineffective at using social media to broadcast the police violence and thus grow support nationally.

Although such police tactics were common, not all student protests were physically confrontational or ended with violence. Indeed, some actions were intended to be humorous, if pointed. In 2005, for example, tired of the inaction of the local government in road maintenance in Gulbarga, students from the All India Democratic Students' Organization (AIDSO) and the All India Democratic Youth Organization (AIDYO) demonstrated with a massive "plant-in." They protested the lack of city infrastructure by planting saplings in the many potholes riddling the city's streets.

Students in India protested on a wide range of issues, and while many were international, such as massive demonstrations against US president George W. Bush and US imperialism led by students of Jawaharlal Nehru University in New Delhi in 2006, by far the majority of them were demonstrations over local or regional issues. Students came out in force, for example, against the multiyear Narmada Valley dam project that would displace thousands of local farmers and residents. They demonstrated against the economic exploitation of locals from the companies working the Assam oil fields, and in the south they battled mining corporations. In eastern India, Kolkata students stopped, emptied, and burned buses and— with thousands of other activists—marched with Nandigram farmers protesting the planned taking of their land for a petrochemical industrial site. Ten of the farmers had been killed by police in pitched battles after the locals, armed with rocks, pickaxes, and machetes, fought security and police troops equipped with guns.

The most populous democracy in the world encompasses multiple ethnicities and religions and centuries of various deeply ingrained traditions, many of them tied to who wields power in society. It has long histories of intercultural strife in many of its regions, many of which are steeped in poverty, and thus at the turn of the millennium it was a country with one foot still firmly planted in the past while attempting nevertheless to cross into modernity. Because it allowed freedom of expression and assembly and media was not overtly censored, large swaths of the population were increasingly influenced by social trends originating in the West. This mix of traditional and progressive ideas, while exciting and revolutionary, has also been chaotic and fueled social turbulence.

In the 2000s, violence was prevalent in many of India's cultures, from everyday occurrences of violence against women to ethnic violence. Violence was often the subject of protests, both on and off campuses, as well. In 2008, for example, after a student named Ashok Karol was beaten to death by seniors at Subodh College in

Jaipur, the Students Federation of India (SFI) and the National Students' Union of India (NSUI) held anti-ragging (anti-hazing) protests and disrupted classes in colleges across the city. They called for university reforms to eliminate such college traditions, claiming that the prolific ragging was condoned and even encouraged by colleges, and the city's universities subsequently announced they would change their policies to try to end the practice.

By the late 2000s, students had grown adept at using the internet and social media to conjure large numbers of supporters to attend rallies and demonstrations, and they broadly proclaimed their successes, such as in the anti-ragging movement. This encouraged more students to try to wield collective power. School administrations and school policies were often the focus of student demonstrations. In Mangaluru (a western coastal city near Bengaluru in the state of Karnataka), students of the SFI and the Democratic Youth Federation of India held massive protests in 2009 and burned in effigy their state education minister, Vishweshwar Kageri, for allowing the gross commercialization of the education system. They claimed that private colleges that had a much higher placement rate in desirable jobs were charging exorbitant admission fees, with a rampant pay-to-play attitude on the part of their private admissions committees, to which the Ministry of Education turned a blind eye. But unlike the ragging protestors, these students were protesting the social status quo, and their cause had no element of unjust violence to attract wider public support. The protests did little to effect significant change; indeed, Kageri would go on to become speaker of Karnataka's legislature.

In southern India, students held protests for political and economic reasons, and they were able to take full advantage of new abilities to organize, network, and tactically launch streets demonstrations that crippled commerce and brought international pressure to bear on government.

In Telangana, a movement for independence galvanized the region. Students initiated a regionwide strike and, through roadblocks, effectively shut down traffic and rail services in Hyderabad, the region's capital and a technology giant, home to international companies such as Motorola and Dell. They protested that under the current administration, the international money pouring into the region was not being reinvested locally but rather funneled out of the province. Local officials brought in thousands of police and hired paramilitaries to violently break up the student protests, but this was a behind-the-times tactical mistake. Students recorded the violence, and images of the beatings went viral and brought more people out to support those already on the streets. Thousands of students were arrested over months of demonstrations intentionally orchestrated to block commerce.

With no indication that the protests would relent, and with heavy pressure on the government by those international corporations, losing millions of dollars daily, to resolve the conflict, the Congress Party conceded to the demonstrations and began to initiate separate-state status, which would officially take effect in 2014. Thus, in support of a regional issue, students were able to organize and launch economically crippling demonstrations, tactically take advantage of police overreactions, and summon greater social support and intense external pressure to bear on the government to force change. They were beaten, arrested, and jailed for their efforts, but they achieved statehood for the region.

The most important issue that India's student population fought for in the past two decades arguably has been for a change in the country's attitudes toward and treatment of women. Violence against women continues to occur often in India—from domestic violence to blatant street attacks to sexual harassment and rape. In the 2010s, this fight for social justice and civil liberties would swell to become a massive movement (and a very public and violent struggle over women's rights and freedoms in many parts of India). The international #MeToo movement was yet to come, but the groundwork for it in India began with chronic gender violence in the 2000s and organizations working to stop it.

In 2004, after acid was thrown in the face of a college girl, students took to the streets in Chennai, calling on police to arrest the perpetrators, who they believed to be connected to mafia entwined with the local government. Public acid attacks on women were not uncommon in India and were on the rise. When police were dismissive of the assault and cracked down on the students rather than arresting the attackers, the protestors called for a statewide *hartal* (strike) and physically vented their anger on police and local officials, pelting troops and government residences with rocks. Battles were waged back and forth across Chennai, with students setting police vehicles ablaze and troops shooting tear gas and charging students with clubs. Order was eventually restored to the city, but by the time the dust settled, many people had been injured.

Women, especially younger urban women, wanted more social freedoms, including the right to choose what they could wear in public, how they wanted to behave, and where they could go. The increasing exposure made possible by the internet and social media to Western ideas of gender equity and current fashions encouraged women to break with conservative ideas of traditional dress and comportment, and this particularly outraged far-right religious groups.

One of India's largest cities and the nation's technological capital, Bengaluru has long been known for its progressiveness, attracting the best and the brightest of India's youth, both men and women, in droves. In the 2000s, one increasingly could see women in the city in jeans and short-sleeved tops during the daytime. But Bengaluru was also famous for its nightlife, and women began leaving their saris at home and exploring current Western fashions, going out to clubs and bars. To traditionalists and extremists who feared the changes in Bengaluru would spread throughout India, this was a symbol of increasing decadence. Indeed, these trends were already clearly spreading to nearby cities in Karnataka.

In 2008, forty members of the extremist Hindu organization Sri Ram Sena (SRS)—the Lord Ram's Army—invaded a nightclub in Mangaluru and beat up every female they could catch. The SRS claimed that the Westernization of India was destroying Indian culture and values and was particularly harmful to young women. Other nearby cities would see similar attacks. The Mangaluru attack by the SRS was, however, videotaped by passersby and transmitted on major media channels throughout the country. Women, students, and youth across the nation, not just in Karnataka, protested for a strong government response. Massive protests followed, but it was hard for gender-justice advocates to gain traction in the face of institutionalized patriarchal attitudes. The outcome of the protests was that the authorities acknowledged that a crime had been committed and claimed the perpetrators would be sought. But they also released statements stressing that women should not be going to pubs and that they should not dress provocatively.

Women and student organizations continued their protests and spread information about the attacks and images of the violence through social media. They used the state's response both to educate and to grow their networks. The social-media barrage continued and was picked up in the news, which repeatedly broadcast images of out-of-control men running down and attacking women in the street, many of whom were wearing saris that night. The general population turned against the traditionalists, women were outraged, and membership levels in women's organizations soared.

When the founder of SRS called for another attack on women in pubs on the upcoming Valentine's Day, a young woman named Nisha Susan launched a Facebook protest that begat the "Loose and Forward" consortium of progressive women, whose numbers immediately swelled into the thousands. Within the year the group had more than sixty thousand supporters. They began the Pink Chaddi campaign, for which women throughout India sent the leader of the SRS a set of their pink underwear, and called for Valentine's Day pub events and demonstrations. These were massively attended and protected by allied groups throughout Bengalaru. The Pink Chaddi campaign garnered international media attention and brought pressure upon India's government to address violence toward women. It also brought popular scorn upon the traditionalists.

Fueled by the pushback, conservatives stepped up their criticisms of liberalism in social media, and correspondingly, lone-wolf attacks increased, many happening in broad daylight. Technologically, the cultural warfare being waged over women's bodies and rights had entered a new phase, with the forces for change beginning to build massive networks and nationwide support. But this growth was also followed by conservative on-air media attacks, right-wing blogging, and cyberattacks, for it wasn't long until the "Loose and Forward" Facebook page and network was hacked and vandalized.

Meanwhile, acid attacks on women were still increasing in number. More than 150 acid attacks were reported in the news during the 2000s, though that many appeared every year in the 2000s in court documents. The only country in the world with more acid attacks on women per year for the 2000s was Bangladesh. Students throughout the decade held numerous protests to try to elevate awareness of the violence being committed against women. But they struggled to get the government to do anything about it. In Anantapur, after two more girls were attacked with acid in 2008, AIDSO and AIDYO staged massive demonstrations decrying the practice. National student protests called for the perpetrators to be arrested and for the government to stop more such attacks through harsher laws and enforcement. But as women sought more liberties, the backlash became stronger, and the number of acid attacks on women continued to rise. Activists demonstrated and then began a social-media campaign to raise awareness internationally, thus bringing international pressure on the national government to do something. Under constant attack for institutionalized sexism, the government would eventually ask its constituent states to regulate over-the-counter acid sales in their respective regions.

The frustration among many young women over their treatment socially—and by their own government—was by the end of the decade palpable, and the challenges women faced in the next decade in seeking to liberalize their societies, to garner civil rights and social justice, had their roots in this one. Long before the #MeToo movement, women in India were frustrated with harassment and fighting for gender justice and institutional changes. Faced with widespread paternalism, they would turn their attention on changing federal laws and the nation's cultural climate around women. The next decade would see incredible progress, but only after increasingly horrific acts of violence perpetrated against women were tirelessly challenged by activists and a nationwide women's movement.

Across much of Asia and Australia, the 2000s were a decade that witnessed tremendous levels of student activism. In many nations, it was a decade of technology-driven experimentation influencing ongoing struggles between activists and authorities in generating and wielding social power. By 2000, many activists were already communicating and organizing through the internet, but as social-media platforms such as Facebook and Twitter caught on and increasingly penetrated into the region toward the end of the decade, students' changed tactics again. The changes in resistance networking and campaigns soon brought technological changes in strategies of suppression, from the censoring of blogs in Bangladesh to the monstrous surveillance programs of China.

In our present moment, we can see that across the world, social activism has radically changed from what it was twenty years ago, and the way that strategies take shape today seems like the natural offshoot of technological advances. Technology spread ideas of democracy and liberalism throughout the world in the 2000s, reaching into previously remote areas in Asia. In addition to inspiration, the new technologies afforded activists the means for greater networking, for gaining wider support, and for disseminating images of and information about injustice. They could help expand national sympathy for a cause and bring international pressure to bear on national governments.

Today, activists struggling in the streets of Hong Kong look in many ways much like activists in Palestine or Venezuela or Seattle, and they organize and show up at demonstrations equipped with many of the same tools, often ordered from the same online retailers. But the similarities and codified ways in which activism occurs today—from Indonesia to Argentina to Canada—were developed through years of innovation and trial and error in the 2000s, and much of it occurred in the East.

6

STUDENT NETWORKING, VIOLENCE, AND SOCIAL UPHEAVAL IN AFRICA

The first decade of the millennium also saw numerous student resistance actions and protests in Africa, and these ranged widely in form due to the vast differences in government systems, cultures, and economic and educational attainment within and among African nations. Like the rest of the world, the region saw growing but extremely uneven exposure to new technology and the new resistance strategies that made use of the internet and social media. Access to new technology was predictably centered on more developed nations and urban areas, in the places where secondary education was based and where people could afford it.

But in the first decade of the twenty-first century, Africa was also the site of numerous regional conflicts, foreign occupations, civil wars, and outbreaks of ethnic violence—all of which pulled youth out of schools and directly into larger, violent struggles. In countries that were not the scene of large-scale politically driven violence, outright war, or extensive ethnic or religious strife, students and young people were often active in agitating for social reforms. But in those nations that lagged behind the rest of the world in terms of economic development and technology, news of resistance efforts, when they occurred, and of the police violence that often suppressed them was not widely disseminated and was often underreported.

In terms of directly challenging authoritarian power, being able to mobilize large numbers means a lot—whether that mobilization occurs in the streets or at polling stations. Even in many of the countries with large swaths of youth not directly enmeshed in larger conflicts, with educational attainment uneven or generally low and access to technology only partial, student activist efforts were often limited to twentieth-century strategies and tactics. Activists had to network by word of mouth and could not form the kind of technology-driven oppositional networks that were sprouting up on the scale that was seen in Eastern Europe, in Central America, or in the more technologically advanced Asian nations. Fighting against authority largely meant putting one's body on the line, and in authoritarian regimes such as those in Somalia or Zimbabwe that could end in horrific violence. Many African countries could, in the 2000s, get away with incredible suppression in ways that were hard to hide in the rest of the world.

In national urban centers such as Lagos, Johannesburg, or Luanda, students had access to current technologies, and these places saw high levels of activism. But even in these places, the means of being able to successfully network and garner larger national public support for a cause remained limited, as was the ability to encourage international pressure on governments. In short, although many were inspired by the Eastern European revolutions, students in Africa were unable to raise the numbers or wield the kind of power in their efforts to catalyze momentum for social reforms that those activists were able to. Thus, rather than an overarching regional narrative of the development of movements, new strategies, and interconnected networks, the region's activist efforts appear more as discrete flare-ups.

That said, students across the continent in the 2000s were not completely isolated, uninformed, or inactive; they formed activist groups, agitated and battled for local social reforms, and through urban areas reached out to form international alliances with students in other nations. Many of the leaders of prodemocracy organizations were indeed inspired by the youth revolutions taking place in Eastern Europe and in the Middle East, and in some cases leaders travelled to neighboring countries to be trained by Otpor and other Eastern European activists. But they were often disadvantaged from the start, playing on a slanted field and struggling against power in the ways students had been doing so for decades. Government corruption was widespread in many of the region's nations, especially in the more impoverished nations. And the use of physical brutality in dealing with opposition activists was rampant.

But even in the least educated nations, students organized and agitated. The UN Development Program's annual report in 2008, for example, ranked the landlocked country of Burkina Faso as having the lowest level of literacy in the world, with even public education well beyond the means of the majority. But student activism was high at a number of schools, including the University of Ouagadougou, the Polytechnic University of Bobo-Dioulasso, the University of Koudougou, the International School of Ouagadougou, and a handful of other private colleges. The largest student organization in the nation is the General Union of Burkina Students (UGEB), of which the National Association of Burkina Students (ANEB) is a part, and it often allied itself in protests with the Burkinabe General Confederation of Labor (CGTB). Growing out of a French Communist ideology from the country's colonial past, these Marxist-oriented student organizations often agitated for social reforms, better material conditions, and social justice. Other student groups opposed UGEB ideology, such as the National Union of Faso Students (UNEF).

Violence in the country was commonplace, and activism in Burkina Faso was a dangerous occupation. Leaders of organizations opposing authority there have a long history of disappearing or turning up dead. Students held protests for years, for example, calling for an honest investigation into the 1998 murder of a journalist and his three colleagues, an investigation that, once started, would drag on until a judge eventually ordered it abandoned in 2006.

In 2000, ANEB called on University of Ouagadougou students to strike repeatedly on a range of issues: to support the students of the Faculty of Health Sciences, who wanted access to internships; to obtain better living and study conditions for students; and to protest dealings with the government, including asking for investigations into the deaths of a roster of slain activists. After one strike at the university lasted for five months, the government simply closed the

University of Ouagadougou, dissolved all its faculties, and invalidated credit for the entire academic year.[46] Student and youth protests in Burkina Faso achieved relatively little during the first decade of the millennium, due in no small part to limited means of widening their networks and battling entrenched authority, though this would change by the beginning of the next decade. In 2014, protests against government corruption would spread from city to city, swelling into a national uprising and eventually a revolution.

Other nations in the 2000s that suffered from economic and educational impoverishment likewise had difficulty generating large movements, though that did not stop students from protesting for social justice and civil rights. But as in Burkina Faso, when one challenges a government that limits rights and has a strongman at the helm, agitation comes with risk. Although a democracy, Djibouti had no independent press and consistently ranked at the bottom among nations in terms of freedom of expression. Corruption was extensive, and although torture was technically prohibited by law, arrested activists and opposition members complained of police torturing them. Nevertheless, students publicly staged protests for local social reforms and against international infractions, including US involvement in Afghanistan and Iraq. In this impoverished nation, protests sometimes consisted of students blocking traffic in the capital, Djibouti, waving signs written on pages torn out of their school notebooks.

Ethiopia was also a country where activism was risky and where protests were brutally suppressed. Under the rule of Meles Zenawi and the Ethiopian People's Revolutionary Democratic Front (EPRDF), which held power from 1995 to 2012, public challenges to authority were simply not tolerated. During his tenure, prime minister and dictator Meles was repeatedly criticized by international human-rights organizations for new and outrageous human-rights abuses committed against activists. His violence in the suppression of political opposition was a feat in a country with an international reputation for chronic and endemically high levels of human-rights abuses. According to the National Committee on Traditional Practices in Ethiopia, nearly seventy percent of the country's marriages were due to "marriage by abduction.[47]

Literacy rates in Ethiopia during the decade hovered around 25 percent, and students protested for better education, improved living conditions, cultural reforms, and social justice. But when protests turned political or grew to any size, police viciously broke them up. Scattered reports throughout the decade of students being killed during small protests appear as minor items in international news feeds, but the government had a suffocating grip on media. Students in Ambo came out in force in 2001, criticizing the government for not addressing bush fires that were raging across the region, but the protests and their suppression went largely unnoticed. Police and an army battalion were deployed against the protests, and they attacked the students. A witness later reported seeing at least one student killed outright and many others injured. About a dozen were listed by family as missing afterwards. Some 1,500 students were arrested in the melee.

Despite the violence, people in Ethiopia continued to protest for social justice and reforms. In 2005, following contested national elections in which the Meles government was seriously challenged, a massive student demonstration originated at Addis Ababa University. It was attacked by police and turned into a full-scale riot. The military was sent in to crush the uprising, resulting in 193 deaths and close to 200 severe injuries. Forty teenagers were among those killed in battles with the military troops. The government immediately blamed the Ethiopian Human Rights Council for making comments that incited the crowd to violence and blamed opposition leaders for inflaming the populace and hijacking student interests.

But at the time, obtaining accurate reports of what happened was impossible, with the true scope of the violence only surfacing later, after a judge leaked an official report before himself fleeing the county for Europe. It turned out that twenty thousand people were initially arrested following the riots, in what grew into a systematic crackdown. What did make it into international news at the time, however, was that after the crackdown, nine desperate

Addis Ababa students who were being hunted by security hijacked a plane, seeking political asylum, and flew it to Khartoum International Airport.

Reports in Kenya also noted that injured students and activists fleeing Ethiopia were arriving in the country and seeking asylum following the riots. As a tactic for controlling such unrest, Kenyan authorities passed national laws criminalizing many forms of expression, including speech that criticized public officials, thus giving the government legal cover for its practice of suppressing demonstrations and arresting activists. Still, idealistic students continued to organize and stage demonstrations, especially in urban areas, even though doing so put them at risk of facing armed police in the streets, probable arrest, and likely torture if arrested. In 2009, following the global trend in countries instituting new antiterrorist laws, Ethiopia passed more restrictive freedom-of-expression laws, including making the reporting on the existence of opposition groups by journalists a crime. The laws were used to prosecute journalists, who would face arrest and possible torture if they dared to cover demonstrations.

A country responsible for many flare-ups of activism was Côte d'Ivoire. Marked by civil war and military coups, and the presence of French troops ostensibly protecting French citizens, the country was a powder keg that exploded repeatedly in the first decade of the millennium. The roles that students played in the country were significant during the 2000s—and complicated. Following President Laurent Gbagbo's rise to power, students and youth, who had been a significant force in his election, continued to be major supporters of Gbagbo, and as such they exerted national influence. Although always asserting that he was a proponent of democracy, Gbagbo increasingly turned authoritarian, and government corruption was rife. In 2003, hundreds of thousands of Ivoirians, including large contingents of students, demonstrated against a French peace plan meant to resolve a standoff between the government and rebel factions in the north of the country through a power-sharing deal. A populist xenophobia that had long been characteristic of Gbagbo supporters surfaced with a vengeance. French citizens were attacked during these protests, and French businesses were burned.

Following the massive demonstrations, Gbagbo rescinded his offer to the rebels, and France deployed security troops in the area. After an Ethiopian air strike on rebels killed French soldiers, the French retaliated by wiping out Côte d'Ivoire's entire air force. Massive, violent anti-French demonstrations flared. And although eventually a peace deal would be made, it would offer only a few years' respite from the violence among the government, rebel opposition, and France. Progovernment students constantly protested French imperialism and the rebels.

When presidential elections that had been postponed from 2005 were held in 2010, leading to the election of Alassane Ouattara over Gbagbo, the sitting president refused to give up power, and violence spiked throughout the nation, sparking the Second Ivorian Civil War. A new prodemocracy movement flared against the tyrant. Gbagbo's security forces began a campaign of killing opposition leaders, abducting thousands of Ouattara supporters and torturing them. The terror campaign by his security included gang rapes of hundreds of women. Gbagbo stepped up the war against the northern rebels, who were mostly Muslim, even hiring Liberian mercenaries who were accused of roaming the region in deaths squads. The United Nations and French forces would eventually intervene and arrest Gbagbo on human-rights violations to face trial by the International Criminal Court for crimes against humanity.

Thus, ironically, it was a student-supported prodemocracy movement, which from the start was inflected with populist xenophobia, that helped seat a strongman who would eventually become the first world leader to be tried for crimes against humanity at The Hague. And it would be a different prodemocracy movement, with student support, that fought to topple him.

Corruption and violence were commonplace in other countries as well. In the Gambia in the 2000s, students were protesting for social justice and against government corruption that was rife at every level under the rule of President Yahya Abdul-Aziz

Jemus Junkung Jammeh. Journalists and activists were increasingly suppressed during the decade, and homosexuality was viciously persecuted. In the first year of the decade, an event took place that would become known as the Gambian Student Massacre. Led by the Gambia Student Union (GAMSU), students were demonstrating after two horrific recent events, asking for local justice from the government. The first crime sparking the protests was the torture and death of a Brikama student after he'd been abducted from campus by government employees. He was stripped, beaten, and forced to drink cement, which killed him. The students pressed for an autopsy, but when the official police report was released it stated his death was due to natural causes. In the midst of this travesty, news spread that a thirteen-year-old girl had been abducted and raped by an armed officer. The local government sandbagged the murder investigation, and GAMSU students filed for a permit to demonstrate for justice in Banjul. Their application was denied and, frustrated with the corruption in the country, they decided to hold a march anyway.

The path of the nonviolent march was blocked by a large police contingent. The marchers stopped, but they continued to chant. Police hit them with tear-gas grenades and a barrage of rubber-coated bullets, forcing them to retreat. They did not, however, disperse but hastily erected barricades across streets and burned tires to stop advancing troops. They then marched in another direction and set a nearby police station on fire. Police followed and began shooting into the crowd with live ammunition, killing fourteen students and wounding dozens more. Following the Gambian Student Massacre, student leaders across the country were arrested and imprisoned. Those not yet caught went into hiding from Jammeh's security forces, and eventually many fled the country. What was left of GAMSU was infiltrated by government agents and informants to root out the remaining vestiges of activism, and a new "pro-government" student union was installed in its place.[48] Although constitutionally protected, freedom of speech and expression continued to be suppressed by the government, and journalists and activists who did not flee were arrested on a wide range of charges, from sedition to defamation.

Liberia began the decade steeped in the violence of the Second Liberian Civil War, with a rebel group in the north challenging the rule of Charles Taylor, known as the "Butcher of Monrovia." He'd earned his moniker after rising to power in Liberia's bloody first civil war, which lasted from 1989 to 1997. Students not directly pulled into the fighting in Liberia agitated for reforms, repeatedly marching on the Ministry of Education in central Monrovia to protest dismal conditions in public schools and the lack of supplies, including chairs. The response they received was to be set upon by city police, who flogged them with whips to drive them off. Frustrated, the students would riot and vent their anger by vandalizing buildings. By 2003, a second rebel group from southern Liberia joined the insurrection, and soon the city of Monrovia itself was under siege. Students in Monrovia openly held anti-Taylor demonstrations, and unrest in the city grew. Besieged and with no hope of battling the insurgency and putting down growing unrest in the capital, much of it student led, the Liberian government negotiated a peace settlement in nearby Accra.

Taylor was also at this time indicted in Sierra Leone for crimes against humanity, for his role in horrors perpetrated in the neighboring country by his special forces. International pressure, including from the United States, for him to give up power increased and, assailed on multiple fronts and with nowhere to turn, Taylor resigned and fled to Nigeria. In 2005, Liberia held open elections, and Ellen Johnson Sirleaf was elected, the first woman president in African history. In 2006, she effected the extradition of Taylor from Nigeria and then handed him over to the Sierra Leone tribunal to be tried in The Hague for his role in horrors committed in the Sierra Leone Civil War. He was convicted of war crimes and sentenced to fifty years in prison.

Alone, without significant networking abilities and unable to mobilize wider public support, Liberian students were often attacked and easily suppressed whenever they demonstrated for reforms. Under the Butcher of Monrovia, an unethical and violent police force set upon student activists with impunity. Nevertheless, students ultimately were a significant factor in deposing Taylor after they joined their efforts within the capital with the external forces bearing down upon the president. But following Taylor's departure, the country would continue to see political turmoil, corruption, and social unrest, with participation in demonstrations sometimes reaching into the thousands, and like many other African nations in the next decade would repeatedly see government-imposed internet blackouts followed by violent police suppression.

In the 2000s, the battles between small, repressive regimes in Africa and limited-scale street protests organized by word of mouth and person-to-person contact was a carryover from the kinds of battles that had historically been waged around the globe, pre–twenty-first century. In order to challenge authoritarians who limited free speech, suppressed journalism, and willingly used violence, students were by necessity forced to form alliances with other groups, whether labor organizations or rebel armies. But as in other repressive regimes in the twenty-first century, such as Belarus or Indonesia, the more violent the government's suppression and the tighter its grip on activism, the more frustrated students would become—and that frustration sometimes led to explosive riots.

In 2001 in Malawi, for example, students from the University of Malawi, along with students from the university's polytechnic branch in Blantyre, rioted in Zomba following the shooting death of a student. The murdered student was part of a demonstration in which students were protesting against police brutality and the deaths of critics of the government while in police custody. The initial demonstrations gained momentum when the students were joined in the streets by local residents, including families with children. Police attacked, firing tear-gas grenades into the crowds, and then began shooting them with live ammunition. News of the student's death spread, and university students and residents together rioted in great numbers, rampaging through the streets of Zomba, pelting police vehicles and a police station with stones and bricks. Rioters vandalized and looted stores and began setting vehicles on fire. Police reinforcements were called in, and—using more tear gas, more rubber-coated bullets, and more live ammunition—they finally quelled the riots.

The need for students to form alliances and gain wider support in battling entrenched power and superior forces was well recognized by activists. Students across Africa had long been adept at these strategies, for this is how students have been waging reform battles for decades. With much of Africa not yet having access to twenty-first-century technology and social-media platforms that could reach youth and students far beyond their local campuses, student activists resorted to generating numbers the old-fashioned way, by building alliances.

In 2003, thousands of Nigerian students joined oil workers and human-rights groups in protesting the planned reduction of citizens' oil subsidies in Nigeria—subsidies that made the cost of fuel for those living in this oil-rich nation bearable. Most Nigerians at the time existed on the equivalent of less than one US dollar a day. The protests were peaceful and lasted for days in cities across the nation, but police and paramilitary mobs working with state security attacked the demonstrators anyway, using tear gas, rubber-coated bullets, and live ammunition. Students erected barricades across streets in Lagos, where more than a dozen activists were killed. Reports of the violence made it to international news media, and international condemnation followed. Heavy-handed police responses drew out more protestors, and the coalition of workers and students, in concert with international pressure brought on by the violence, was able to force the Nigerian government to back off the proposed reforms. Still, the cost was extremely high, for in addition to the deaths and injuries in the streets, many student activists, striking workers, and journalists were, in the aftermath, beaten or arrested and abused while in custody.

Small protests in countries such as Somalia rarely made international news in the early 2000s, especially prior to the global explosion of social media, but those that did are revealing in what they say about local social conditions in their nations and what happened when students protested against low-level authorities or those who had weapons. They also reveal the challenges and risks that students faced in places remote from the eyes and influence of other nations. In 2004, for example, the Al-fajr School in Mogadishu spontaneously issued new fees for students, charging them for the two months when they are traditionally on vacation. The students refused to pay and staged a loud demonstration against the administration on campus. School security guards, who were allowed to carry guns, opened fire on the students, killing one and wounding others. Prior to the widespread social-media networking to come in the next decade, incidents such as this often went unreported, which allowed security forces to mete out violence with impunity. Activists often found themselves isolated, fearful, and unable to find support beyond their immediate environs and family. Such violence against localized protests like the example from Mogadishu was common and fairly ubiquitous across much of Africa. The brutality in one country encouraged brutality in another.

At the turn of the new millennium, students were also staging protests in Sudan against the government and its treatment of arrested student activists. Demonstrations spread from Khartoum to Omdurman and in the Nile and Northern states. As the demonstrations caught on, Sudanese authorities responded by unleashing police troops armed with tear gas and clubs on the protestors. This was the go-to response by the government to student protests during the entire decade. In 2007 and 2008, Sudanese students protesting the treatment of detained students massed in large gatherings in Khartoum and other cities and were again brutally set upon by police, who beat, arrested, and detained yet more students, setting off another turn in a chronic cycle of demonstrations followed by violent suppression and arrests, followed by more demonstrations and more violence and arrests.

Authoritarian violence against activists and opposition groups was widespread and common across much of the continent. Togo ramped up a crackdown on activism and protests at the turn of the century, and numerous international human-rights organizations criticized the government's use of terror in silencing citizens, particularly ahead of the OAU (Organization of African Unity) summits. Investigations revealed that in Togo, dozens of journalists, political activists, and students were arrested, beaten, and tortured by police on a whole host of charges. Amnesty International published findings that listed extrajudicial executions, torture, arbitrary arrests, imprisonment in horrendous conditions, and "disappearances" of those critical of the government as common practices used by authorities to compel silence among the general populace. It specifically noted the arrest and imprisonment of Koumoyi Kpelafia and Hanif Tchadjobo, two student leaders of an organization called the Student Council of the University of Benin (CEUB).

But even facing horrible repression, students continued to protest in Togo. For example, in 2000, they held a large demonstration against the presence of security forces on campuses and new rules limiting students' abilities to call a strike. The protesting students were violently beaten by security, and the student organizers were arrested and imprisoned. More protests and arrests followed. Subsequently, student leaders of the demonstrations, whether arrested or still at large and in hiding, were convicted in show trials and sentenced to lengthy prison terms. The Togolese government then passed new laws making defaming the state a crime punishable by imprisonment.

The terror campaigns and crackdown on freedoms of the press in Togo were effective, and little news of subsequent protests or activism escaped the nation. The BBC reported the University of Lomé, in the nation's capital, was closed in 2005 following "campus disturbances," which were student protests. But news agencies could offer no substantive details.[49] Another report smuggled out of the country surfaced internationally in 2011. The university was again closed after a demonstration was violently attacked by security, with the protest leaders arrested and charged with organizing an illegal gathering. This kind of control over the population was possible, however, only as long as the general populace was kept impoverished and terrorized, and as long as the opposition was without access to the technologies that could disseminate reports and images or could make networking on a large scale possible.

In Kenya, students also faced violent suppression, but nevertheless they protested often. Ongoing demonstrations ushered in the new millennium; in 1999, Moi University had erupted in student riots after a monthslong series of protests fueled by a student leader claiming he'd been abducted and tortured by local police. Adding to student anger were repeated school closures and several clashes with armed locals. During the worst of these, female students reported, they had been raped by security. The university responded to the demonstrations by banning leading student organizations from campus, and more protests and riots broke out, with students smashing windows and destroying buildings. Local police were called in to control the students, and attacked them.

In 2000, student unrest continued to spread, and four major universities were closed due to demonstrations and violent clashes with police. Students protested against educational fees, against the establishment of competing educational programs, against the government, against police brutality and student deaths in conflicts with police. They demonstrated against a whole host of other related issues. The ongoing police brutality spawned violence in the student demonstrators, and what would begin as peaceful marches often would end with students in the streets hurling stones at passing cars, and then at the police they knew were coming to attack them. Such violent student demonstrations became common in Kenya.

In 2002, a small group of protesting students from Kenya's University of Nairobi was confronted by police, who in arresting them managed to kill one of the protestors. In response, university students poured out of the university and rampaged through the district, throwing stones and driving back security troops, who retreated to a police station after they ran out of live ammunition and tear gas. Nairobi was brought to a standstill as students jammed the city's major roads, smashing windows and destroying cars. Police set up barricades outside the city to redirect traffic, to keep drivers from being stoned by the students holding the streets.

Seeing the effectiveness of tangling traffic and the police's response, which was to move troops out of the city to the roadblocks, students made this a common strategy of disruption over the decade. At Kenya Polytechnic and then at the Eldoret National Polytechnic, students rioted in October 2002, taking to the streets and throwing stones at cars and buildings. The next decade was similarly marked by violent student demonstrations on a whole range of issues, from wage disputes to students being killed by police to universities serving stale bread in cafeterias. Students destroyed property, took to the streets, and stoned vehicles until police arrived to teargas and disperse them. Kenyatta University would remain closed for months following particularly furious riots in 2003.

Occasionally students were killed outright in clashes with Kenyan police, which then sparked massive riots. In Nairobi, for example, a 2009 protest over the death of a student shot by police was spearheaded by the Student Organization of Nairobi University (SONU) and was initially planned to be nonviolent. But what started as a peaceful protest gave way to angry students once again stoning passing cars and chanting antigovernment slogans. Riot police were trucked in and unleashed on the students, and the area around the university erupted into running battles between police troops and students. This cycle in Kenya, with violence on both sides, would continue well into the next decade.

Roadblocking and stone throwing at cars to stop traffic were adopted as tactics by students in other countries as well, though in Zambia it was developed into a greater strategy to force change by strangling commerce. At the University of Zambia (UNZA) in Lusaka, student protests made international news yearly in the first decade of the millennium.[50] Most of these protests had to do with educational governance and reforms, with students protesting the high cost of education, delays in meal-plan allowances, fee hikes, and in one case a student's death while trying to cross the highway next to the university. In protests, UNZA students typically blocked the Great East Road, building barricades to stop traffic and then stoning any approaching cars. Police were slow to respond, but when they arrived they discharged copious amounts of tear gas and dispersed the students, who fled back onto campus. Similar roadblocking protests over fee hikes and meal plans also occurred during the decade at the Copperbelt University in Kitwe, with students similarly taking over roads and stoning cars until police dispersed them.

In Tanzania, students at the University of Dar Es Salaam held a protest against a new government rule that tied eligibility for student loans to tangible collateral, thus making loans far beyond the reach of the poor. Riot police attacked the demonstration, and fifty students were arrested. The university was closed while officials investigated the incident, using the investigation to identify the organizers and then charging them under laws against threats to social order. In Tunisia, students staged numerous demonstrations for social justice and government reforms, particularly in the southern regions. Throughout the decade, protestors faced police suppression and mass arrests, and students often reported being beaten by police after they had surrendered. Police interrogations included torture, and the leaders of protests were prosecuted and imprisoned. Tunisian students would rise up in a massive prodemocracy movement at the beginning of the new decade, and their suppression in the 2000s was part of the reason for that revolt.

Zimbabwe also saw a lot of student resistance in the first decade of the millennium, much of it predicated on the country's increasingly dire economic state, and like many of its neighbors, the state responded with violence. Thirty-seven years under President Robert Mugabe and the Zimbabwe African National Union–Patriotic Front took a country that had a 5 percent GDP growth rate and a budget surplus in 1980 (mostly due to agricultural exports) and bankrupted it. The government increasingly relied on bureaucratic corruption to maintain the state as the country nose-dived into poverty. At the turn of the century, students at the University of Zimbabwe, in Harare, began a protest against the government's pitiful support of students, which did not even cover the cost of the annual meal plan. The protestors marched off campus, and demonstrations grew and morphed into general protests against the government, the ongoing financial collapse of the nation, and corruption. Students chanted slogans that pointed out the bureaucrats were getting rich while students starved. Police shock troops surrounded these demonstrations and repeatedly hit them with tear gas and baton charges.

The economic crisis spawned all kinds of crises for students. In 2001, a female student committed suicide after having to enter into a relationship with a "sugar daddy" to support herself, a practice that had become common. With education the only way out of poverty for many Zimbabweans, predatory men of means took advantage of the disparity between what students were given as allowances and the high cost of attending university. Following the suicide, University of Zimbabwe students held a series of massive protests against the practice, waving placards that drew attention to the nation's HIV infection rate and claiming the older, often infected wealthy "sugar daddies" were spreading the disease. The roads onto campus were blocked, and approaching cars were overturned or stoned. In response to the demonstrations, police troops raided the campus, firing tear gas into the residence halls and violently beating any student they could catch. At least one student was beaten to death, and others were seen jumping from upper-story windows to escape the violence.

A lot of the economic crisis was due to Mugabe's actions following a failed strategy to purchase and redistribute lands from the nation's white minority; approximately .5 percent of the population held 70 percent of the best farmland. When the landholders refused to take Mugabe's proposed buyouts, he simply took their land by force, in actions that brought crippling international sanctions on the country. The landgrabs crippled agricultural production and, combined with international sanctions, fueled widespread famine. Student unions, which are particularly strong in the country, protested against Mugabe's policies in demonstrations that drew thousands. And although the "sugar daddy" student protests were not taken seriously, by middecade, the HIV crisis had to be, for an estimated 25 percent of all Zimbabweans were infected with HIV.

Mugabe would hold on to power for some time, though, and although students protested repeatedly for economic reforms and against widespread corruption, their demonstrations could not gain wider traction. When they occurred, they were often brutally suppressed. Mugabe would continue to rule as a dictator, falsifying election results when necessary, until a military coup deposed him in 2017.

In the 2000s, authoritarians across Africa used violence to crush demonstrations, terrorize their populaces, and silence opposition. But the suppression tactics used in Zimbabwe and Togo paled by comparison to the horrific violence used to suppress a peaceful prodemocracy demonstration in Guinea. Guinea was marked by instability in the early part of the millennium, especially as its neighbors were embroiled in civil wars. And it was not a stranger to authoritarian violence. In 2008, a military junta led by Moussa Dadis Camara seized control of the government, and in 2009, brutality against opposition activists reached a new level under his tenure, culminating in what has become known as the September 28 Massacre.

On that day in 2009, tens of thousands of prodemocracy demonstrators, many of them students, gathered in a stadium in Conakry for a peaceful demonstration to hear prodemocracy speakers, forge connections among groups, and voice their support for democratic rule. Presidential Guard members (known for the red berets they wear), police, and nonuniformed security agents arrived outside the stadium by the truckload after the rally began, and while the attention of those inside was focused on the speakers, they sealed off all the exits, trapping those inside. Then they launched a barrage of tear-gas grenades over the walls and into the structure. Shock troops wearing gas masks entered the arena in waves and began openly firing on the crowds with live ammunition, killing more than 150 and wounding thousands. When the panicked civilians ran for exits, they found Red Berets and armed paramilitaries waiting for them with guns raised. They shot all who approached, and when the troops ran out of ammunition, they began bayoneting their victims.

With no avenues of escape, protestors began scaling the upper walls of the arena ringing the top rows of seats and jumped, many breaking their legs as they hit the ground. With all exits sealed and in complete command of the arena, groups of Red Berets began openly gang-raping women caught in the stadium, taunting them while doing it because they were Peuhl (the majority ethnic group of the opposition, which is also largely Muslim). The flagrant rapes occurring on the ground among the scattered dead and dying added to the general horror of the scene. Survivors of the massacre reported that some women were shot in the head after being raped. Other women died from wounds suffered during the assaults, for witnesses later reported to human-rights investigators numerous instances of women being vaginally impaled with sticks, bayonets, and the barrels of rifles (which were sometimes discharged during the assaults). Captured opposition leaders were forced to watch the atrocities. Other women were abducted and moved to nearby houses, where they were subsequently raped for days.

Following the massacre, Red Berets closed off the area, removed bodies from the stadium, and buried them in mass graves. As rumors of the attack, then actual news reports, and finally a few photos of the massacre began to leak out, international condemnation of the government followed. Camara denied the extent and details of the massacre, though human-rights groups had already begun to document the violence. Due to massive international pressure, Camara agreed to return Guinea to civilian control, and elections were held in 2010. Alpha Condé, leader of the opposition, was elected to lead Guinea.

Although reforms were promised and to some extent implemented, Guinea's future would be marred by more corruption and repression. Occasionally prodemocracy demonstrations would flare, and in 2013 there were notably large protests, but in a country in which up to 95 percent of women were subjected to female genital mutilation, "human rights" and "abuse" remained relative terms.[51] Repeatedly in 2018 and 2019, demonstrations in Guinea would end with police violence and protestors' deaths.

While police and security violence was often the end result of activist efforts in many countries in Africa in the 2000s, it was not the case in all of them. On the other end of the spectrum from Togo or Guinea, students and activists were successful in peacefully demonstrating for reforms in Ghana. The decade saw a lot of student activity in the country, but unlike many protests across the continent, the majority of demonstrations in this nation remained nonviolent, and student resistance often resulted in modest reforms. In 2001, for example, University of Ghana students frustrated with student loan funds not being issued marched in Legon. Dressing in red or sporting red armbands, they blocked traffic and held officials and workers hostage inside Accra's Gulf House until the protestors secured a promise that their loans would be processed and released. They weren't violent, they just refused to let officials leave. Police were present but did not react aggressively, and the students left after about five hours. By the following week, the loans were disbursed. Encouraged by success, students peacefully protested on a range of issues in Ghana during this decade, from fee hikes to politics. Most demonstrations were over local issues or connected to local incidents and thus relatively limited in size, but they largely occurred without incident, with both students and authorities showing restraint.

Postapartheid South Africa has had among the highest numbers of protests in the world annually. Many of the networks and groups formed during the antiapartheid demonstrations continued on and turned their attention to other reforms. In the 2000s, student organizations joined other groups fighting for social or economic justice, against corruption, and against chronic economic disparity between the rich and the poor. Students marched with workers in urban streets, and they camped with villagers in land occupations. The numbers of protests in the nation steadily increased during the first half of the decade, and they surged higher following the 2008 economic crisis. For students concerned with educational reforms, with so much protesting occurring in the country, it was hard to get media coverage of student actions unless students were victims of particularly violent police suppression. By 2010, a dozen protests were happening on any given day of the year.

Police were not averse to using force in South Africa to break up protests, and they used it often, but relative to the number of protests occurring in the nation and the brutality of police violence in nearby authoritarian regimes, the degree of force used was low. Students protested against high costs of education, continued racial discrimination in schools, and the slowness of educational reforms. Enormous protests occurred at the University of Limpopo, Mangosuthu University of Technology, Tshwane University of Technology, and Vaal University of Technology. And yet, even though membership in activist organizations was high, and the country hosted numerous student networks that were continuously demonstrating for reforms by holding strikes, boycotts, and marches and setting up roadblocks, it wouldn't be until the middle of the next decade that they summoned and wielded significant international pressure on their government. The lack of national media coverage of their protests in the 2000s would be offset by extensive international media coverage made possible by new technology in the next decade.

Across Africa in the 2000s, there were tens of thousands of protests, a great many of them student led. But many of the countries were under the grip of authoritarian regimes or quasidemocracies rife with high- and low-level corruption. And many countries were terribly impoverished and war torn and enduring widespread disease and famine. Although some students in urban centers had access to modern technology and some international media, the bulk of the continent lagged far behind much of the rest of the world in terms of new personal technology and cutting-edge strategies for networking, communicating, and disseminating information. The protests tended to rely on twentieth-century strategies and so often remained isolated and easy to suppress. In many countries, this insulated dictators, and they could suppress dissent with overwhelming force and brutality. Because many of these nations had state-controlled media and limitations on freedom of expression and assembly, they could use terror, arrests, torture, kidnappings, incarceration, and killings to keep their citizens from rising up. Without international organizational networks and ways of getting information to the rest of the world, which could bring international aid or pressure, many activist organizations were on their own, fighting against more powerful forces.

Africa in the 2000s serves as a foil against which we can see how much technology in the twenty-first century had already begun to transform activism in the rest of the world. The disparities between how students were waging campaigns for reforms in Eastern Europe and how they were doing it in much of Africa during the 2000s highlights just how much technology changed social activism and its outcomes. The changes also show how much technology has empowered individuals by connecting them to vast networks. When media was controlled and protests smashed with brute force in Africa, it was hard for opposition groups to generate larger movements. In the coming decade in Africa, with the spread of cell phones and access to social-networking platforms, activism would surge to unprecedented levels. New tactics and new capabilities in mobilizing massive numbers, combined with the ability to spread captured images of police violence internationally and thus bring international pressure to bear on oppressors, would radically transform the way activism occurred.

Of course, authoritarians, and their police and security forces, would for some time try to respond as they historically have, with acts of violence. But soon, they would find that such acts could no longer be hidden so easily from the world, and that widely disseminated images of violence against ordinary people often sparked a groundswell of local support for opposition causes. They could also bring international condemnation, crippling economic sanctions, and even UN intervention. In the next decade, activism and suppression in Africa would undergo a sea change in terms of strategies, tactics, and outcomes.

7

INTERNATIONAL NETWORKS, INDIGENOUS PEOPLES' RIGHTS, AND ECONOMIC JUSTICE IN MEXICO, CENTRAL AMERICA, SOUTH AMERICA, AND ISLAND NATIONS

Student activism was extremely high throughout Latin America and neighboring island nations in the first decade of the new millennium. Many countries had long histories of student agitation, including pronounced levels of activity in the 1990s, and activism only increased in the 2000s. Particularly notable for the region in the first decade of the millennium are the networks that student organizations formed among countries and the solidarity among students agitating in neighboring nations. In the 1990s, students were already forming extensive networks and coordinating demonstrations, and when new affordable technology swept the regions in the 2000s, these networks transitioned to internet and social-media platforms. In terms of the use of new technology in protest strategies (and in terms of a mix of authoritarian and democratic governmental contexts), student activism in Central and South American nations was in many ways similar to that occuring in Eastern

Europe. Otpor and CANVAS would develop a number of direct connections to Central and South American student organizations. In addition to prodemocracy protests, though, the demonstrations in Latin America typically concerned institutionalized corruption, demands for social justice, or economic or education reforms. Students also protested against police violence.

Some student activities in Latin America had an outsized influence on those in other nations, and Mexico's organizations were some of the most influential. At the dawn of the new millennium in Mexico, National Autonomous University of Mexico (UNAM) students were striking, barricading the main entrance to the flagship campus in the capital and occupying buildings, after administrators released plans for a tuition hike from almost nothing (the constitution guaranteed citizens a free education) to the equivalent of around 160 US dollars a year for tuition. The strike closed the university system of 270,000 students for eight months while student leaders and officials negotiated terms. At one point, administrators scrapped the plans, thinking this would end the strikes, but the students presented a list of entirely new demands, including the elimination of lab fees and further reforms that would establish a student presence in administrative decisions.

The students remained nonviolent, and police dispatched to control students often went unarmed. If insensitive to their demands, the government was nonetheless sensitive to the risk of violence and wanted no modern analogies drawn to the 1968 student massacre when troops machine gunned down protesting students in the Tlatelolco neighborhoood of Mexico City. Only a few clashes with police broke out, and this occurred off UNAM grounds when police physically removed students striking in solidarity from occupied high schools. Ultimately UNAM's tuition was not raised, though the students were unsuccessful in their other demands. Student activism at the main UNAM campus remained high throughout the decade, though it would be in Oaxaca that the next major movement would start, and the struggle would center on police violence, state politics, and corruption.

In 2006, Oaxaca students, leftist activists, and opposition leaders joined the region's already demonstrating teachers who had set up union camps in the city. The teachers had been brutally set upon by local police, and the wider support followed media reports of the violence. The city was filled with protestors for months, and demonstrators repeatedly battled with local police. The police attacked again and again, and levels of violence continued to escalate as more and more people joined the demonstrations. The crowds grew large enough to bring the capital city of the state to a standstill.

After three people were killed in a single day's raids (one was a New York journalist), President Vicente Fox ordered federal troops to quell the uprising, which was no longer only about teacher pay but also about police violence, corruption, and contested state elections. Thousands of troops were bused to the city. Alerted that they were coming, demonstrators dispatched a large contingent to form a blockade across the main highway in Nochixtlán, just northwest of the city. Their stand bought time for those in the city to prepare, to build barricades across city streets and arm themselves. The Nochixtlán defenders suffered for what they did, however, for they were attacked by the federals. Many were wounded or killed outright. Caught demonstrators were arrested, and a number of those arrested disappeared forever. Students, activists, and reporters at the scene photographed dead bodies in the streets and piled in the back of military trucks and posted them on blogs, spreading the images through the internet and international news media.

Those inside Oaxaca saw those blogs and communiqués and knew what was coming, but the sacrifice of their colleagues galvanized the resistance, and they defied the arriving troops. After the delayed federal forces arrived at the city, the onslaught commenced. Troops began systematically, violently retaking the city, block by block. Demonstrators pushed buses and cars across city streets and set them on fire, manned barricades, and threw bricks and Molotov cocktails at the advancing lines, retreating grudgingly as security used tear gas and fired rubber-coated bullets and occasionally live ammunition at them. The federal troops used military armor and bulldozers to clear the streets of the burning barricades.

University students then sent out a call to students through multiple media platforms to occupy the Benito Juárez Autonomous University of Oaxaca. They used the internet, social media, and student news media to spread the word. A group of students barricaded themselves in the student radio station in order to keep broadcasting throughout the attack. An autonomous university forbids police from entering campus grounds, so the university became a sanctuary for demonstrators from the larger protests. It was, however, officially closed and sealed, ringed off by federal troops. Still broadcasting, the student radio station (Radio Universidad) was subsequently hit with multiple rounds from high-powered rifles, though the source of the gunfire was never revealed.

Demonstrations would repeatedly break out in various parts of the city only to meet with suppression, and students in other cities and towns launched protests in solidarity. Eventually the leaders of the demonstrations would negotiate with the federal government to end them, but after seven months of violent protests in the city dozens of citizens had been killed and hundreds wounded. Corruption and police brutality in the region remained a problem, despite government assurances it would be cleaned up. During the decade, there were numerous claims by residents of police and political intimidation, kidnappings, torture, and assassinations of opposition leaders by hired thugs or paramilitary groups working for corrupt government officials. Such allegations by residents were repeatedly supported by the coincidental burning of sympathetic local media outlets. The protests would serve as background for the violence against students by corrupt officials and federal troops in the region in the 2010s.

Costa Rican students, like many of their neighbors, saw a radical evolution in student networking abilities and in demonstration strategies and tactics at the turn of the millennium. In the first few years of the decade, students repeatedly led rallies opposing the US war in Iraq, but it was not until a 2004 event that students realized the power they wielded in the country. In that year, a nationwide demonstration of truck drivers against a Spanish-owned monopoly that inspected vehicles successfully blocked all the major roads in the country. The effectiveness of the action in stopping commerce encouraged other organizations to challenge the government, and many student groups launched their own strikes, roadblocks, and marches. They asked for educational reforms, an end to the Central America Free Trade Agreement (CAFTA) among the United States and five Central American nations (Costa Rica, El Salvador, Guatemala, Honduras, and Nicaragua) plus the Dominican Republic, and for legislation protecting the environment. Others protested for clean water, lower taxes, and more education funding. Still others called for an end to US imperialism, the cleaning up of Costa Rican government corruption (which was rampant and chronic), and the ceasing of pineapple-farm expansions.

The truckers' strike eventually ended without resolution, though the pressure of tens of thousands of truckers, students, and residents marching in the streets of San Jose and elsewhere did serve notice on the Costa Rican government that many Costa Ricans were unhappy with its current policies and performance. While demonstrators were frustrated in the short term, they did have a tremendous impact upon activism levels and the country's policies going forward. In 2008, there was a notable demonstration in the north by students and activists who gathered to protest a planned open-air gold mine of some 477 acres, which would result in the clearcutting of the surrounding area. The festival-like atmosphere of the demonstration—complete with live music, food vendors, and dancing—belied the seriousness of the activists and their determination. They networked and formed alliances with other groups invested in tourism, clean water, and the environment. The demonstrations would be constant, with large ones occurring annually.

For three years, activists battled the government-backed plan, and through a massive media campaign, a national education campaign, and alliances with Nicaraguan student and activist groups who protested the mine on the grounds that it would pollute the countries' shared rivers, they finally forced the government to ban all open-pit gold mining. Costa Rican activists were particularly good not only at staging demonstrations but at educating the general population and the government about the importance of Costa Rica's natural resources in attracting tourist dollars.

In Honduras, protests for government reforms and on a wide variety of issues were common and, as in other area nations, students in the 2000s were expanding their networks and experimenting with social media as a tool for building protest numbers quickly. In 2006, students demonstrated in massive numbers against President Manuel Zelaya after he signed the free trade agreement with the United States and neighboring nations. They were joined in their protests by farmers and workers, and although they couldn't get the nation to withdraw from CAFTA, they did exert tremendous pressure on the government and, in doing so, realized the power they could wield.

Three years later, however, Zelaya had garnered much support in the country among students, for he shifted leftward during his presidency. Following a military coup that ousted the president, students marched in support of the displaced leader. They cited improvements under Zelaya over the past four years to the nation's infrastructure, to education (which was made free to young children), and in the form of increased wages for workers. Protest attendance swelled into the thousands, and in addition to challenging the military for its power grab, demonstrators heavily criticized neighboring countries and the United States for standing idly by while a military coup overthrew a democratically elected president.

Using modern technology and working in tandem with networks established with other groups in previous fights for reform, students came out in force, protesting alongside workers and residents, but they were no match for the country's police and military. Police in full riot gear, supported by military troops in armored vehicles and light tanks, roughly suppressed the demonstrations with tear gas, water cannons, and baton charges. Zelaya would eventually return

from exile to thousands of awaiting supporters, though his time of
leading the country was over. He returned to a country on the brink
of ruin, in the hands of authoritarian Porfirio Lobo Sosa, who continued to use troops to brutally suppress demonstrations and whose
forces arrested, imprisoned, and tortured activists, political opponents, and journalists.

In Nicaragua, a country with high levels of violence, university
students came out in support of a number of other groups demonstrating for reforms. They often employed arson against government
property, and in some cases fired homemade missiles at security
forces. Doctors protesting and striking for higher wages nationally in 2003, for example, found themselves supported by a large
force of students from Central American University (UCA) who
set cars and vans on fire. President Enrique Bolaños Geyer asserted
the vandalism did not help further the negotiations. Other student
demonstrations were peaceful, but there was a faction of Nicaraguan student activists that was drawn to violence. When fuel prices
pushed transportation costs up, students wearing masks blocked
major highways and roads, manning them with homemade mortars
that they used to bomb approaching vehicles. Using Molotov cocktails, they set fire to buses and cars that tried to run the blockades.

In 2006, the Sandinistas retook control of the government under
leftist President Daniel Ortega, an authoritarian who subsequently
violently suppressed peaceful demonstrations. Suppression of
demonstrations was so vicious that protesting university students
and opposition activists were forced to go into hiding. As in those
nations under the yoke of Eastern European strongmen in the 1990s
or dictators in Africa in the 2000s, public protests against the government in Nicaragua dwindled out of fear. That didn't stop effigies
of government officials from being hanged under bridges or burned
publicly.

Protestors were forced to adopt guerilla-style tactics, demonstrating and attacking government figures when they ventured out in
public or when they passed in motorcades, then quickly dispersing
before troops arrived. Human-rights watch groups have consis-

tently noted the government's violence toward indigenous peoples and its abuse of citizens' civil rights. As the decade progressed, Nicaraguan activists would increasingly turn to the internet and social media to protest and to launch guerilla-style virtual attacks on the government, similar to Russia's Voina activists.

Argentina has a long and storied history of committed student activism, and at the turn of the century students were already protesting in massive force as the country careened into economic crisis. President Carlos Saúl Menem had, in early 1999, announced huge reductions in the federal budget to keep the country's enormous deficit in check, in accordance with rules imposed by the International Monetary Fund. The equivalent of hundreds of millions of US dollars were cut from the education budget; the proposed radical tightening of universities' purses threatened to shut down programs, cut wages, and decimate student allowances and resources. This brought tens of thousands of students to the streets. They were joined by residents and allied opposition groups in demonstrations so large they forced the president to cancel his educational reforms. The students, however, did not stop protesting but rather joined growing protests against the government breaking out across the country. [52] The civil unrest grew. Menem resigned rather than fight the uprising, and in December 1999, Fernando de la Rúa's administration took over a country plummeting toward defaulting on its IMF debt.

By the end of 2001, the banking system of Argentina was in a panic, and limits on the amount of personal cash withdrawals were imposed. Massive demonstrations erupted in every sizeable city, in protests characterized by the banging of empty pots and pans; these were called the *cacerolazo* protests. As they grew in size and intensity, demonstrations began to be hit by riot police. The protestors fought back, and images of the violence quickly spread through national and international media. The crowds swelled, and the chronic violence used against them led to widespread rioting. De la Rúa imposed a national state of emergency and deployed the military to restore order. Despite the use of the military, the protests nevertheless continued, as did the rioting, and with no available options left, the government resigned.

The country's financial woes only worsened, and students and other activists continued protesting for economic help for the poor and against the government's failed economic policies as the crippled government flailed about. In 2002, Argentina defaulted on its international debt, and its economy failed. Government assistance for the poor fell drastically, unemployment skyrocketed, and food and fuel shortages followed. Citizens responded with more protests, and crowds became a constant feature before government buildings and banks. Students marched waving flags with Che Guevara's image on them and called for revolution. Police repeatedly used tear gas, baton charges, and barrages of rubber-coated bullets to disperse the more unruly protests, but this only sparked rioting, looting, and retaliatory violence on police units caught alone or in small groups.

For weeks, columns of protestors marched through city streets, setting fires and erecting barricades. In intense urban battles with police and security forces, dozens of people were killed. Police and military troops staked out defensive positions around government buildings, banks, businesses, and supermarkets to protect them, and troops hunkered down before or repelled angry mobs. The protests died down some after Néstor Carlos Kirchner assumed the presidency in 2003 and began to try to turn the economy around, but they did not disappear completely.

Things got better economically for the nation, but in 2004, close to 50 percent of Argentina's population still lived below the poverty line. Even as the economy slowly recovered (in great part due to the willingness of international institutions to renegotiate and forgive a huge portion of the country's debt), protests against the government's handling of its finances, unemployment, and poverty continued. Students and activists repeatedly blocked roads with burning tires, manned barricades, and in some cases doused themselves with gasoline and struck matches in acts of self-immolation meant to attract media attention. As the decade wore on, the economy recovered, and citizens grew tired of the constant social unrest; gradually, the levels of protest across the nation dropped off. Through the rest of the decade activism was for many an ingrained part of student identity, and they continued to agitate for reforms, but by 2010, most demonstrations in the country had become non-violent.

Inspired by social unrest in neighboring nations, Bolivia was also rocked by student protests for economic justice during this decade. In April 2000 in Cochabamba, thousands of students and activists protested in the city's streets when the government decided to increase water rates and charge peasants for water taken from local wells. Demonstrations swept across Bolivia, with students coming out in every city in support of the poor and against the government's economic plans. In La Paz, the protests were enormous, enough so that the government called a state of emergency and used the military to suppress them. The state of emergency allowed security troops to operate however they saw fit, and they hit the protestors hard. They gassed them and beat them with batons; they unloaded barrages of rubber-coated bullets into gathered crowds. Demonstrators responded by throwing bricks and rocks. Running battles between security and demonstrators raged throughout La Paz for a week, until government and protest leaders negotiated a settlement. The government dropped the water-fee plan, and the protest leaders told civilians and students to return home.

Students and activists had swelled demonstrations for weeks in cities, towns, and villages throughout the country, blocking roads and sometimes fighting the military over the initial water-rights issue, but their demands had in the process grown to include a range of desired government reforms, from stopping unrestricted mining to the end of abuses of local land rights and the need for minority representation in government. They were energized by the protests, and even after the resolution on the water issue, they continued to agitate for reforms. Numerous student groups, for example, held demonstrations in solidarity with Aymara natives who had blocked roads and held their own protests over land use and natural-gas extraction that ended in battles with soldiers that left half a dozen Aymara dead and dozens of protestors injured.

2003 was yet another tumultuous year for Bolivia. Striking police in La Paz were attacked by military troops called in to suppress them, resulting in shootouts between the armed parties that left fourteen dead. This brought students and civilians out en masse to protest the killings and in support of the police against the military. Fire was set to half a dozen government buildings, which burned to the ground as local firefighters joined striking police in solidarity. When students attempted to overrun the government palace, however, they were cut down by military troops firing barrage after barrage of rubber-coated bullets.

The uprising was violent, but it was surpassed seven months later in El Alto, when citizens of the poverty-stricken shanty town demonstrated against the government's proposal to export extracted gas to the United States and to Mexico through a pipeline running through Chile. The demonstrations ended in violence when security and protestors faced off and troops opened fire with live ammunition. The city streets erupted into mayhem as troops chased down the fleeing protestors and beat them. Sixteen people were killed in the attacks, and many more were severely wounded.

Students across the country immediately protested against the brutality. They also protested the plight of the nation's poor and the government's support of corporations that were exploiting Bolivia's resources without any benefit to the Bolivian masses. Students and activists marched in massive crowds in Cochabamba. Thousands more, joined by indigenous people and miners, marched in the streets of La Paz for days, some erecting barricades across main avenues and others carrying protest signs, clubs, or rocks. The miners joining the demonstrations brought along sticks of dynamite, which they lit and threw when police approached. The protests grew and quickly morphed into antigovernment demonstrations, calling on President Gonzalo Sánchez de Lozada to resign.

Instead, Sánchez de Lozada called in the military and deployed entire battalions in the city streets, supported by armored vehicles and tanks. While some troops took up defensive positions around government buildings, others were unleashed on the protestors. Military aircraft airlifted foreigners out of the country. But rather than quelling the unrest, the violence fueled it. Images of troops brutally beating protestors, and of people dying in the streets, were recorded and disseminated by students through social media and by journalists through international news media. This brought more people into the streets. With every sign suggesting that the conflict would only escalate, Sánchez de Lozada resigned. By the end of the demonstrations, referred to afterwards as "Bloody October," more than seventy people had been killed and thousands injured.

Six months later, in 2005, the streets of La Paz, Cochabamba, and Santa Cruz de la Sierra were once more filled with students, indigenous people, and miners (again bringing dynamite) protesting for the nationalization of the oil industry. These demonstrations were sparked by the high price of fuel and unwanted changes to the country's constitution. They called for the resignation of President Carlos Mesa. The split between the well-heeled of Bolivia (most of whom were tied in some way to international capitalist ventures and corporations) and indigenous peoples, the poor (64 percent of the population lived below the poverty line), and the working class continued to increase, and the majority of the people of Bolivia were angry about it. The military threatened to intervene once again, but eventually the protests brought down another president. Mesa resigned by the end of the year.

Violence and protests in Bolivia often went hand in hand, and the brutality wasn't only coming from the side of authority. In El Alto in 2006, several hundred leftist students stormed a university administration council meeting and beat the administrators gathered there. Afterwards, the students threatened more violence if the administrators did not resign, which they promptly did. Violence would break out repeatedly over the next few years as students and activists continued to push for constitutional reforms and were met in the streets by riot police.

Not all student demonstrations ended in violence in Bolivia, though. In El Alto, students demonstrated against local brothels and bars in 2008 that catered to prostitution, asking the government to shut them down. Although pimping is outlawed in Bolivia, prostitution itself is legal. The students increased their pressure on the government through a publicity campaign and by going on a hunger strike. Feeling the pressure from the activists, who had been joined by residents, the mayor closed the brothels. In a counterprotest, sex workers went on a hunger strike of their own. A group of them dramatically sewed their own lips shut, while another three dozen or so fasted and held signs claiming their right to make a living. As dramatic as the sex workers' protests were, they lost the brothel battle. Although they were a brief spectacle for the media, they did not have the widespread social support the students did and couldn't counter the sustained pressure the students wielded on the government through their extensive social networks.

In the eastern regions of Bolivia in 2008, right-wing youth and students repeatedly protested against leftist president Evo Morales, the first indigenous president of the country, who enjoyed popular support in the majority-indigenous nation. (He would win subsequent reelection in 2009, 2014, and 2019 at the head of the Movement for Socialism party.) Protests for greater autonomy in these resource-rich lowland districts, often sponsored by wealthy nonindigenous landowners and capitalists, were sometimes led by student organizations, and they included the scaling of security fences to occupy natural-gas facilities. Over the coming years, the protests would lead to a full-fledged separatist movement, with international financial support (especially from the United States) backing the demonstrators. The Morales government would face increasing protests throughout the country in the decade to come as it faced a series of economic crises and accusations of corruption. After clearly fraudulent election results were announced following the 2019 presidential election in a blatant attempt by Morales to hold onto power, massive protests would erupt across the entire nation and he would be forced from office.

In the 1990s, Brazil had been rocked by student protest activity, from antigovernment marches to demonstrations for land reform. When residents and workers joined the students, attendance at protests in the nineties swelled to numbers exceeding 150,000. Many of the demonstrations ended in clashes with security, resulting in thousands of injuries and numerous deaths. In the 2000s, students' concerns trended to include economic and international issues. In 2001, for example, students protested Canada's ban on beef imports from Brazil due to fear of mad cow disease. Restaurant and bar owners dumped Canadian whisky and other products throughout the country, and the protests made international news when students delivered a live cow to the Canadian embassy in Brasilia, suggesting the Canadian ambassador barbecue it, since unlike in more developed nations Brazilian beef was pasture raised, not grown on protein feed made up of ground-up cow parts (which is how mad cow disease is spread).

Although the governments of Brazil and the United States had good relations with one another, in 2003 there were both peaceful and violent student protests in Brazil against the US war in Iraq. Peaceful protests, like those organized by the Revolutionary Popular Students Movement (MEPR), were common, and these tended to be sit-ins and occupations. The more violent marches on government buildings were met and suppressed by security forces. As in the Canadian protests against the war, students vented their anger on things associated with the Untied States. In Rio de Janeiro, students marched through the heart of the city, throwing stones and Molotov cocktails at the US consulate, at banks, at a McDonald's, and at a passing military patrol unit. They didn't get far, though, before they were attacked and arrested by security forces.

Anti–United States sentiment was a common feature of student resistance action in the country, for many viewed the imperial giant to the north as meddling too much in foreign affairs. Ahead of a visit by US president George W. Bush to Sao Paulo in 2007, thousands of demonstrators took to the main street of the financial district in what started out as a peaceful demonstration. Students, environmentalists, leftists, unionists, and others from a whole slew of organizations marched waving hammer-and-sickle flags and posters of Bush sporting a Hitler mustache, and shouting antiwar, anti-imperialist, and anti–United States slogans. Police forces clad in riot gear struck the protestors with tear gas and baton charges, driving them into side streets. Participants reported a small contingent of extremists had thrown rocks at police and that the violent police charge on the main demonstrations was an overreaction. Other protests were planned in three other countries on Bush's "Latin America tour," and student organizations had linked networks to orchestrate demonstrations internationally as he travelled from country to country. These events all had similar outcomes, with security attacking the demonstrations. The anti-Bush march in Colombia would be suppressed with violence.

As access to the internet and social-media platforms increased, so too did the international nature of protests in Brazil, both in that their messaging began reaching a wider audience and in that they began to tackle international issues and politics. Students in Brazil, as in many Central and South American nations, became more worldly in terms of activism. So while it may have been surprising to tourists on vacation, in terms of student resistance it was not surprising at all that in 2009, Jewish students marched on the beautiful sands of Ipanema Beach in Rio de Janeiro protesting the visit to Brazil of Iran's president, Mahmoud Ahmadinejad, the. Chanting Jewish students powered down the beach, parting the crowds, waving Israeli flags, and brandishing signs decrying Iran's president and his denial of the Holocaust.

Chilean students similarly held international protests in the 2000s, though they supported the other side of the Israeli-Palestinian conflict from their neighbors in the Brazilian beach protests. Thousands of Chilean students and activists marched in pro-Palestine demonstrations beginning in 2001, waving Palestinian flags and touting images of Yasser Arafat, chanting for the creation of a Palestinian state. To a visitor of the country, this may have seemed as unusual as the Brazilian Jewish student protests, but hundreds of thousands of Chileans can trace their ancestors back to Palestine. Palestinian business leaders were also responsible for helping modernize Chile's economy, and three of Chile's elite schools are Palestinian, promoting Arab culture and language. University students actively demonstrated regarding political issues and economic reforms and against US imperialism.

Inspired by effective student movements happening across the world, by middecade high school students in Chile were testing their power. In 2006, students connected through social-media networks called for a nationwide high school strike to protest against the government's support of neoliberal policies. Known as the "Penguin Revolution," for the students' black-and-white school uniforms, the students occupied schools across the country to draw attention to growing economic inequality and the government's embrace of the corporate elite. Although the protests were largely symbolic, they effectively energized a new generation of students, youth who in the coming decade would continue to organize and agitate on university campuses. They helped build an activist culture that by 2019 would challenge the government, launch battles with security for control of city streets across the nation, and swell a demonstration to over a million people on the streets of Santiago.

The fever for activism raged in many nations in the region. Across Colombia there were violent student protests already underway at the start of the decade. In 2000, masked students demonstrated nationally when US president Bill Clinton visited Cartagena. Armed FARC and National Liberation Army (ELN) rebels set off bombs and blocked highways. The student demonstrations were attacked all across Colombia by security forces. During Clinton's visit, the unrest was kept out of Cartagena, for the city was under tight security. Thousands of military and police troops patrolled the streets, military helicopters flew overhead, and warships moved into the area.

As the battles among leftist rebels, right-wing militants, and the US-backed military began to escalate in Colombia in 2000, violence erupted on college campuses, with politically aligned students taking increasingly extremist positions. Some began embracing violence as a tactic, attacking opposing groups and targeting professors

whose ideologies they opposed. By 2001, five university professors
had been assassinated and others shot, attacked, or kidnapped. Violence throughout the country had become common, and protests
were often met with police violence. In 2001, students protesting
the US bombing of Afghanistan were set upon by security forces,
and when tear gas didn't disperse them, troops opened fire with
live rounds, killing one of the demonstrators and wounding others.
Anti–United States demonstrations became common, with students protesting against the growing US presence in Colombia
and US support of the Colombian military. They also opposed the
superpower's spraying of toxic chemicals over Colombian lands in
its "War on Drugs" and its financial backing of paramilitary death
squads that hunted and killed FARC sympathizers, union leaders,
and human-rights workers.

In 2007, ahead of the visit by US president George W. Bush on his
"Latin America tour," hundreds of masked students demonstrating
against him were attacked by an equal force of security troops who
hit them with tear-gas grenades, water cannons, and baton charges.
The students responded by throwing stones and homemade explosives made of gunpowder wrapped in tinfoil known as "potato
bombs." The pitched battle lasted until security reinforcements
arrived and the student lines were eventually broken.

The larger population of Colombia eventually grew tired of the
constant brutality and the disruptions of everyday life, becoming
particularly disenchanted with political student activists whose protests ended in property damage, battles with police, and lingering
clouds of tear gas. After images of dozens of caged, often starving
kidnap victims held in the jungle by FARC rebels spread through
news media, public sympathy for the rebels dropped. The emaciated
victims included foreigners, some of whom had been hostages for
a decade. In 2008, hundreds of thousands of Colombians marched
in major cities calling for the end of FARC. Even though by the end
of the decade, student activists could use sophisticated technology
to network, having lost support among the general population, student protests declined.

In Ecuador during the decade, students were also experimenting with the use of technology and social media to summon large numbers of people and forming alliances with other groups for reforms. In 2000, the government declared a state of emergency after students, workers, and indigenous peoples started large-scale protests, clogging traffic in the capital, over government policies. Under the leadership of President Jamil Mahuad, the value of the nation's currency had dropped 30 percent in a single year. Demonstrations went on for weeks across the county. In major cities, students marched and occupied parks, and in rural areas where people were protesting for indigenous people's rights, activists erected barricades across roads to halt commerce. Workers and students marching on the presidential palace in Quito were hit hard by security firing tear-gas grenades and rubber-coated bullets at them. The protests grew to enormous proportions, and the military conducted a coup, forcing the president to resign. In 2001, his replacement, President Gustavo Noboa, faced still more demonstrations by students and indigenous peoples who were protesting the high cost of living.

In 2005, the next leader, President Lucio Gutiérrez, also faced massive protests after he disbanded the nation's supreme court and appointed new members to the bench who promptly absolved a number of politicians facing corruption charges, including an unpopular ex-president who was in exile. In the capital, thousands came out against the moves, many of them young students unhappy with the direction the country was taking. Police and armored security forces attacked demonstrators with water cannons and tear gas, and battles erupted in the streets. Gutiérrez declared a state of emergency, but his plan of being able to use the military to quell the uprisings backfired. The military withdrew its support of Gutiérrez, and he was forced to flee the country.

Feeling their strength, students and activists also began protesting for the oil companies drilling in the country to pay revenues to support the nation's infrastructure maintenance. The companies initially balked but soon agreed to the demands after demonstrations, occupations, and roadblocks brought oil production to a

standstill. And when socialist president Rafael Correa was elected
in 2007, demonstrations against the oil companies' exploitation of
Ecuador continued, with activists pressing for the nationalization
of the country's oil industry, which happened in 2010.

At the start of the millennium in Peru, under constant pressure
by students who continuously staged demonstrations in which they
often painted their hands white to symbolize government corruption, President Alberto Fujimori withdrew security forces that had
been stationed on university campuses since the late nineties. Even
so, his campus reforms left the government securely in charge of
educational institutions, which made him unpopular among students. In 2000, students and workers banded together to protest
against him in force after he claimed victory in national elections for
an illegal third term. Demonstrators burned government buildings
and, in the process, killed half a dozen government workers. Troops
were deployed and crushed the initial uprising, but images of their
violence widely circulated in the media, bringing more residents
into the streets in support of the protests. Students and activists
used the images and their national networks to call for reinforcements to come to Lima for more protests. Following the president's
inaugural address, up to a hundred thousand Peruvians marched in
the capital in a new prodemocracy movement. Although Fujimori
tried to dismiss the protests as the workings of his political opponent, Alejandro Toledo, legitimate corruption allegations against
the government surfaced. Under investigation by the country's
National Intelligence Service, and beset on all sides, Fujimori fled
the country.

Prior to the next elections in Peru, students did not quietly return
to their studies but instead continued to network and demonstrate
for changes. They wanted a free press in the nation, economic
growth, and anticorruption reforms. Notably, students and activists working with Amnesty International explicitly called for the
end of torture by security and police forces—a widespread practice
up until then. In 2001, Toledo won the presidency on a platform of
reform, though soon his government would also face massive pro-

tests. Under his presidency, the economy grew, but the effects were not felt by everyday Peruvians who were struggling to make a living wage. When workers, teachers, transport labor, and students went on strike in 2003, Toledo chose to respond as his predecessors had, with violence. He called a state of emergency, putting twelve of the nation's regions under military control; banned protests; and gave troops the right to enter homes, arrest suspects, and use whatever force necessary to maintain social order.

In Puno, security forces opened fire with live ammunition on students who refused to end their demonstrations, killing one and injuring fifty. Giving low-level military troops discretionary powers quickly became a media nightmare for the government, as more and more incidents of violence were recorded and disseminated online. As the brutality continued, video began to make international news. Students used social media to expose the viciousness of the soldiers and called for international aid. In the city of Arequipa, troops fired tear gas and rubber-coated bullets into a group of marching teachers—an act that never plays well on the nightly news.

Toledo's presidency became a nightmare, even for him. A devastating earthquake, his unpopular reforms, and his handling of the economy left him with an approval rating below 10 percent. Eventually the strikes ended, through a combination of sheer military suppression and moderate government reforms that led protest leaders to call them off. From then on, that combination would become a standard in Peru's playbook for stopping strikes and demonstrations. The government would hit protestors with physical force, followed by minor concessions with the promise of larger reforms to come.

This did not, however, preclude all activism, and Peru saw other violent civil actions later in the decade, though over different issues. In 2009, students came out in force to support indigenous peoples and to fight against the government-supported exploitation of the Amazon rainforest through oil and gas leases after a violent confrontation in Amazonia in early June. Local demonstrators had been attacked by police and fought back in a battle that left more than thirty dead. Police officers were killed by spears and arrows, and the local civilians died from gunshot wounds. Following the violence, tens of thousands of students, activists, workers, and indigenous people marched together in groups throughout the nation. They marched in the streets of the capital and other major cities, and they marched in towns and villages, protesting more planned leases and excessive police violence. A number of the marches were violently attacked by security forces. Police in the capital thwarting a march on Peru's congress were particularly violent, with troops using armored vehicles, tear gas, water cannons, and rubber-coated bullets against demonstrators, who responded by throwing rocks and Molotov cocktails. As images of the battles spread through social media, more students poured off campuses to support the demonstrations. The protests forced the government to make concessions to indigenous people, granting them some power in the resource exploration process and promising them financial gains from any leases granted. In the next decade, supported by student groups, indigenous people would be protesting again when the government failed to make good on its promises.

Venezuela was another country controlled at the turn of the millennium by a strongman unafraid to use force on his opponents. Nevertheless, the nation saw civil unrest and much student protest in the 2000s. In 2001, thousands of students, teachers, and parents protested President Hugo Chávez's educational reforms, claiming they were nothing more than leftist indoctrination programs that would destroy the country's educational system. Chávez was a hero to the poor of the country; however, the middle and upper classes saw his reforms as a severe threat to the country's economy, culture, educational traditions, and future. The challenges against the populist dictator achieved little, though, and campuses also began to see violence from pro-Chávez groups who disrupted professional classes and clashed with students trying to complete their degrees. In 2002, Chávez was briefly ousted in a military coup following public demonstrations, though afterwards he was returned to power following larger protests by the country's poor. He would remain in office for the rest of the decade, surviving a recall referendum and many protests, which were often suppressed with violence perpetrated by his troops and by government-equipped paramilitary mobs.

In Cuba, the government took the opportunity to crack down on dissent on the island nation while the rest of the world watched and squabbled over the US invasion of Iraq in 2003. Security rounded up dozens of activists and journalists in what became known as the "Black Spring"; they were arrested, convicted on various charges, and imprisoned. This effectively drove most antigovernment critique in the nation underground. Public dissent was extremely dangerous, though it continued to surface, notably in Cuban rap music. The genre itself was originally banned by the government, but seeing the style was so popular that it couldn't be stamped out by simple decree, the government moved to co-opt it on state-run television and radio, thinking by doing so it would gain the support of the younger generation. Once rap was legalized, the music's popularity and the number of Cuban rap groups exploded far beyond what was endorsed by state sponsorship. With danger and defiance prime elements in the "street cred" of the genre, rap groups in Cuba naturally gravitated toward including protest in their lyrics. They challenged the United States and protested against international events, against social injustice and police violence, and, eventually, against the government.

In something that sounds more like a Hollywood film script for a comedic espionage thriller than anything else, in 2009, a US government contractor, inspired by Otpor's effectiveness in raising mass revolts in Serbia, enlisted help from Serbian revolutionaries in a scheme to use a Serbian record producer to approach rappers in Cuba to write and perform songs that would foment youth revolt. At the same time, through shell companies and intermediaries, conservative US NGOs began underwriting Cuban hip-hop festivals.[53] Programmatic US efforts to infiltrate the Cuban hip-hop scene went on for years and understandably made international news when the project was eventually revealed.

In Haiti, small demonstrations by students and activists against
the government of President Jean-Bertrand Aristide in the early
2000s faced severe brutality at the hands of police and paramilitary government supporters who would attack demonstrators while
police simply looked on. In 2003, however, Haitians came out in
force to protest against Aristide. One massive anti-Aristide demonstration led by thousands of students marching in Port-au-Prince
was joined by residents and swelled into the tens of thousands.
Spin-off demonstrations lasted for days. While police fired tear gas
at approaching crowds and closed ranks around government buildings, Aristide recruited and armed paramilitary thugs to attack the
protestors. Armed and paid, they repeatedly attacked unarmed
protestors, sometimes indiscriminately firing into crowds with live
ammunition. This was too much, and the marches in the streets of
the capital turned into full-scale riots. Aristide unleashed the military, and dozens were killed in the subsequent violence. Under
heavy suppression and fatigue, the demonstrations would eventually burn out.

In 2004, an armed insurgency began in the north of Haiti, while
university students continued to lead nonviolent demonstrations
calling for Aristide's resignation in the capital. When a thousand
university students marched in Port-au-Prince against the president
in late February, they were attacked by pro-Aristide paramilitaries
armed with rocks, machetes, and guns. But using paramilitaries
came with risk for the government, for they tended to be overzealous
in their attacks. The student demonstration was being covered by
international news media, and the raiding mob launched an attack
on the reporters, which was simultaneously broadcast on international news streams. The Untied States urged all US citizens to leave
the country as quickly as possible, and international airports were
packed with fleeing foreigners. The uprising, however, couldn't be
stopped by thugs or troops, and as the nation continued to erupt,
Aristide fled the country. The United Nations stepped in to enforce
order and remained in Haiti until after the 2006 presidential elections, in which René Préval was elected.

The chaos and violence attending many of the protests in Latin America weren't unique among the regions of developing nations in the world. The variety of governments, cultures, and political ideologies, ranging from extreme left to extreme right, and widespread economic instability across the continent all but guaranteed turbulence among and within those nations. What was unique was the extent of the student networks already in place, developed through the previous decade of student and youth protests. When new technologies allowed students and activists to expand their networks even further, students were ready to capitalize on the opportunity. They made the most of being able to broadcast widely, through social media, images of police violence when it occurred and to launch effective real-time calls for demonstrations.

In the coming decade, they would add more technology and new tactics to their arsenal of protest weapons, including computer hacking of government networks, international social media–based movements to bring external ipressure to bear on governments, and encrypted cell-phone broadcasting of troop movements in order to warn protestors on the streets or launch their own counterattacks. For Latin America, the decade was one of social turbulence, but it was nothing like the chaos to come.

THOUGHTS ON THE TRANS-
FORMATION AND POWER OF
STUDENT RESISTANCE

Activist organizations, strategies, and demonstrations were growing across the world in the first decade of the millennium thanks to the internet and, like rhizomes, they spread in every direction and would erupt forth in the 2010s like never before. While most demonstrations remained locally or nationally focused in the early 2000s (apart from campaigns against US wars, imperialism, and unethical investments), the concerns of citizens across nations often ran in parallel. Thus student organizing and protest in the 2000s set the stage for the coming revolution in activism that would flourish in the 2010s, when advances in social-media technology would facilitate massive unrest and the proliferation of movements around the world on an unprecedented scale, fueled by a sharp rise in authoritarianism, xenophobia, and nationalism.

The United States and Europe in the first decade of the millennium witnessed domestically oriented demonstrations against corporate greed and exploitation, racism, and education reforms, and they hosted significant antiwar movements and early demonstrations for climate-change awareness. Importantly, students in the West at this time were experimenting with social-media networking to organize protests and spread information. They began forming international virtual networks and tried disseminating information on a global scale, especially as Western nations increasingly provided sanctuary to activists fleeing violent suppression elsewhere. Significantly, many of these activists arriving in the West used the internet to garner support for their causes and continued to organize and agitate for improvements in their home countries, leading to an increase in diasporic activism globally. International hacktivist groups in Europe also launched cyberattacks on multinational corporations and authoritarian governments; more than any other region, the European Union witnessed this shift to technology-driven activism and an experimentation with new tactics that would soon come to much of the rest of the world. The European Union was the first to see the sophisticated computer organizing strategies and networking that anticipated the global shift to social-media and cell-phone networking, and the development of resistance tactics taking advantage of live-stream video recording, instantaneous data dissemination, and flash mobbing. These experiments in new activism tactics immediately began to be picked up by and to affect resistance efforts in other regions.

At the same time in the early 2000s, Eastern Europe witnessed the student and youth-driven color revolutions, and those struggles found a receptive international student audience, contributing as much as anything to the coming youth culture of resistance of the 2010s across the globe. Resistance movements that flared up across Eastern Europe included Otpor in Serbia, KAN in Kosovo, Gong in Croatia, Kmara in Georgia, Mjaft! in Albania, and Pora! in Ukraine. Youth resistance in the region grew as the 2000s progressed, and although these student activists did not yet have the lightning-speed tools of social media, their relative successes were watched by the world. Experimenting with computer technology and new forms of dissent, from performance art to video protests to early forms of flash mobbing, they changed the methods of modern protest, especially as they spread information through international networks and online platforms. This fostered an international youth culture of resistance that would develop into an international style associated with protest in the 2010s. Following the lead of many of Eastern Europe's countries in the 2000s, movements and revolutions would flare in the 2010s throughout Asia, the Middle East, Africa, and South America.

Asia would become one of the hotbeds of student resistance, and student protest actions occurred there in every conceivable form in the 2010s. The region's wide variety of cultures and governments ranged from Western-style democracies to absolute dictatorships to constitutional monarchies. But none escaped the effects of an ever-increasing economic globalism, the growing proliferation of affordable technology, and the constantly expanding international reach of Western popular culture. Even in self-isolating authoritarian nations, the transmission of Western media and culture spread, and the prodemocracy revolutions in Eastern Europe in the 2000s encouraged many seeking democracy elsewhere to try their hand at organizing movements against authoritarian regimes in the 2010s. These movements were greeted by robust dictatorial countermeasures—both physical and virtual—especially in China and North Korea, but by the end of the 2010s, many of Asia's nations were seeing ever larger spikes in youth resistance, networking, and peaceful activism that were paired with matching increases in violent government suppression and new authoritarian laws, like a macabre dance between beauty and beast.

Starting in the 2000s, the Middle East also saw increases in activism—predictably reflected in anti–United States war demonstrations, a rise in anti-Western sentiment, and continued protests over Israel's occupation of the West Bank and Gaza—that would continue in the 2010s. The region also saw backlashes of cultural conservatism as Western pop culture spread globally early in the decade, but this trend was increasingly challenged by youth and students excited to be plugging into international media and social networks and learning about what youth in more culturally liberal countries were doing and the freedoms they enjoyed. As the 2000s wore on, students in the Middle East increasingly began adopting the strategies for organizing resistance movements used, especially in 2003, in the Eastern European color revolutions, the leaders of which were broadcasting their ideas and tactics for social, cultural, and political revolution worldwide—setting the stage for the coming Arab Spring, with its astonishing early successes, and then the slow grind back to power of authoritarian and military governments over the course of the 2010s.

Africa in the 2000s saw tens of thousands of protests, and a great many of them were student- and youth led, but other than in major urban areas, affordable technology, information, and new strategies of resistance were slow to penetrate the region. Many African nations remained under the grip of authoritarian regimes or quasi-democracies rife with corruption. Much of the continent was impoverished, a good bit of it war torn, and many people were suffering from famine and disease. Protests in Africa in the 2000s tended to rely on twentieth-century strategies and for the most part remained locally isolated and easy to suppress by military-backed regimes who were likewise using tried-and-true twentieth-century tactics of suppression. In the 2010s, however, resistance strategies and methods in many African nations would follow trends established in Europe, Asia, and the Middle East and inspired by the successful revolts in Tunisia and Egypt that led to the Arab Spring.

In Latin America, the adoption of extensive online activist networks and new methods of protesting happened at a pace just behind that of Europe and the United States in the 2000s, though the resulting linkages were in some ways more extensive, building on decades of established international Latin American student networks. In terms of the use of new technology in protest strategies (and a mix of authoritarian and democratic governmental contexts), student activism in Central and South American nations was in many ways similar to that occuring in Eastern Europe, and, not surprisingly, organizations such as Otpor and CANVAS established direct connections to Central and South American student organizations. In addition to prodemocracy protests, demonstrations in the region typically concerned institutionalized corruption, demands for social justice, indigenous people's rights, and economic or education reforms. The region saw tremendous political chaos during the 2000s, and many of the battles waged would set up the Latin American Spring revolts that would sweep across the entirety of the region and neighboring island nations with an ever-spiraling intensity in the next decade.

In terms of student and youth resistance, the 2000s were thus a watershed decade for developing new strategies and tactics driven by technological innovations that allowed for vast networking and the dissemination of information over the internet. The decade was a time of great experimentation in terms of protest, and the successes of specific movements—especially those in Eastern Europe—would then inspire movements around the world deeply into the 2010s. Young people were inspired by the Eastern European color revolutions that had yielded both new countercultural cachet and political successes. International networks proliferated, movements jumped national boundaries, and acts of hacktivism became common. That said, most of the actual protesting that occurred during the decade was relatively traditional twentieth-century-style marching, rallies, and occupations based on local, culturally specific organizing efforts, though certainly aided by the internet. It would not be until the international rise of social media in the 2010s and the proliferation of cheap cell phones that came with a camera and the ability to upload video that student and youth resistance would fully transform into the global force it would become.

If the 2000s revolutionized thinking about resistance and what was possible, the 2010s would revolutionize revolution itself. Activists using new methods and strategies of resistance, armed with new technology, agitated on an unprecedented scale, and social movements erupted around the world, changing entire societies and the geopolitical landscape. There would be the Arab Spring, the African prodemocracy revolts, the Sunflower Movement, the Hong Kong Umbrella Movement, the Occupy movements, many international women's-rights movements, the Latin American Spring, Black Lives Matter, and the Global Climate Strike movement. The hundreds of thousands of protests staged during the 2010s would become the foundation of a new way of making change in contemporary society, and in many regions, student-led movements played significant roles in government reform and cultural change.

Student resistance today is very different than it was at the start of the millennium; it has an international culture, plus highly effective and flexible tactics and strategies for documenting abuses and combating suppression with instantaneous international reach and support. There are international organizations devoted to giving workshops and information on how to do grassroots and community organizing in different areas of the world, for conducting effective protests designed for specific cultures, for countering police and even military tactics, for navigating local laws and local courts if arrested, and for reaching news media organizations and international human-rights groups to report abuses. And as new as today's resistance movements are, even at this moment student resistance is evolving yet again. The staging of protests is growing more and more sophisticated. Contemporary movements are unfurling complex battle campaigns challenging entrenched authority on multiple fronts, through many channels and mediums simultaneously. Student resistance today clearly has the potential to wield more power, and to generate that power faster, than ever before.

NOTES

Specific sources are cited in the Notes when quotations, statistics, and isolated perspectives on events are referenced in the text. Incidents lacking secondary confirmation were generally excluded from the text, except where noted.

This book could not have been written without technological advances in research made available in the last decade and a team of researchers adept in using these research tools. Large databases and sources we accessed included: International Newsstream (which accesses the contents of more than six hundred newspapers internationally, including the major papers in most nations), InfoTrac, *New York Times* Historical Newspapers, *Times of London* Digital Archive, US Newsstream, the *Chronicle of Higher Education*, JSTOR, Historical Abstracts, and the Global Nonviolent Action Database, as well as individual major news media archives (current and historical) and the various physical and virtual archives listed in the Acknowledgements.

When contradictions in reports could not be resolved, I relied on larger news agencies with international distribution and recognized, reliable fact-checking practices, but noted contrasting reports in the text where warranted. The object of this book is to tell the story and characterize the tremendous scope of recent student resistance actions (within their immediate contexts), but such an endeavor is certain to contain flaws and errors as new details of events emerge over time.

1   I employ the terms "left" and "right" in this book, but we should remember their meanings differ from nation to nation and may individually be inclusive of a range of ideologies, many of them at odds one with another. I also use the term "democracy," but please keep in mind that it means something very different in Beijing from in Hong Kong, in Iran from in Egypt, and in Latin America from in the United States. As much as possible, I'll contextualize such terms culturally and historically when I use them.

2   See Willis Rudy, *The Universities of Europe, 1100–1914* (Rutherford, NJ: Associated University Presses, 1984).

3   In his researching of the event through interviews and government documents, Zheng Yi—who himself both had been a Red Guard in 1968 and was later arrested for participating in the pro-democracy movement and 1989 Tiananmen Square

uprising—identified a lineage of cannibalism in the region's history, noting the effect of three years of famine, vicious factionalism, and local corruption as contributing factors. But there are also allegorical parallels for what the powerful in his country in the 1990s were doing to its own citizens. Zheng Yi, *Scarlet Memorial: Tales of Cannibalism in Modern China*, ed. and trans. T. P. Sym (New York: Perseus, 1998).

4   "Canada: Mass Protests Against War on Iraq," World Socialist Web Site, January 20, 2003, https://www.wsws.org/en/articles/2003/01/cana-j20.html.

5   Andy Riga, "Students Get Stuck: Concrete Protest before Strike Tomorrow by Associations Representing 25,000," *The Gazette* (Montreal), February 23, 2005.

6   Tim McSorely, "Student Strike Was Successful but Fresh Battles Loom," *Canadian Dimension* 30, no. 4 (July–August 2005): 13.

7   "Around the Nation," *Houston Chronicle*, November 19, 2009, 3.

8   See "Harvard Students Campaign for a Living Wage, 1998–2002," Global Nonviolent Action Database, accessed December 13, 2020, https://nvdatabase.swarthmore.edu/content/harvard-students-campaign-living-wage-1998-2002.

9   "Swarthmore Students Campaign for Card Check Neutrality in Workers' Unionizing, 2006," Global Nonviolent Action Database, accessed December 13, 2020, https://nvdatabase.swarthmore.edu/content/swarthmore-students-campaign-card-check-neutrality-workers-unionizing-2006.

10   "Lots of Speculation around Coke's New CEO," *Tribune* (Welland, Ontario), April 22, 2004, A7.

11   Margaret Webb Pressler, "Human Rights Charges Still Gnaw at Coca-Cola; Protesters Convene at Stockholders Meeting," *Washington Post*, April 22, 2004, E.01.

12   Gregg Sherrard Blesch, "Opposed To War—Dozens of Local Students Protest," *Columbian* (Vancouver, WA) March 6, 2003, C1.

13   "Between 500,000 to 2 Million Take to the Streets of L.A. to Demonstrate Against Anti-Immigrant Bill," *Democracy Now*, March 27, 2006, transcript available at http://www.democracynow.org/2006/3/27/between_500_000_to_2_million.

14   Matt Krupnick and Doug Oakley, "Thousands Protest Tuition Hikes, Layoffs at University of California," McClatchy-Tribune News Service, September 24, 2009, https://www.mercurynews.com/2009/09/24/5000-at-uc-berkeley-protest-tuition-increases-furloughs-layoffs/.

15   *Human Rights Watch World Report, 2003*, Human Rights Watch, 2003, https://www.hrw.org/legacy/wr2k3/.

16   Michel Chossudovsky and Finian Cunningham, *The Iraq War Reader: A History of War Crimes and Genocide: The Unleashing of America's New Global Militarism*, online interactive i-book, (Montreal: Global Research, 2012), https://www.globalresearch.ca/the-iraq-war-reader-a-history-of-war-crimes-and-genocide-the-unleashing-of-america-s-new-global-militarism/31067.

17   "Iran: July 1999 Demonstrations in Tehran." Research Directorate, Immigration and Refugee Board, Ottawa, Canada, December 2000, https://docplayer.net/79661424-Chronology-iran-july-1999-demonstrations-in-tehran.html; Elahe Sharifpour-Hicks, "Heading Into Iran's Winter of Discontent," *Wall Street Journal* (Europe), September 23, 1999; "Police Enforce Calm after Worst Iranian Riots in 20 Years," CNN, July 13, 1999.

18   "Fatah Activist Killed by Palestinian Executive Force, Armed Group," BBC, May 18, 2007, 1.

19   "Pakistani Women March in Rape Row," *BBC News, September 29, 2005, http://news.*

bbc.co.uk/2/hi/south_asia/4294840.stm.

20   "Crowds Gather to Protest Bush Visit to Austria," *Irish Examiner* (Cork, Ireland),
      June 21, 2006, https://www.irishexaminer.com/world/arid-30264277.html.

21   Karin Strohecker, "Deportations Spark Immigration Uproar in Austria; A
      15-Year-Old Albanian Girl Whose Parents Were Kicked Out Has Threatened Suicide,"
      Vancouver Sun (Vancouver, BC), October 10, 2007, A13.

22   Donald MacLeod, "To the Barricades: Political Protest in France Reflects Growing
      Discontent in Universities," *The Guardian* (London), April 30, 2002, https://www.
      theguardian.com/education/2002/apr/30/internationaleducationnews.france.

23   Suzanne Daley, "Anti-Le Pen Protests Draw a Million into Streets in France," *New
      York Times*, May 2, 2002, https://www.nytimes.com/2002/05/02/world/anti-le-pen-
      protests-draw-a-million-into-streets-in-france.html.

24   Alex Duval Smith, "France's Global Warning," *The Observer* (London), March 19,
      2006. https://www.theguardian.com/world/2006/mar/19/france.alexduvalsmith.

25   Molly Moore, "Millions in France Protest Law, Leadership; Opposition to Labor Bill
      Widens into Protest of Government Deemed Out of Touch," *Washington Post*, April
      5, 2006, A17.

26   Elaine Sciolino, "Paris Suburb Riots Called 'a Lot Worse' than in 2005," *New York
      Times*, November 27, 2007, https://www.nytimes.com/2007/11/27/world/europe/27i-
      ht-riots.4.8500200.html.

27   Kate Connolly, "Nuclear Protest: German Activists Block Train," *The Guardian*
      (London), November 14, 2001, 1.19.

28   Keith B. Richburg, "Italian Police Feel Backlash from G-8 Summit Violence; EU Offi-
      cials Urge Thorough Probe, Propose New Force," *Washington Post*, August 11, 2001,
      A14.

29   Daniel Williams, "Anti-War Activists Protest in Florence; Thousands Denounce U.S.
      Iraq Policy," *Washington Post*, November 10, 2002, A26.

30   "Millions Unite in Grief and Anger on Streets of Madrid," *Evening Times* (Glasgow,
      Scotland), March 13, 2004, 6.

31   Keith B. Richburg, "Millions in Spain Decry Attacks; Marchers Jam Streets; Govern-
      ment Still Focused on Basque Separatists," *Washington Post*, March 13, 2004, A01.

32   Mark Steel, "We Will Not Be Moved," *The Independent* (London), February 11, 2003,
      4, 5.

33   "Serbian Students Warn 'Regime' to Expect 'More Open Rebellion,'" BBC Monitoring
      Europe, October 16, 1999, 1.

34   Peter Ford, "How the Balkan Strongman Was Toppled: Yugoslavia Activists——with
      Foreign Help——Offer a Textbook Case on Dislodging a Dictator Without Firing
      a Shot," *Christian Science Monitor*, January 27, 2003, https://www.csmonitor.
      com/2003/0127/p12s01-usmi.html.

35   *Srdja Popovic and Matthew Miller, Blueprint for Revolution: How to Use Rice Pudding,
      Lego Men, and Other Nonviolent Techniques to Galvanize Communities, Overthrow
      Dictators, or Simply Change the World (New York: Spiegel & Grau, 2015).*

36   Irina Sandul, "Kuchmagate, Two Years On," *Time* (Odessa), September 26, 2002,
      http://content.time.com/time/world/article/0,8599,354919,00.html.

37   Peter Wilson, "Orange Revolutionaries' Democracy Lessons," *The Australian* (Can-
      berra, ACT), December 3, 2004, 8.

38   "Ukrainian Opposition Youth Group Vows Nationwide Protests," BBC Monitoring
      Newsfile, October 26, 2004, 1.

39   C. J. Chivers, "How Top Spies in Ukraine Changed the Nation's Path," New York Times, January 17, 2005, https://www.nytimes.com/2005/01/17/world/europe/how-top-spies-in-ukraine-changed-the-nations-path.html.

40   Claudia Ciobanu, "Students Demand an Environment for Education," Inter Press Service, December 26, 2008, http://www.ipsnews.net/2008/12/bulgaria-students-demand-an-environment-for-education/.

41   "Polish Weekly Profiles Nationalist Party, Rival Groups," BBC Monitoring Europe, May 21, 2008.

42   Cathy Young, "Putin's Young 'Brownshirts,'" Boston Globe, August 10, 2007, http://archive.boston.com/news/globe/editorial_opinion/oped/articles/2007/08/10/putins_young_brownshirts/; Mark Ames and Alexander Zaitchik, "Skinhead Violence Rising in Russia," The Nation, September 10, 2007, https://www.thenation.com/article/archive/skinhead-violence-rising-russia/.

43   Nick Sturdee, "Don't Raise the Bridge: Voina, Russia's Art Terrorists," The Guardian (London), April 12, 2011, https://www.theguardian.com/artanddesign/2011/apr/12/voina-art-terrorism.

44   Nick Sturdee, "Russia's Robin Hood," Index on Censorship 40, no. 3 (October 4, 2011): 92, https://doi.org/10.1177/0306422011418758.

45   Adam Lusher, "Where Are They Now? At Least 10,000 People Died in Tiananmen Square Massacre, Secret British Cable from the Time Alleged," The Independent (London), December 24, 2017.

46   Alpha Barry, "Pas d'état de grâce," Jeune Afrique/L'Intelligent, no. 2079 (November 14–20, 2000); Ousmane Sow, "Coup de torchon à l'université," Jeune Afrique/L'Intelligent (Paris), October 17–23, 2000.

47   "Youth in Crisis: Coming of Age in the 21st Century," UN Office for the Coordination of Humanitarian Affairs, February 23, 2007; "UNICEF Supports Fight to End Marriage by Abduction in Ethiopia," UNICEF press release, UN Office for the Coordination of Humanitarian Affairs, November 9, 2004, https://reliefweb.int/report/ethiopia/unicef-supports-fight-end-marriage-abduction-ethiopia.

48   Alieu Darboe, "The Gambia: 1994–Present," International Center on Nonviolent Conflict, February 2010, https://www.nonviolent-conflict.org/wp-content/uploads/2016/04/darboe_the_gambia.pdf; "Gambia: Cold Commemoration of Gambia's Student Massacre." Gambia News, 2007, http://www.afrol.com/articles/25032.

49   "Togolese University Said Closed Following Student Protests," BBC Monitoring Newsfile, February 7, 2005, 1.

50   The fact that even small protests in Zambia made it into international news (whereas incidents in neighboring countries often did not) had much to do with the country's relationship with the outside world. Formerly the northern region of Rhodesia, Zambia has since its colonization been a largely Christian nation, where English is the official language of education and business. During the 2000s, the country became economically stable and saw massive foreign investment, and thus drew international interest in what was happening in the area.

51   Country Reports on Human Rights Practices for 2011: Guinea, Bureau of Democracy, Human Rights and Labor United States Department of State, 2012, https://2009-2017.state.gov/j/drl/rls/hrrpt/2011humanrightsreport/index.htm?dlid=186203#wrapper.

52   Cristina Bonasegna Kelly, "Argentina Drops Plan to Cut Education Funds," Chronicle of Higher Education, May 21, 1999, https://www.chronicle.com/article/argentina-drops-plan-to-cut-education-funds/.

53   Tracy Wilkinson, "Young Cuban Artists Testing the Boundaries of Dissent," *Los Angeles Times*, March 3, 2015, http://www.latimes.com/local/great-reads/la-fg-c1-cuba-dissident-music-20150303-story.html.

BIBLIOGRAPHY

The research and writing of this book relied mainly on scholarly and academic studies and reports by various governmental and nongovernmental organizations and international human rights organizations. Thus, this bibliography represents more of a parallel track and a starting point for deeper inquiry than an exhaustive list of references.

The bulk of the research conducted for this book involved collecting and compiling a massive database of primary documents and reports and (because much of the material is too recent to have made it into academic studies) hundreds of thousands of newspaper articles—far too many to list individually. In addition to undertaking primary research, we also combed through three decades' worth of coverage in more than a thousand different newspapers from around the world. News articles and reports on student actions were sorted and annotated for political leanings and vantage points, and cross-checked and compared with other reports. Our research team also plowed through thousands of smaller newspapers, journals, websites, artifacts, blogs, flyers, and one-off publications—again, too many to note here individually.

But there were also a certain number of books, articles, and reports that were on the cutting age of awareness of the global student resistance movement of the last twenty years and that thus accompanied and guided our work, as reflected in the bibliography that follows.

Al-Mughrabi, Nidal. "Israeli Troops Kill Seven Palestinians on Day of Heightened Gaza Border Protests: Medics." Reuters, 6 April 2018. https://www.reuters.com/article/us-israel-palestinians-protests/israeli-troops-kill-seven-palestinians-on-day-of-heightened-gaza-border-protests-medics-idUSKCN1HD0OG.
Altbach, Philip G., ed. *Student Political Activism: An International Reference Handbook*. Westport, CT: Greenwood Press, 1989.
———, ed. *Student Politics: Perspectives for the Eighties*. Metuchen, NJ: Scarecrow Press, 1981.

Altbach, Philip G., and Robert Cohen. "American Student Activism: The Post-Sixties Transformation." *Journal of Higher Education* 61, no. 1 (1990): 32–49. https://doi. org/10.2307/1982033.

Ames, Mark, and Alexander Zaitchik. "Skinhead Violence Rising in Russia." *The Nation*, 10 September 2007. https://www.thenation.com/article/archive/skinhead-violence-rising-russia/.

Amin, Julius A. "Cameroonian Youths and the Protest of February 2008." Translated by Jen Bircher. *Cahiers d'Études Africaines* 53, no. 211 (2013): 677–97. https://doi.org/10.4000/etudesafricaines.17459.

Amnesty International. *China: The Massacre of June 1989 and Its Aftermath*. London: Amnesty International, 31 March 1990. https://www.amnesty.org/download/Documents/200000/asa170091990en.pdf.

Amutabi, Maurice N. "Crisis and Student Protest in Universities in Kenya: Examining the Role of Students in National Leadership and the Democratization Process." *African Studies Review* 45, no. 2, Special Issue: African Universities in Crisis and the Promotion of a Democratic Culture (September 2002): 157–77. https://doi.org/10.1017/S0002020600031474.

"Analysts, Activists Say Even Though Dangerous Street Protests Are Still a Viable Tool Against Mugabe," *All Africa*, 15 November 2015. https://allafrica.com/stories/201511160826.html.

"Anti-U.S. March in Tehran." *New York Times*, 5 November 5 1999.

"Around the Nation." *Houston Chronicle*, 19 November 2009, 3.

Associated Press, "50,000 Children in Yemen Have Died of Starvation and Disease So Far This Year, Monitoring Group Says." *Chicago Tribune*, 16 November 2017. https://www.chicagotribune.com/nation-world/ct-save-the-children-yemen-20171116-story.html.

Ayyar, Kamakshi. "The Men Accused of Raping and Murdering an Eight-Year-Old Girl in India Are Standing Trial. Here's What to Know." *Time* (India), 27 April 2018. https://time.com/5255375/kathua-india-rape-case-trial/.

Babu, Kimberley B. "Arrests End in Riot in Hartford." *Boston Globe*, 4 March 1991.

Barry, Alpha. "Pas d'état de grâce." *Jeune Afrique/L'Intelligent*, no, 2079 (14–20 November 2000).

Beaty, Thalia. "Strike to Win: Can Polish Feminists Turn Protest into Power?" *Dissent* 64, no. 3 (Summer 2017): 125–33. https://www.dissentmagazine.org/article/poland-feminists-strike-manifa-razem-protest-power.

Beck, Carlton E., ed. *Perspectives on World Education*. New York: Wm. C. Brown, 1970.

"Belarusian Opposition Rallies against President's Participation in Election." BBC Monitoring Former Soviet Union, 25 November 2010.

Benedikter, Roland, Katja Sieppman, and Migue Zlosilo. "Chile: Country or Change?: Backgrounds of Chilean Politics After the Elections," *Harvard International Review* 35, no. 3 (Winter 2014): 63–68. https://www.jstor.org/stable/42772694.

Bennani-Chraïbi, Mounia, and Mohamed Jeghllaly. "The Protest Dynamics of Casablanca's February 20th Movement." Translated from the French by Sarah-Louise Raillard. *Revue Française de Science Politique* [English edition] 62, no. 5–6, Arab Uprisings, Reflections on Revolutionary Situations in Context (2012): 103–30. https://doi.org/10.3917/rfsp.625.867.

"Between 500,000 to 2 Million Take to the Streets of L.A. to Demonstrate Against Anti-Immigrant Bill." *Democracy Now*, 27 March 2006. http://www.democracynow.org/2006/3/27/between_500_000_to_2_million.

Bibliography

Blake, John. "Students Return to AU Center." *Atlanta Journal and Constitution*, 26 August 1992.

Bollag, Burton. "Czech Students' Protest over Crackdown by Police Leads to Biggest Demonstration in Twenty Years." *Chronicle of Higher Education*, 29 November 1989. https://www.chronicle.com/article/czech-students-protest-over-crackdown-by-police-leads-to-biggest-demonstrations-in-20-years/.

———. "Eastern Europe Finds University Reform Is a Long, Hard Task." *Chronicle of Higher Education*, 31 July 1991. https://www.chronicle.com/article/eastern-europe-finds-university-reform-is-long-hard-task/.

———. "20 Years after the Islamic Revolution, Iran's Campuses Begin to Loosen Up." *Chronicle of Higher Education*, 10 March 2000. https://www.chronicle.com/article/20-years-after-the-islamic-revolution-irans-campuses-begin-to-loosen-up/.

Boren, Mark Edelman. *Student Resistance: A History of the Unruly Subject.* New York: Routledge, 2001.

———. "A Revolutionary Learning: Student Resistance? Student Power." In *Radical Experiments in Utopian Pedagogies*, edited by Mark Cote and Richard Day, 76–92. Toronto: University of Toronto Press, 2007.

———. "Students Show the Power and Future of Democracy." *News and Observer* (Raleigh, NC), 27 March 2018, A3.

Boudreaux, Richard. "Russian Protester Finds Another Path to Change." *Wall Street Journal*, 09 March 2012. https://www.wsj.com/articles/SB10001424052970203961204577269241996622920.

Bousquet, Marc. "Occupy and Escalate." *Academe* 96, no. 1 (January–February 2010): 29–33. https://www.aaup.org/article/occupy-and-escalate#.X-jpO9hKi-Y.

Boyer, LaNada. "Reflections on Alcatraz." *American Indian Culture and Research Journal* 18, no. 4 (1994): 75–92.

Bowers, John W., Donovan J. Ochs, and Richard J. Jensen, and David P. Schultz. *The Rhetoric of Agitation and Control.* 3rd ed. Long Grove, IL: Waveland Press, 2009.

Bradley, Kimberly. "Gowns, Wurst and Protesters: It's Ball Season in Vienna." *New York Times*, 4 February 2018. https://www.nytimes.com/2018/02/04/world/europe/vienna-ball-season.html.

Brindle, Andrew. "A Corpus Analysis of Discursive Constructions of the Sunflower Student Movement in the English-Language Taiwanese Press," *Discourse and Society* 27, no. 1 (2016): 3–19. https://doi.org/10.1177/0957926515605957.

Brown, Sarah. "Harvard Students Build 'Resistance School' to Harness Anti-Trump Sentiment." *Chronicle of Higher Education* 21 April 2017. https://www.chronicle.com/article/harvard-students-build-resistance-school-to-harness-anti-trump-sentiment/.

Brown, Wendy. *In the Ruins of Neoliberalism: The Rise of Antidemocratic Politics in the West* (New York: Columbia University Press, 2019).

Bullock, Clifford A. "Fired by Conscience: The 'Black 14' Incident at the University of Wyoming and Black Protest in the Western Athletic Conference, 1968–70." *Wyoming History Journal* 68, no. 1 (Winter 1996): 4–13.

Bureau of Democracy, Human Rights and Labor. *Country Reports on Human Rights Practices for 2011: Guinea.* United States Department of State, 2012. https://2009-2017.state.gov/j/drl/rls/hrrpt/2011humanrightsreport/index.htm?dlid=186203#wrapper.

Burg, David F. *Encyclopedia of Student and Youth Movements.* New York: Facts on File, 1998.

Calhoun, Craig. "Protest in Beijing: The Conditions and Importance of the Chinese Student Movement of 1989." *Partisan Review* 56, no. 4 (1989): 563–80.

Chauvin, Lucien O. "Students in Peru Channel Protests into a New Political Party." *Chronicle of Higher Education*, 25 June 1999. https://www.chronicle.com/article/students-in-peru-channel-protests-into-a-new-political-party/.

Chen, Rou-lan. "Chinese Youth Nationalism in a Pressure Cooker." In *Taiwan and China: Fitful Embrace*, edited by Lowell Dittmer. Berkeley: University of California Press, 2017.

Chen, Ya-chen. "Queering Women in Taiwan." *American Journal of Chinese Studies* 23, no. 2 (October 2016): 239–56. https://www.jstor.org/stable/44289157.

Cheng, Chu-yuan. *Behind the Tiananmen Square Massacre: Social, Political, and Economic Ferment in China*. Boulder, CO: Westview Press, 1990.

Chivers, C. J. "How Top Spies in Ukraine Changed the Nation's Path." New York Times, 17 January 2005. https://www.nytimes.com/2005/01/17/world/europe/how-top-spies-in-ukraine-changed-the-nations-path.html.

Chomiak, Laryssa and John P. Entelis. "The Making of North Africa's Intifadas." *Middle East Report*, no. 259, North Africa: The Political Economy of Revolt (Summer 2011): 8–15. https://merip.org/2011/06/the-making-of-north-africas-intifadas/.

Chossudovsky, Michel, and Finian Cunningham. *The Iraq War Reader: A History of War Crimes and Genocide: The Unleashing of America's New Global Militarism*. Online interactive i-book. Montreal: Global Research, 2012. https://www.globalresearch.ca/the-iraq-war-reader-a-history-of-war-crimes-and-genocide-the-unleashing-of-america-s-new-global-militarism/31067.

Ciobanu, Claudia. "Students Demand an Environment for Education." Inter Press Service, 26 December 2008. http://www.ipsnews.net/2008/12/bulgaria-students-demand-an-environment-for-education/.

Clarke, Killian. "Unexpected Brokers of Mobilization: Contingency and Networks in the 2011 Egyptian Uprising." *Comparative Politics* 46, no. 4 (July 2014): 379–97. https://www.jstor.org/stable/43664115.

Cohen, Roger. "The Unlikely Road to War." *New York Times*, 17 March 2014. https://www.nytimes.com/2014/03/18/opinion/cohen-the-unlikely-road-to-war.html.

Congdon, Matt. "Endangered Scholars Worldwide." *Social Research* 79, no. 3, The Future of Higher Education (Fall 2012): v–xvii. https://www.jstor.org/stable/23350029.

Connell, Dan. "Refugees, Ransoms and Revolt: An Update on Eritrea." *Middle East Report*, no. 266, Iraq: Ten Years Later (Spring 2013): 34–39. https://merip.org/2013/03/refugees-ransoms-and-revolt/.

Connolly, Kate. "Nuclear Protest: German Activists Block Train." *The Guardian* (London), 14 November 2001, 1.19.

Contreras, Raoul. "Chicano Movement Chicano Studies: Social Science and Self-Conscious Ideology." *Perspectives in Mexican American Studies* 6 (1997): 20–51. http://hdl.handle.net/10150/624827.

Cox, Laurence. "Challenging Toxic Hegemony: Repression and Resistance in Rossport and the Niger Delta." *Social Justice* 41, no. 1/2 (135–136), Special Issue: Bhopal and After: The Chemical Industry as Toxic Capitalism (2014): 227–45. https://www.jstor.org/stable/24361599.

Craig, Tim. "Pakistan's Prime Minister Is Defying the Clerics–Very Carefully." *Washington Post*, 8 March 2016. https://www.washingtonpost.com/world/

pakistans-prime-minister-is-defying-the-clerics--very-carefully/2016/03/08/
a6ecea88-e450-11e5-a6f3-21ccdbc5f74e_story.html.

"Crowds Gather to Protest Bush Visit to Austria." *Cork* (Cork, Ireland), 21 June 2006.

Dağtaş, Mahiye Seçil. "'Down With Some Things!' The Politics of Humour and Humour as Politics in Turkey's Gezi Protests." *Etnofoor* 28, no. 1, Humour (2016): 11–34. https://www.jstor.org/stable/43823940.

Daley, Suzanne. "Anti–Le Pen Protests Draw a Million into Streets in France." *New York Times*, 2 May 2002. https://www.nytimes.com/2002/05/02/world/anti-le-pen-protests-draw-a-million-into-streets-in-france.html.

Daneshvar, Parviz. *Revolution in Iran*. London: Palgrave Macmillan, 1996.

Darboe, Alieu. "The Gambia: 1994–Present." International Center on Nonviolent Conflict, February 2010. https://www.nonviolent-conflict.org/wp-content/uploads/2016/04/darboe_the_gambia.pdf.

Day, Elizabeth. "#Blacklivesmatter: The Birth of a New Civil Rights Movement." *The Guardian* (London), 19 July 2015. https://www.theguardian.com/world/2015/jul/19/blacklivesmatter-birth-civil-rights-movement.

DeConde, Alexander, ed. *Student Activism: Town and Gown in Historical Perspective*. New York: Scribner's, 1971.

DeGroot, Gerard J., ed. *Student Protest: The Sixties and After*. London: Addison-Wesley, 1998.

Desruisseaux, Paul. "Anti-American Protests in China Prompt Several Colleges to Cancel Student Trips." *Chronicle of Higher Education*, 21 May 1999. https://www.chronicle.com/article/anti-american-protests-in-china-prompt-several-colleges-to-cancel-student-trips/.

Diuk, Nadia. "Euromaidan: Ukraine's Self-Organizing Revolution." *World Affairs* 176, no. 6 (March/April 2014): 9–16. https://www.jstor.org/stable/43555086.

"Famous Quebec Student Protester Gets His Sentence: 120 Hours' Community Service," *Canadian Press* (Toronto), 5 December 2012. https://globalnews.ca/news/316134/famous-quebec-student-protester-gets-his-sentence-120-hours-community-service/.

"Fatah Activist Killed by Palestinian Executive Force, Armed Group." BBC, 18 May 2007, 1.

Favela, Mariana. "Redrawing Power: #YoSoy132 and Overflowing Insurgencies." *Social Justice* 42, no. 3/4 (142), Special Issue: Mexican and Chicanx Social Movements (2015): 222–36. https://www.jstor.org/stable/24871336.

Flores, Juan. "Latino Studies: New Contexts, New Concepts." *Harvard Educational Review* 67, no. 2 (1997): 208–21. https://doi.org/10.17763/haer.67.2.9wxl957q7x716706.

Fluri, Jennifer L. "Feminist-Nation Building in Afghanistan: An Examination of the Revolutionary Association of the Women of Afghanistan (RAWA)." *Feminist Review* 89, no. 1 (2008): 34–54. https://doi.org/10.1057/fr.2008.6.

Fogg Davis, Heath. "Sex-Classification Policies as Transgender Discrimination: An Intersectional Critique." *Perspectives on Politics* 12, no. 1 (March 2014): 45–60. https://doi.org/10.1017/S1537592713003708.

Ford, Peter. "How the Balkan Strongman Was Toppled: Yugoslavia Activists—with Foreign Help—Offer a Textbook Case on Dislodging a Dictator without Firing a Shot." *Christian Science Monitor*, 27 January 2003. https://www.csmonitor.com/2003/0127/p12s01-usmi.html.

"France: French Students Lead Fight against Police Brutality, Tear Gas Used to Disperse Protesters." *Asia News Monitor* (Bangkok), 28 February 2017.

Fuentes-Nieva, Ricardo and Gianandrea Nelli Feroci. "The Evolving Role and Influence and Growing Strength of Social Movements in Latin America and the Caribbean." In *Alternative Pathways to Sustainable Development: Lessons from Latin America*, International Development Policy series No.9, edited by Gilles Carbonnier, Humberto Campodónico, and Sergio Tezanos Vázquez, 323–38. Boston: Graduate Institute Publications, Brill-Nijhoff, 2017. https://journals.openedition.org/poldev/2378.

Galioto, Katie and Megan Uekert. "Students Participate in 42nd March for Life." UWire. com, 25 January 2015.

"Gambia: Cold Commemoration of Gambia's Student Massacre." *Gambia News*, 2007. http://www.afrol.com/articles/25032.

Gambino, Lauren. "Native Americans Take Dakota Access Pipeline Protest to Washington." *The Guardian*, 10 March 2017. https://www.theguardian.com/us-news/2017/mar/10/native-nations-march-washington-dakota-access-pipeline.

Gerbaudo, Paolo. *Tweets and the Streets: Social Media and Contemporary Activism*. London: Pluto Press, 2012.

Giroux, Henry A. "The Quebec Student Protest Movement in the Age of Neoliberal Terror." *Social Identities* 19, no. 5 (2013): 515–35. https://doi.org/10.1080/13504630.2013.835510.

Gohel, Sajjan M. "Bangladesh: An Emerging Centre for Terrorism in Asia," *Perspectives on Terrorism* 8, no. 3 (June 2014): 84–91. http://www.terrorismanalysts.com/pt/index.php/pot/article/view/348/691.

Hammond, Ken. "From Kent State to Tiananmen: Some Personal Reflections." *Vietnam Generation* 2, no. 2 (1995): 127–31. https://digitalcommons.lasalle.edu/cgi/viewcontent.cgi?article=1081&context=vietnamgeneration.

Henry, Samuel. "Echoes of 1968 as French Students Take to the Streets to Join Protests." *Daily Telegraph* [Edition 2] (London), 13 October 2010: 20.

Hertling, James. "Students Join Protests as Hong Kong Returns to Chinese Control." *Chronicle of Higher Education*, 11 July 1997. https://www.chronicle.com/article/students-join-protests-as-hong-kong-returns-to-chinese-control/.

Hertz, Rosanna, and Susan M. Reverby. "Gentility, Gender, and Political Protest: The Barbara Bush Controversy at Wellesley." *Gender and Society* 9, no. 5 (1995): 594–611. https://www.jstor.org/stable/189898.

Herszenhorn, David. "Ukraine's Forces Move Against Protesters, Dimming Hopes for Talks." *New York Times*, 9 December 2013. https://www.nytimes.com/2013/12/10/world/europe/ukraine-unrest.html.

Hill, Symon. *Digital Revolutions: Activism in the Internet Age*. Oxford: New Internationalist, 2013.

Hine, William C. "Civil Rights and Campus Wrongs: South Carolina State College Students Protest, 1955–1968." *South Carolina Historical Magazine* 97, no. 4 (1996): 310–31. https://www.jstor.org/stable/27570185.

Hirsch, Eric L. "Sacrifice for the Cause: Group Processes, Recruitment, and Commitment in a Student Social Movement." *American Sociological Review* 55, no. 2 (1990): 243–54. https://doi.org/10.2307/2095630.

Hmed, Choukri. "Abeyance Networks, Contingency and Structures: History and Origins of the Tunisian Revolution." Translated from the French by Sarah-Louise Raillard. *Revue Française de Science Politique* [English edition] 62, no. 5–6, Arab Uprisings, Reflections on Revolutionary Situations in Context (2012): 31–53. https://doi.org/10.3917/rfsp.625.797.

Bibliography

Honig, Bonnie. *Emergency Politics: Politics, Law, Democracy.* Princeton, NJ: Princeton University Press, 2009.

Hooghe, Marc. "Taking to the Streets: Economic Crises and Youth Protest in Europe." *Harvard International Review* 34, no. 2 (Fall 2012): 34–38. https://www.researchgate.net/publication/264467275_Taking_to_the_Streets_Economic_Crises_and_Youth_Protest_in_Europe.

Hosking, Taylor. "The Changing Landscape of Student Protest in Higher Education." *The Atlantic,* 20 December 2017. https://www.theatlantic.com/education/archive/2017/12/the-changing-landscape-of-student-protest-in-higher-education/548867/.

Hoyle, Ben. "Ukraine Future in Balance as 500,000 Take to Kiev Streets." *Times* [Edition 2] (London), 02 December 2013, 30.

Huggler, Justin. "Outrage as Austrian Politician Linked to 'Holocaust Songbook.'" *Telegraph* (London), 25 January 2018. https://www.telegraph.co.uk/news/2018/01/25/outrage-austrian-politician-linked-holocaust-songbook/.

Human Rights Watch. *Human Rights Watch World Report, 2003.* Human Rights Watch, 2003. https://www.hrw.org/legacy/wr2k3/.

Immigration and Refugee Board, Research Directorate. "Iran: July 1999 Demonstrations in Tehran." Immigration and Refugee Board (Ottawa, ON), December 2000.

"India: Police in Indian-Controlled Kashmir Use Pellet Guns to Shoot Protesters in Eye." *Asia News Monitor* (Bangkok), 30 August 2016.

Isidore, Chris and Robert Mclean. "University of California Dumps Private Prison Stocks after Student Protests." CNN Money, 29 December 2015. https://money.cnn.com/2015/12/29/investing/university-california-private-prison-stocks/.

Iskandar, Adel. "Teaching the Arab Uprisings: Between Media Maelstrom and Pedantic Pedagogy." *Political Science and Politics* 46, no. 2 (April 2013): 244–47. https://doi.org/10.1017/S104909651300022X

Jacobsen, Christine M. and Mette Andersson. "'Gaza in Oslo': Social Imaginaries in the Political Engagement of Norwegian Minority Youth." *Ethnicities* 12, no. 6 (December 2012): 821–43. https://doi.org/10.1177/1468796812451097.

Jewkes, Rachel, Emma Fulu, Tim Roselli, and Claudia Garcia-Moreno. "Prevalence of and Factors Associated with Non-partner Rape Perpetration: Findings from the UN Multi-country Cross-sectional Study on Men and Violence in Asia and the Pacific." The Lancet 1, no. 4 (October 1, 2013): E208–E218. https://doi.org/10.1016/S2214-109X(13)70069-X.

Jones, Denisha and Jesse Hagopian, eds. *Black Lives Matter at School: An Uprising for Educational Justice* (Chicago: Haymarket Books, 2020).

Jordan, Miriam. "Stanford University Sexual-Assault Case Prompts Backlash," *Wall Street Journal,* 7 June 2016. https://www.wsj.com/articles/stanford-university-sexual-assault-case-prompts-backlash-1465343570.

Kapur, Ratna. "Brutalized Bodies and Sexy Dressing on the Indian Street," *Signs: Journal of Women in Culture and Society* 40, no. 1 (Autumn 2014): 9–14.

Kassow, Samuel D. *Students, Professors, and the State in Tsarist Russia.* Berkeley: University of California Press, 1989. http://ark.cdlib.org/ark:/13030/ft9h4nb67r/.

Kelly, Cristina Bonasegna. "Argentina Drops Plan to Cut Education Funds." *Chronicle of Higher Education,* 21 May 1999. https://www.chronicle.com/article/argentina-drops-plan-to-cut-education-funds/.

Kigotho, Wachira. "Academics in Ethiopia Are Again Under Siege." *Chronicle of Higher Education*, 18 May 2001. https://www.chronicle.com/article/academics-in-ethiopia-are-again-under-siege/.

Klein, Naomi. *This Changes Everything: Capitalism vs. the Climate*. New York: Simon and Schuster, 2014.

Kowsmann, Patricia. "Portuguese Workers Strike to Say Austerity Has Gone Too Far; Nationwide Work Stoppage Is Fourth Since 2011." *Wall Street Journal*, 27 June 2013. https://www.wsj.com/articles/SB10001424127887323419604578570874072424636.

Kroll, Andy. "Betsy DeVos' New Proposal Aligns Her with For-Profit Colleges Over Debt-Saddled Students." *Rolling Stone*, 25 July 2018. http://www.rollingstone.com/politics/politics-news/betsy-devos-borrower-defense-7035421.

Krupnick, Matt and Doug Oakley. "Thousands Protest Tuition Hikes, Layoffs at University of California." McClatchy-Tribune News Service, 24 September 2009. https://www.mercurynews.com/2009/09/24/5000-at-uc-berkeley-protest-tuition-increases-furloughs-layoffs/.

"Large Pro-EU, Anti-Government Protest Held in Poland." *MaltaToday* (San Gwann, Malta), 7 May 2016.

Lemay, Violaine, and Marie-Neige Laperrière. "Student Protests and Government Somersaults: The Quebec Spring from a Law and Society Perspective." *Canadian Journal of Law and Society/ Revue Canadienne Droit et Société* 27, no. 3 (2012): 339–50. https://muse.jhu.edu/article/504384/pdf.

Lewis, Jerry M. "Black Day in May." *American History Illustrated* 25, no. 2 (1990): 34–35.

Lloyd, Marion. "Violence Recedes at U. of Karachi, but Pakistani Politics Persists." *Chronicle of Higher Education*, 26 March 1999. https://www.chronicle.com/article/violence-recedes-at-u-of-karachi-but-pakistani-politics-persists/.

"Lots of Speculation around Coke's New CEO." *Tribune* (Welland, ON), 22 April 2004, A7.

Lusher, Adam. "Where Are They Now? At Least 10,000 People Died in Tiananmen Square Massacre, Secret British Cable from the Time Alleged." *The Independent* (London), 24 December 2017.

Macintyre, Donald. "In Jerusalem, an Embassy Opens. In Gaza, at Least 58 Die on Bloodiest Day in Years." *The Independent* (London), 14 May 2018. https://www.independent.co.uk/news/world/middle-east/gaza-protests-latest-palestinians-killed-border-embassy-jerusalem-trump-a8351761.html.

MacLeod, Donald. "To the Barricades: Political Protest in France Reflects Growing Discontent in Universities." *The Guardian* (London), 30 April 2002. https://www.theguardian.com/education/2002/apr/30/internationaleducationnews.france.

MacLeod, Fiona. "Protest Students: 'Police Tried to Turn Us into Informants.'" *The Scotsman* (Edinburgh), 31 January 2011.

Mangcu, Xolela. "Shattering the Myth of a Post-Racial Consensus in South African Higher Education: 'Rhodes Must Fall' and the Struggle for Transformation at the University of Cape Town," *Critical Philosophy of Race* 5, no. 2 (2017): 243–66. https://doi.org/10.5325/critphilrace.5.2.0243.

Marques de Morais, Rafael. "A Journey for Rights and Dignity: A Participant's Observation." Maka Angola, 22 November 2017. https://www.makaangola.org/2017/11/a-journey-for-rights-and-dignity-a-participants-observation/.

Matthews, Anne. *Bright College Years: Inside the American Campus Today*. Chicago: University of Chicago Press, 1997.

Bibliography

McCarthy, Michael A. "Occupying Higher Education: The Revival of the Student Movement." *New Labor Forum* 21, no. 2 (Spring 2012): 50–55.

McSorely, Tim. "Student Strike Was Successful but Fresh Battles Loom." *Canadian Dimension* 30, no. 4 (July–August 2005): 13.

Magner, Denise K. "Duke Agrees to Student Demands on Code of Conduct for Clothing Manufacturers." *Chronicle of Higher Education*, 12 February 1999. https://www.chronicle.com/article/duke-agrees-to-student-demands-on-code-of-conduct-for-clothing-manufacturers/.

Medoff, Rafael. "'Retribution Is Not Enough': The 1943 Campaign by Jewish Students to Raise American Public Awareness of the Nazi Genocide." *Holocaust and Genocide Studies* 11, no. 2 (1997): 171–89. https://doi.org/10.1093/hgs/11.2.171.

"Millions Unite in Grief and Anger on Streets of Madrid." *Evening Times* (Glasgow, Scotland) 13 March 2004, 6.

Mina, An Xiao. *Memes to Movements: How the World's Most Viral Media Is Changing Social Protest and Power.* Boston: Beacon Press, 2019.

Mitra, Durba. "Critical Perspectives on SlutWalks in India." *Feminist Studies.* 38, no. 1 (Spring 2012): 254–261. https://www.jstor.org/stable/23269181.

Moore, Molly. "Millions in France Protest Law, Leadership; Opposition to Labor Bill Widens into Protest of Government Deemed Out of Touch." *Washington Post*, 5 April 2006, A.17.

Mosse, George. *The Image of Man: The Creation of Modern Masculinity.* New York: Oxford University Press, 1996.

Mufson, Claire. "Montpellier Dean Detained, Suspended after Masked Men Attack Students." France 24, 29 March 2018. https://www.france24.com/en/20180329-france-montpellier-dean-suspended-letting-masked-attackers-law-school.

Munro, Robin. "Remembering Tiananmen Square: Who Died in Beijing, and Why." *The Nation*, 11 June 1990, https://www.thenation.com/article/archive/remembering-tiananmen-square/.

Mydans, Seth. "Zigzag in Jakarta: General Is Suspended." *New York Times*, 14 February 2000. https://www.nytimes.com/2000/02/14/world/zigzag-in-jakarta-general-is-suspended.html.

Nadeau, Barbie Latza. "Italy's Lost Generation: Youth Unemployment Hits Nearly 50 Percent." Daily Beast, 7 June 2014. https://www.thedailybeast.com/italys-lost-generation-youth-unemployment-hits-nearly-50-percent.

Nadeau-DuBois, Gabriel. *In Defiance.* Translated from the French by Lazer Lederhendler. Toronto: Between the Lines, 2015.

Nelson, Dean. "Delhi Rape Was a Small Incident, Says Minister." *Telegraph* [Edition 2] (London), 22 August 2014. https://www.telegraph.co.uk/news/worldnews/asia/india/11050649/India-minister-sparks-outrage-over-small-gang-rape-comment.html.

"New Protests After Suicide of 16-Year-Old Gang-Raped Twice in Calcutta." *Telegraph* (London), 1 January 2014.

Ng, Vitrierat and Kin-man Chan. "Emotion Politics: Joyous Resistance in Hong Kong." *China Review* 17, no. 1 (February 2017): 83–115. https://www.jstor.org/stable/44160410.

Nikolayenko, Olena. "Origins of the Movement's Strategy: The Case of the Serbian Youth Movement Otpor." *International Political Science Review / Revue Internationale De Science Politique* 34, no. 2 (March 2013): 140–58. https://doi.org/10.1177/0192512112458129.

"OCCRP announces 2015 Organized Crime and Corruption 'Person of the Year' Award."
Organized Crime and Corruption Reporting Project, 2015. https://www.occrp.org/
en/poy/2015/.

Office for the Coordination of Humanitarian Affairs. "Youth in Crisis: Coming of Age
in the 21st Century." United Nations Office for the Coordination of Humanitarian
Affairs, 23 February 2007.

Osborne, Samuel. "Father of Indian Girl Who Was Gang-raped, Bricked to Death and Fed
to Dogs Tells of Moment He Found Her." *The Independent* (London), 18 May 2017.

"Pakistani Women March in Rape Row." BBC News, 29 September 2005. http://news.bbc.
co.uk/2/hi/south_asia/4294840.stm.

Palacios-Valladares, Indira. "With or Without Them: Contemporary Student Movements
and Parties in the Southern Cone." *Latin Americanist* 60, no. 2 (June 2016): 243–68.
https://doi.org/10.1111/tla.12076.

Phillips, Tim. "New Report on Human Rights Violations During Turkey's Response
to Gezi Park Protests." Activist Defense, 4 October 2013. https://activistdefense.
wordpress.com/2013/10/04/new-report-on-human-rights-violations-during-turkeys-
response-to-gezi-park-protests/.

"Police Enforce Calm after Worst Iranian Riots in 20 Years." CNN, 13 July 1999.

"Polish Paper Profiles Organizers of Anticounterfeit Protest Movement Publication." BBC
Monitoring Europe, 1 February 2012.

"Polish Weekly Profiles Nationalist Party, Rival Groups." BBC Monitoring Europe, 21 May
2008.

Popovic, Srdja, and Matthew Miller. *Blueprint for Revolution: How to Use Rice Pudding,
Lego Men, and Other Nonviolent Techniques to Galvanize Communities, Overthrow
Dictators, or Simply Change the World.* New York: Spiegel & Grau, 2015.

Prasse-Freeman, Elliott. "Power, Civil Society, and an Inchoate Politics of the Daily in
Burma/Myanmar," *Journal of Asian Studies* 71, no. 2 (May 2012): 371–97. https://www.
jstor.org/stable/23263426.

Press, Robert M. *Ripples of Hope: How Ordinary People Resist Repression Without Violence.*
Protests and Social Movements. Amsterdam: Amsterdam University Press, 2015.

Rachik, Abderrahmane. *Les mouvements de protestation au Maroc: De l'émeute à la mani-
festation.* Forum des Alternatives Maroc (FMAS), 26 May 2015.

Rennie, David. "Two Solo Protests Mark Tiananmen 10th Anniversary." *Daily Telegraph*
(London), 5 June 1999.

Revesz, Rachael. "New Delhi and Sao Paolo Worst Places in the World for Sexual Violence
Against Women, Shows Study." *The Independent* (London), 16 October 2017. https://
www.independent.co.uk/news/world/asia/new-dehli-sao-paolo-women-sexual-vio-
lence-worst-place-world-india-capital-brazil-a8002541.html.

Rhee, Foon. "Vanguards and Violence: A Comparison of the U.S. and Korean Student
Movements." *Korean Studies* 17 (1993): 17–38. https://www.jstor.org/stable/23720039.

Richburg, Keith B. "Millions in Spain Decry Attacks; Marchers Jam Streets; Government
Still Focused on Basque Separatists." *Washington Post*, 13 March 2004, A.01.

———. "Italian Police Feel Backlash from G-8 Summit Violence; EU Officials Urge Thor-
ough Probe, Propose New Force." *Washington Post*, 11 August 2001, A.14.

Riga, Andy. "Students Get Stuck: Concrete Protest before Strike Tomorrow by Associations
Representing 25,000." *The Gazette* (Montreal), 23 February 2005.

Rowen, Ian. "Inside Taiwan's Sunflower Movement: Twenty-Four Days in a Student-Oc-
cupied Parliament, and the Future of the Region." *Journal of Asian Studies* 74, no. 1
(February 2015): 5–21. https://doi.org/10.1017/S0021911814002174.

Rúdólfsdóttir, Annadís G. and Ásta Jóhannsdóttir. "Fuck Patriarchy! An Analysis of
Digital Mainstream Media Discussion of the #freethenipple Activities in Iceland in March 2015." *Feminism & Psychology* 28, no. 1 (2018): 133–51. https://doi.
org/10.1177/0959353517715876.

Rush, Curtis. "Cop Apologizes for 'Sluts' Remark at Law School," *Toronto Star* (Toronto) 2
February 2018. https://www.thestar.com/news/gta/2011/02/18/cop_apologizes_for_
sluts_remark_at_law_school.html.

Sandul, Irina. "Kuchmagate, Two Years On." *Time* (Odessa), 26 September 2002. http://
content.time.com/time/world/article/0,8599,354919,00.html.

"Saudi Arabia: Has the Rate of Executions Doubled?" BBC News, 8 March 2018. https://
www.bbc.com/news/uk-43316987.

Saunders, Joseph. "Signs of Intellectual Freedom Begin to Emerge in Indonesia." *Chronicle
of Higher Education*, 17 April 1998. https://www.chronicle.com/article/signs-of-intel-
lectual-freedom-begin-to-emerge-in-indonesia/

Scherer García, Julio, and Carlos Monsiváis. *Parte de Guerra: Tlatelolco 1968*. Mexico City:
Aguilar, 1999.

Schmidt, Katherine A. "Germans Fight for College Funds." *USA Today*, 18 December 1997.

Sciolino, Elaine. "Paris Suburb Riots Called 'a Lot Worse' Than in 2005." *New York
Times*, 27 November 2007. https://www.nytimes.com/2007/11/27/world/europe/27i-
ht-riots.4.8500200.html.

Seymour, Richard. "Quebec's Students Provide a Lesson in Protest Politics." *The Guardian*
(London), 7 September 2012. https://www.theguardian.com/commentisfree/2012/
sep/07/quebec-students-lesson-protest-politics.

"Serbian Students Warn 'Regime' to Expect 'More Open Rebellion.'" BBC Monitoring
Europe, 16 October 1999, 1.

Shafak, Elif. "The View from Taksim Square: Why Is Turkey Now in Turmoil?" *The
Guardian* (London), 3 June 2013. https://www.theguardian.com/world/2013/jun/03/
taksim-square-istanbul-turkey-protest.

Sharifpour-Hicks, Elahe. "Heading into Iran's Winter of Discontent." *Wall Street Journal*
[Europe], 23 September 1999.

Sherkat, Darren E., and T. Jean Blocker. "The Political Development of Sixties Activists:
Identifying the Influence of Class, Gender, and Socialization on Protest Participation." *Social Forces* 72, no. 3 (1994): 821–42. https://doi.org/10.1093/sf/72.3.821.

Sherrard Blesch, Gregg. "Opposed to War—Dozens of Local Students Protest." *Columbian*
(Vancouver, WA), 6 March 2003, C1.

Slater, Dan. "Revolutions, Crackdowns, and Quiescence: Communal Elites and Democratic Mobilization in Southeast Asia." *American Journal of Sociology* 115, no. 1 (July
2009): 203–54. https://doi.org/10.1086/597796.

Slocum, Jenée, and Robert A. Rhoads. "Faculty and Student Engagement in the Argentine
Grassroots Rebellion: Toward a Democratic and Emancipatory Vision of the University." *Higher Education* 57, no. 1 (January 2009): 85–105. https://doi.org/10.1007/
s10734-008-9134-4.

Smith, Alex Duval. "France's Global Warning." *The Observer* (London), 19 March 2006.
https://www.theguardian.com/world/2006/mar/19/france.alexduvalsmith.

Soule, Sarah A. "The Student Divestment Movement in the United States and Tactical Diffusion: The Shantytown Protest." *Social Forces* 75, no. 3 (1997): 855–83. https://doi.org/10.2307/2580522.

Sow, Ousmane. "Coup de torchon à l'université." *Jeune Afrique/L'Intelligent*, 17–23 October 2000.

Statland de López, Rhona. "Mexico's Largest University Ends Semester amid Student Occupation of the Campus." *Chronicle of Higher Education*, 23 July 1999. https://www.chronicle.com/article/mexicos-largest-university-ends-semester-amid-student-occupation-of-the-campus/.

Steel, Mark. "We Will Not Be Moved." *The Independent* (London),11 February 2003, 4, 5.

Strohecker, Karin. "Deportations Spark Immigration Uproar in Austria; A 15-Year-Old Albanian Girl Whose Parents Were Kicked Out Has Threatened Suicide." *Vancouver Sun* (Vancouver, BC), 10 October 2007, A13.

Sturdee, Nick. "Russia's Robin Hood." *Index on Censorship* 40, no. 3 (4 October 2011): 92. https://doi.org/10.1177/0306422011418758.

———. "Don't Raise the Bridge: Voina, Russia's Art Terrorists." *The Guardian* (London), 12 April 2011. https://www.theguardian.com/artanddesign/2011/apr/12/voina-art-terrorism.

"Swarthmore Students Campaign for Card Check Neutrality in Workers' Unionizing, 2006." Global Nonviolent Action Database. https://nvdatabase.swarthmore.edu/content/swarthmore-students-campaign-card-check-neutrality-workers-unionizing-2006.

Tavernise, Sabrina. "The Fight for Pakistan's Future, Violently Reflected on Campus." *New York Times*, 21 April 2010, A1. https://www.nytimes.com/2010/04/21/world/asia/21university.html.

Taylor, Astra. *Democracy May Not Exist, but We'll Miss It When It's Gone*. New York: Metropolitan Books, 2019.

Taylor, Keeanga-Yamahtta. *From #BlackLivesMatter to Black Liberation*. Chicago: Haymarket, 2016.

Taylor, Kate. "Mattress Protest at Columbia University Continues Into Graduation Event." *New York Times*, 19 May 2015. https://www.nytimes.com/2015/05/20/nyregion/mattress-protest-at-columbia-university-continues-into-graduation-event.html.

"Teen Girls with Stones New Threat in Kashmir." *Balochistan Times* (Quetta, Pakistan), 2 May 2017.

Terada, Rei. "Out of Place: Free Speech, Disruption, and Student Protest." *Qui Parle* 20, no. 1 (Fall/Winter 2011): 251–69. https://doi.org/10.5250/quiparle.20.1.0251.

"Thousands Protest in South Korea." *Phoenix Gazette* (Phoenix, AZ), 1 December 1993.

"Three Hundred Forty Arrests at Protest over Trident Nuclear Missiles." *Irish Times* (Dublin), 13 February 2001, 10.

"Togolese University Said Closed Following Student Protests." BBC Monitoring Newsfile, 7 February 2005, 1.

Traynor, Ira. "Belgrade Rally Says Milosevic Must Go," *The Guardian* (London), 19 June 1992.

Tremlett, Giles. "Dispatch Madrid: How Corruption, Cuts and Despair Drove Spain's Protesters on to the Streets." *The Observer* (London), 22 May 2011. https://www.theguardian.com/world/2011/may/21/spain-reveals-pain-cuts-unemployment.

Trevor, Ian. "Ukraine's Bloodiest Day: Dozens Dead as Kiev Protesters Regain Territory from Police." *The Guardian* (London), 21 February 2014. https://www.theguardian. com/world/2014/feb/20/ukraine-dead-protesters-police.

Tully, James. *Public Philosophy in a New Key*. Volumes 1 and 2. Ideas in Context. Cambridge: Cambridge University Press, 2008.

Tunbridge, Louise. "Kenyan Higher Education Faces Collapse Due to Repression." *Chronicle of Higher Education*, 5 April 1996. https://www.chronicle.com/article/kenyan-higher-education-faces-collapse-due-to-repression/.

"Ukrainian Opposition Youth Group Vows Nationwide Protests." BBC Monitoring Newsfile, 26 October 2004, 1.

UNICEF. "UNICEF Supports Fight to End Marriage by Abduction in Ethiopia." Press release, UN Office for the Coordination of Humanitarian Affairs, 9 November 2004. https://reliefweb.int/report/ethiopia/unicef-supports-fight-end-marriage-abduction-ethiopia.

"UWI Removes Students from Register." BBC World News, 4 October 2010.

Van der Werf, Martin. "Sweatshop Issue Escalates with Sit-Ins and Policy Shifts." *Chronicle of Higher Education* 10 March 2000. https://www.chronicle.com/article/sweatshop-issue-escalates-with-sit-ins-and-policy-shifts/.

Van Gyampo, Ransford Edward. "Student Activism and Democratic Quality in Ghana's Fourth Republic." *Journal of Student Affairs in Africa* 1, no. 1/2 (2013): 49–66. https://www.researchgate.net/publication/307772564_Student_activism_and_democratic_quality_in_Ghana's_Fourth_Republic.

Vignati, Rinaldo and David Bull. "Chronology of Italian Political Events, 2010." *Italian Politics* 26, Much Ado about Nothing? (2010): 1–42. https://www.jstor.org/stable/43486777.

Webb Pressler, Margaret. "Human Rights Charges Still Gnaw at Coca-Cola; Protesters Convene at Stockholders Meeting." *Washington Post*, 22 April 2004, E.01.

"Wedding Joy Marred by Catalan Resentment." *Herald* (Glasgow, Scotland), 4 October 1997.

White, Ben. "Update on Conflict and Diplomacy 16 May–15 August 2014," *Journal of Palestine Studies* 44, no. 1 (Autumn 2014): 204–37. https://doi.org/10.1525/jps.2015.44.2.116.

Wilkinson, Tracy. "Young Cuban Artists Testing the Boundaries of Dissent." *Los Angeles Times*, 3 March 2015. http://www.latimes.com/local/great-reads/la-fg-c1-cuba-dissident-music-20150303-story.html.

Williams, Daniel. "Anti-War Activists Protest in Florence; Thousands Denounce U.S. Iraq Policy." *Washington Post*, 10 November 2002, A.26.

Wilson, Peter. "Orange Revolutionaries' Democracy Lessons." *The Australian* (Canberra, ACT), 3 December 2004, 8.

Woodard, Colin. "Student Movement in South Korea Becomes Quiescent under New Government." *Chronicle of Higher Education*, 17 April 1998. https://www.chronicle.com/article/student-movement-in-south-korea-becomes-quiescent-under-new-government/.

Wright, Robin. "We Invite the Hostages to Return." *New Yorker*, 8 November 1999. https://www.newyorker.com/magazine/1999/11/08/we-invite-the-hostages-to-return.

Wu, Leon. "Columbia Students Protest Trump Election on College Walk." UWire, 9 November 2016.

Young, Cathy. "Putin's Young 'Brownshirts.'" *Boston Globe*, 6 December 2008. http://
archive.boston.com/news/globe/editorial_opinion/oped/articles/2007/08/10/putins_
young_brownshirts/.
Youngers, Coletta. "The Peru We Built Is Fighting Back." *Washington Post*, 23 April 2000.
Zahid, Farhan. "Radicalisation of Campuses in Pakistan." *Counter Terrorist Trends and
Analyses* 9, no. 11 (November 2017): 12–15. https://www.jstor.org/stable/26351567.

INDEX

Abkhazia 125
Accra 197
Action Command of Indonesian Students (KAMI) 17
Addis Ababa University 193–194
Afghanistan 44, 48, 54, 68, 71, 81, 105, 118, 145, 192, 227
Afghan Northern Alliance 54
Agha-Soltan, Neda 63
Aghhajari, Hashem 61
Ahmadinejad, Mahmoud 61–62, 64
Alabama 18
Al-Aqsa Martyrs Brigade of the Fatah 68
Al-Aqsa University 68
Albania 32, 111, 114, 116, 119, 132
Alcatraz Island 26
Al-fajr School in Mogadishu 200
Algeria 16
Alianza Popular Revolucionaria Americana (APRA) 13
Aliyev, Heydar 116
Aliyev, Ilham 116, 119
Aliyev, Turan 118
All Burma Monks' Alliance 155
Alliance for Change 109
All India Democratic Students' Organization (AIDSO) 180, 186
All India Democratic Youth Organization (AIDYO) 180, 186
All India Students Congress 16
All India Students' Federation (AISF) 178
al-Qaeda 54
Al-Ummah College 67
American Chamber of Commerce 164
American Student Union 14
Amnesty International 159, 201
Anaithu Kalloori Maanavar Kootamaippu 180
Anantapur 186
Anhui Province 173
An-Najah National University 68
Arab Spring 53, 237–239
Arafat, Yasser 68, 225
Arequipa 230
Argentina 13, 16, 144, 187, 218–219
Aristide, Jean-Bertrand 233
Armenians 130
Arroyo, Maria Gloria Macapagal 156–157
Article 66 of the Lao Penal Law 149
Asia-Pacific Economic Cooperation (APEC) 165
Association of Secondary Teachers, Ireland (ASTI) 93
Atma Jaya Catholic University 144
Aung San Suu Kyi 156
Australia 135, 137–138, 141–142, 187
Austria 11, 77–78, 88

Austria-Hungary 12
Autonomous Web of Liberation 140
Awami League (AL) 154
Azerbaijan 116, 117–118, 124
Azeris 118, 30
Aznar, José Maria 97

Baku 119
Baku State University 117
Ball State University 46
Bălți 127
Bangkok 162
Bangladesh 142, 153–155, 186–187
Bangladesh Nationalist Party (BNP) 153
Bangladesh Student League 153
Banjul 196
Barcelona 97
Bard College 44
Basilica of Saint Mary 128
Basirli, Ruslan 118
Battle of Morningside Heights 24
Beijing 29, 170, 173
Beijing University 12
Beirut 70
Belarus 119, 122, 198
Belarusian KGB 120
Belarusian Pro-Independence Bloc 122
Belgrade 36, 108–110, 173
Belgrade Agreement 116
Bengalaru/Bengaluru 182, 184
Benito Juárez Autonomous University of Oaxaca 214
Berisha, Sali 112
Berlin 11, 86, 88
Berlusconi, Silvio 95–96
Bethlehem 66
bin Laden, Osama 54, 68
Black Hand 12
Black Lives Matter 52, 239
Black Spring 232
Blair, Tony 101–102
Blanqui, Louis-Auguste 11
Bloody October 222
Bloody Sunday Massacre (1905) 12
Blueprint for Revolution (Popović) 111
Bolivia 61, 220–223
Bologna 9
Bologna Process 77, 88, 90, 98, 100, 105
Books Not Bombs 45, 140
Bosnia-Herzegovina 12
Bowie State 24
Bracks, Steve 141
Brandenburg Gate 86, 88

Brasilia 224
Brazil 16, 19, 31–32, 223–225
Brazilian Jewish 225
Brisbane 140–141
Brown University 42
Bucharest 32
Bulgaria 122
Burkinabe General Confederation of Labor (CGTB) 191
Burkina Faso 191–192
Burschenshaften (German political student group) 10–11, 87
Bush, George W. 35, 45, 54–55, 78, 97, 145, 165, 181, 224–225, 227
Butcher of Baghdad 57
Butcher of Monrovia see Taylor, Charles

cacerolazo protests 218
California State University 46
Camara, Moussa Dadis 206–207
Cambodia 148, 160
Camp Humphreys 164
Canada 35–37, 187, 224
capitalism 51, 79–80, 104, 129–130
capitalist fascism 129
Cartagena 226
Cassette Scandal 113
Castro, Fidel 19–20
Center for Applied Nonviolent Action and Strategies (CANVAS) 111, 143, 150, 212, 238
Central America 16, 23, 190, 225
Central America Free Trade Agreement (CAFTA) 215–216
Central American University (UCA) 217
Champs-Élysées in Paris 21
Charest, John James 36
Chaudhry, Mahendra 142
Chávez, Hugo 231
Chennai 179–180, 183–184
Chiang Kai-shek 13
Chicago 25, 46, 47
Chicano Caucus 47
Chile 13, 221, 225–226
China 13, 29–31, 33, 61, 135–136, 144, 149–150, 161, 168–179, 187, 237
Chinese Communist Party 13, 29
Chirac, Jacques 82–84
Chronicle of Higher Education 42
Circassians 130
Clinton, Bill 226
Coalition de l'Association pour une Solidarité Syndicale Étudiante Élargie (CLASSÉÉ) 36–37
Coca-Cola 43–44
Cochabamba 220–222
College Democrats of America 46
College Republicans 45, 47
Colombia 14, 16, 19, 43, 225–227
Columbia University 14, 24, 47
Columbus, Christopher 98
Communist Party of Vietnam (CPV) 160
Condé, Alpha 207

Congress of Racial Equality (CORE) 18–19, 25
Congress Party 183
Connery, Sean 102
Copperbelt University in Kitwe 204
Cornflower Revolt 121
Correa, Rafael 229
Cossacks 12
Costa Rica 215–216
Côte d'Ivoire 194–195
Croatia 78
Cuba 16, 19, 232
Cuban rap 232
Cultural Revolution 15
cyberinfiltration 105
cyberlinking 4
cybernetworks 87
cyber-resistance attacks 33
cybersurveillance 175
cyberterrorism 76
Czechoslovakia 18, 28
Czech Republic 123

Dáil Éireann 93
Dalai Lama 176
Dalga (Wave) movement 118
Dartmouth College 41
Dartmouth Review 41
December Ninth Movement 13
de Gaulle, Charles 21
de la Rúa, Fernando 218
de la Sierra, Santa Cruz 222
de Lozada, Gonzalo Sánchez 221–222
Democratic Convention in Chicago (1968) 25
Democratic Opposition of Serbia (DOS) 110
Democratic Progressive Party (DPP) 168
Democratic Socialists of America 44
Democratic Youth Federation of India (DYFI) 178, 182
Democrats 45
Denim Revolution 121
Denmark 79–80
desegregation 16, 18–19, 24
détournement (protest tactic) 38, 110
Dhaka 153
Día de la Hispanidad (Spain) 98
District of Columbia 44
Djibouti 192
Dominican Republic 19, 215
Drugaya Rossiya (Other Russia) coalition 129
D'Souza, Dinesh 41
Dublin 93–94
Ðukanović, Milo 116
Duke University 38

East China Sea 174
Eastern Europe 6, 11, 14, 32, 59–60, 62, 74, 107, 111, 115, 121, 123, 127–128, 132, 134–135, 137–138, 143 190, 210–212, 237–239
East Timor 143, 146–147
Ecuador 13, 19, 228–229
Egypt 58, 238
Eisenstein, Sergei 132

Index

Ejército de Liberación Nacional (ELN) 43
El Alto 221–223
Eldoret National Polytechnic 203
El Salvador 215
EMVest 43
England 11, 100–101
Estrada, Joseph 156
Ethiopia 192–194
Ethiopian Human Rights Council 193
Ethiopian People's Revolutionary Democratic Front
  (EPRDF) 192
Europe 9–11, 16, 28, 33, 26, 56, 75–106, 123, 135,
  235–236, 238
European Union 75, 77, 81, 90, 100, 95, 105–106, 110,
  115, 122, 125–126, 236
Euskadi Ta Askatasuna (ETA) 97
Executive Force 68
ExxonMobil 102

Facebook 103, 126, 139, 185–187
Fatah Youth Movement 68
Fédération Étudiante Collégiale du Québec (FECQ)
  36–37
Fédération Étudiante Universitaire du Québec
  (FEUQ) 36–37
Ferdinand, Franz 12
Feyziyev, Namiq 118
Fidelity Investments 43
Fighting Sioux mascot 39, 41
Fiji 142
Finland 80
Fisk University 24
flash mobbing 4, 76, 133, 137, 236
Follen, Karl 10
Fort Benning 46
Fournier, Jean-Marc 37
Fox, Vicente 213
Fox News 52
France 11, 20, 22, 83, 85, 95, 99, 195
Frankfurt (Germany) 10
Freedom Riders program 18
Freedom Summer 18
Free Education for Everyone protest 94
Free Republic movement 45
Free Speech Movement 19
Free Tibet student activists 167
French Revolution 20
Friends of the Earth 140
Fuerzas Armada Revolucionarias de Colombia
  (FARC) 43, 226–227
Fujimori, Alberto 229

G8 protests 89–90
Galway 93
Gambian Student Massacre 196
Gambia Student Union (GAMSU) 196
Gandhi, Mahatma 16
Gandhi, Sonia 179
Gavrilo Princip (student radical group) 12
Gaza 28, 237
Gaza Strip 65

Gbagbo, Laurent 194–195
General Union of Burkina Students (UGEB) 191
Generation Students Group 156
Genoa 95
George Mason University 47
Georgia 32, 121, 124–125, 129–130
Germany 3, 10–11, 26, 78, 85–90, 95
Geyer, Enrique Bolaños 217
Ghana 208
Gilchrist, Jim 47
Global Climate Strike movement 239
globalism 96, 135–136, 237
Goddess of Democracy (statue) 29–30
Gong (Croatia) 117
Gongadze, Georgiy 113
Gorbachev, Mikhail 29
Göttingen (Germany) 10
Great Britain 100, 103
Great East Road 203
Great Land Grab speculation 43
Greece 90, 92, 99, 122
Greenland 104
Green Party 26, 44–45
Greensboro (North Carolina) 18
Grigoropoulos, Alexandros 91
Guangxi 15
Guangzhou 175
Guantánamo 55
Guatemala 19, 215
Guevara, Che 19, 219
Guinea 61, 206–208
Gulbarga 180
Guomindang (KMT) 15, 168
Gusmao, Xanana 146
Gutiérrez, Lucio 228
Gyanendra (King) 152–153

Haarder, Bertel 80
Habibie, B. J. 146
Haiti 19, 233
Halifax 35
Hamas militants 65–66, 68
Hambach (Germany) 10
Han Chinese 176–178
Hanchongnyon (Federation of Student Councils) 164
Harvard Club 41–42
Hasina, Sheikh 154
Hezbollah 70
Hiroshima 166
Holocaust 225
Honduras 39, 215–216
Hong Kong 6, 90, 169–171, 187
Hong Kong Umbrella Movement 239
Howard, John 138, 141
Howard University 24
Hunan Province 175
Hungary 3, 14
Hussein, Saddam 56–57
Hyderabad 182

Iceland 104–105

Iliescu, Ion 32
imperialism 144, 170, 195, 215, 226
  anti–US 56
  anti-Western 27
  in China 170
  economic 28, 51, 75, 135
  in France 195
  in Japan 13, 174
  Western 55–56, 58, 60, 93, 111
Independence Intifada 70
India 3, 5, 11, 16, 136–137, 141, 178, 181, 183–184
Indonesia 17, 32, 142–145, 187, 198
Indonesian Communist Party (PKI) 17
Internal Security Act (ISA) 150–151, 158
International Court of Justice 115
International Criminal Court 195
International Labor Rights Fund 43
International Monetary Fund (IMF) 126, 218
International Republican Institute 110
International School of Ouagadougou 191
International Socialist Organization 47, 140
Intifada 28
Ipanema Beach 225
Iran 18, 27, 32, 59–64, 69, 118
Iraq 35, 45, 48, 51, 56–58, 88, 93, 96–98, 102, 105, 118,
  140, 145, 151, 161, 166, 192, 214, 224, 232
Ireland 92-94, 102
Islamabad 72
Islamophobia 178
Israel 28, 64, 66–67, 69, 237
Italy 20–22
Izz-ad-Din al-Qassam Brigades 68

Jabiluka Action 140
Jakarta 17, 143–146
Jamia Hafsa madrassa 72
Jammeh, Yahya Abdul-Aziz Jemus Junkung 195–196
Japan 12–14, 22, 88, 136, 163–167
Jawaharlal Nehru University, New Delhi 181
Jayalalitha, Jayaram 179
Jeans for Freedom 121
Johannesburg 190
Johns Hopkins 42
Jordan 69
Jovanovic, Milja 110

Kabul 55
Kageri, Vishweshwar 182
KAN (Kosovo Action Network) 107, 117, 236
Kanteper, Nejla 101
Karnataka 184–185
Karol, Ashok 181
Karzai, Hamid 55
Kent State University 25
Kentucky Fried Chicken (KFC) 58, 93
Kenya 16, 32, 194, 202
Kenya Polytechnic 203
Kenyatta University 203
Khamenei, Ayatollah Ali 59–61
Khan, Ayub 22
Khartoum International Airport 194

Khatami, Mohammad 59–60, 62
Kim Dae-jung 163
Kim Jong-un 138
Kirchner, Néstor Carlos 219
Kmara (Georgia) 117, 236
Koizumi, Junichiro 157, 164, 166, 174
Kolkata 181
Korea 17, 136
Kosovo Action Network 115–116
Kosovo Liberation Army (KLA) 115
Kpelafia, Koumoyi 201
Kuchma, Leonid 113
Ku Klux Klan 19
Kurdistan Workers' Party (PKK) 101
Kuwait 57

labor unions 21–22, 84–85
Lagos 190
Lahoud, Émile 70
Lake Forest College 44
Lal Masjid 72
Laos 149–150, 157, 160
Lao Students Movement for Democracy 149
La Paz 220–222
Las Ramblas 97
Latin America 13, 16, 19–20, 27, 31, 43, 211–212, 234,
  238
Latin American Spring 14, 239
Latvia 126
Lebanon 70
Lee Myung-bak 166
Left Bank 21
Legon 208
Le Pen, Jean-Marie 82
Levi Strauss factory 39
Lewis & Clark College 43
LGBTQ protests 52
Lhasa 176
Liberia 197
Liberty Square 169
Limerick 93
Living Wage Campaign (LWC) 41–42
Loja (Macedonia) 117
London's West End 101
Lord Ram's Army 184
Los Angeles 46
Luanda 190
Lukashenko, Alexander 119–121, 133
Luther, Martin 10
Lu Ts'ui 13

M1 Alliance 140–141
Mahuad, Jamil 228
Maidan Nezalezhnosti (Independence Square) in
  Kiev 113
Malacanan Presidential Palace 157
Malawi 198
Malaysia 137, 150–151
Mandalay 155
Mangaluru 182, 184
Mangosuthu University of Technology 209

Index

Maoists 152
Mao Zedong 13, 15, 29
Maple Spring (Canada) 37
Martyr Yasser Arafat Bloc 68
May '68 Revolution in France 21
May Fourth Movement (1919) 12–13
May Thirtieth Movement 13
Medvedev, Dmitry 131
Melbourne 140–141
Menem, Carlos Saúl 218
Mesa, Carlos 222
#MeToo movement 5, 183, 186
Mexico 13, 19, 31, 39, 139, 212, 221
Mexico City 23, 27, 212
Middle East 11, 20, 32, 35, 53–75, 93, 101, 108, 133, 151, 190, 236–237
Milošević, Slobodan 32, 36, 108–110
Minuteman Project 47
Mississippi 18
Mjaft! (Enough!) movement 59, 111–113, 117, 236
Mogadishu 200
Moi University 202
Moldova 126
Molotov cocktails 21, 23, 29, 56, 73, 84, 91, 213, 217, 231
Monrovia 197
Montenegro 116
Montreal 35–37
Morales, Evo 223
Moscow 11, 115, 129–130
Moscow McDonald 131
Mount Royal Cross 36
Moussavi, Mir Hussein 62
Mozambique 32
Mubarak, Hosni 58
Mugabe, Robert 204–206
Munich 11
Musavi, Hadi 118
Musharraf, Pervez 70–73
Myanmar 149, 154–155, 159

Nagasaki 166
Nagoya 166
Nairobi 202–203
Nanchang 175
Nandigram 181
Nashi (Ours) (youth group) 129–130
National Association of Burkina Students (ANEB) 191
National Autonomous University of Mexico (UNAM) 23, 212
National Awakening Movement of South Azerbaijan (NAMSA) 118–119
National Awami Party (NAP) 153
National Collegiate Athletic Association (NCAA) 40
National Committee on Traditional Practices 192–193
National Democratic Institute 110
National Democratic Party of Germany (NPD) 86
National Endowment for Democracy 110
National Guard 25–26
National Guard Memorial Building 43
National Intelligence Service 229
nationalism 54, 65, 74, 81, 106, 111, 235

Nationalist Student League 153
nationalization 222, 229
National League for Democracy 156
National Liberation Army (ELN) 226
National Network Opposing the Militarization of Youth 47
National Polytechnic Institute 23
National Renewal of Poland movement 127–128
National Student League (NSL) 14
National Students' Union of India (NSUI) 182
National Technical University of Athens 91
National Union of Faso Students (UNEF) 191
National Union of Students (NUS) 100–101, 140
NATO 55, 110–111, 114–116
Naval Station (NAVSTA) 97
neoliberalism 37, 79–81, 93, 96, 105
Nepal 152–153
Netanyahu, Benjamin 65
Newsweek 55
New York 24
Nicaragua 19, 215, 217–218
Nigeria 32, 197, 199
Nihon University 22
Noboa, Gustavo 228
Nochixtlán 213
North America 35–52
North Dakota 39
Northern Alliance 55
North Korea 150–151, 159–160, 163, 167, 237
Novi Sad 109

OAU (Organization of African Unity) 201
Oaxaca 212–214
Obama, Barack 50–51, 56
Occupy demonstrations 51
October (Eisenstein) 132
October Massacre 23
October Square in Minsk 121
O'Keeffe, Batt 94
Okinawa 166
Omdurman 200
Orange Revolution (Ukraine) 113–114, 121, 128
Ordaz, Díaz 23
Organization for Islamic Propagation 60
Ortega, Daniel 217
Osaka 166
Otpor ("Resistance") 36, 59, 107, 110–112, 117, 143, 190, 212, 232, 236, 238
Ottawa 35
Ouattara, Alassane 195
Oxford 10

Pakistan 22, 70–72
Palestine 44, 66–69, 187, 226
Palestine Liberation Organization (PLO) 68
Palestinian Authority 66
Pan-Blue coalition 168
Papua New Guinea 142, 145
Paraguay 16
Paris 20–21, 82–85
Paris Nanterre University 20

Student Resistance in the Age of Chaos:
Book 1, 1999–2009

Patil, Pratibha 179
Patriots Rally for America 45
Penguin Revolution 226
Pentagon (United States) 19, 26
People for the Ethical Treatment of Animals (PETA) 93
People's Park (China) 177
Persian Gulf War 32
Perth 141
Peru 13, 19, 229–231
Peuhl 207
Philippines 137, 156–157
Pine Ridge Reservation 26
Pink Chaddi campaign 185
Pinochet, Augusto 28
Plaza de las Tres Culturas 23
Poland 3, 11, 14, 127–128
Polytechnic University of Bobo-Dioulasso 191
Pope Benedict XVI 96
Popović, Srdja 111
Pora! (It's Time) 59, 113–114, 117, 236
Port-au-Prince 233
Portugal 104
Prague Spring 18, 28
Presidential Guard 206
Préval, René 233
Privy Council 162
pro-Chinese students 167
Progressive Student Labor Movement (PSLM) 41–42
Prophet Muhammad 55
Proryv (Breakthrough) 125
Puno 230
Pusan 164–165
Pussy Riot 12
Putin, Vladimir 128–129, 131, 133, 138
Pyeongtaek 165

Quebec 36–37
QUEER (Queers United to Eradicate Economic Rationalism) 140
Quito 228

raasta roko (road blocking) 180
racism 40–42, 47–48, 51–53, 74, 86, 100, 106, 235
Rally for the Republic (RPR) 82
Rcheulishvili, Vakhtang 124
Reagan, Ronald 25
Red Army 13
Red Berets 207
Red Guard 15
Republican Party 40, 47, 52
Resistance Archive 7
Revolutionary Popular Students Movement (MEPR) 224
Revolutionary Students Front (RSF) 178
Rhodesia 27
Riga 126
Rio de Janeiro 224–225
Rizal, José 157
Romania 32
Rose Revolution 121, 124

Russell Athletic 39
Russia 11–12, 122, 125–126, 128, 130–132, 138, 149
Russo-Georgian War 125

Saakashvili, Mikheil 124–125
Saffron Revolution 155
Saint Petersburg 11, 130
Saint Scholastica's Day Riot (1354) 10
Sand, Karl 10
San Francisco 25, 46, 89
Santiago 226
São Paulo 224
Sarajevo 12
Sarkozy, Nicolas 85
Save Free Education 101
School of the Americas 46
Schröder, Gerhard 88
Schwarzenegger, Arnold 49
Scotland 100
Scottish Campaign for Nuclear Disarmament 102
Seattle 89, 187
Second Ivorian Civil War 195
Second Liberian Civil War 197
Second Sino-Japanese War 174
Second World War 14, 16, 163–164
Self-Determination Movement 115
Seoul 163–165
Serbia 61, 108, 110–111, 114–116, 119, 124, 129, 132, 232, 236
Seventh Facet 120
sexual violence 5, 71, 83, 165, 179
Shaanxi 174
Shalit, Gilad 65
Shamali, Ali 68
Shanghai 13, 173
Shinawatra, Thaksin 162
Sierra Leone Civil War 197
Singapore 6, 157–159
Sirleaf, Ellen Johnson 197
"Sleep Outside in the Cold" campaign 94
Socialist Alliance 140
social justice 17, 18, 33, 74, 77, 108, 193
social liberalization 17
Somalia 190, 199
Somphone, Sombath 150
Sorbonne 20–21
Sosa, Porfirio Lobo 217
South Africa 16, 27, 32, 208–209
South America 16, 23, 108, 225, 236
South Carolina State University 24
Southern Negro Youth Congress 14
South Korea 17, 28, 136, 162–166
South Ossetia 125
Soviet Union 32
Spanish Socialist Workers' Party 97–98
Sri Ram Sena (SRS) 184–185
Studenski Grad 122–123
Student Afro-American Society 24
Student Council of the University of Benin (CEUB) 201
Student Labor Alliance (SLA) 42

Index

Student League for Industrial Democracy (SLID) 14
Student Nonviolent Coordinating Committee (SNCC) 18
Student Organization of Nairobi University (SONU) 203
Student Peace Coalition 45
Students Against War 47
Students Federation of India (SFI) 178, 182
Students for a Democratic Society (SDS) 19, 46
Student Youth Movement 68
sub-Saharan Africa 43
Sudan 200
Suharto (Indonesian president) 17, 32, 146
Sukarno (Indonesian president) 17
Sukarnoputri, Megawati 145
Summer Olympic Games in 1968 (Mexico City) 23
Sunflower Movement 239
Supreme Court of Pakistan 73
Susan, Nisha 185
Swarthmore College 42
Swarthmore Labor Action Project 42
Sweden 98–99
Switzerland 104
Syngman, Rhee 17
Syntagma Square 92
Syria 70

Taiwan 168, 171
Taliban 55
Tamil Nadu Agricultural University 179
Tanzania 204
Tarnowskie Gory 127
Taylor, Charles 197–198
Tbilisi 125
Tchadjobo, Hanif 201
Tehran 60, 62
Telangana 182
Thailand 161–162
Thammasat University 161
Tiananmen Square 29, 31, 61, 170–172
Tibet 142, 170, 176
Timiryazev State Biological Museum 131
18 Tir 59–60
Tlatelolco Massacre 24
Togo 201, 206, 208
Tokyo 14, 163, 166
Toledo, Alejandro 229–230
Toronto 35
Transnational Radical Party 149
tribalism 142
Trident Ploughshares 102
Trump, Donald 52, 133, 138
Tshwane University of Technology 209
Tsinghua University 13
Tunisia 16, 204, 238
Turin Fiat factory 21–22
Turkey 32
Twitter 6, 126, 139, 187

Uighurs 149, 170, 176–177
Ukraine 32, 113–114, 116, 121, 128–129, 132

UN Development Program 191
UN Interim Administration (UNIA) 115–116
Union Nationale des Étudiants de France 20–21
Union of Students in Ireland (USI) 94
Unitas (Montenegro) 59, 117
United Civic Party 120
United Malays National Organization 151
United National Front of Democracy against Dictatorship (UDD) 162
United National Movement 124
United Nations 115, 146–147, 160, 195, 210
United States 11, 20, 24, 111, 122, 125, 133, 135, 165, 174, 197, 221, 226, 235, 238
    alt-right student groups in 3
    antiwar demonstrations in 25, 75
    conservative ideology in 51
    desegregation efforts in 24
    domestic issues 14
    embassy in Tehran 27
    government linking 9/11 terrorist strikes with Iraq 35
    invasion of Afghanistan 44, 68, 71, 81, 105, 118, 145, 192, 227
    invasion of Iraq 35, 58, 81, 88, 97, 105, 118, 140, 145, 151, 161, 192, 214, 224, 232
    operations in Colombia 44
    recession of 2008 48
    September 11 terrorist attacks 87
    South Korea's students protests in 28
    standoff between Iran and 27
    student activists in 11, 14, 16, 18, 19, 36, 39
    worker unions and organizations in 38
United Students Against Sweatshops (USAS) 38
Universities and Colleges Act 151
University of Belgrade 108
University of Bucharest 32
University of California, Berkeley 14, 19, 25, 38, 42, 49
University of California, Santa Cruz 47
University of Dar Es Salaam 204
University of Dhaka 153–154
University of Florida 38
University of Georgia 42
University of Ghana 208
University of Hawaii 38
University of Indonesia 17
University of Jordan 69
University of Koudougou 191
University of Limpopo 209
University of Lomé 201
University of London 101
University of Malawi 198
University of Nairobi 202
University of North Dakota Student Political Action Network 39
University of Ouagadougou 191–192
University of Technology Sydney (UTS) 139
University of Tehran 59, 61–62
University of Texas 38
University of the South Pacific 142
University of Tokyo 22
University of Virginia 42

Student Resistance in the Age of Chaos:
Book 1, 1999–2009

University of Wisconsin 38, 46
University of Zagreb 79
University of Zambia (UNZA) 203
University of Zimbabwe in Harare 204–205
University Square (in Bucharest) 32
Ürümqi 177–178
USAID 110
US Cavalry 26

Vaal University of Technology 209
Vancouver 35
Veliaj, Erion 112
Velvet Revolution 29
Venezuela 13, 16, 187, 231
Vienna 11, 78
Vietnam 19, 148–149, 160–161
Vietnam War 18, 25–27
Voina (group) 12, 131–132, 218
Voronin, Vladimir 126
Vorotnikov, Oleg 131
Voting Rights Act of 1965 19

Wahid, Abdurrahman 144
Walk for Reconciliation across Sydney Harbour
    Bridge 139–140
Walking Without Putin 129
Warmbier, Otto 160
War on Drugs 43
Washington 18, 25, 56
Washington, DC 19, 46
Washington Monument 44
Waterloo Bridge 101
weapons of mass destruction (WMDs) 57
Weather Underground (underground terrorist
    group) 25
Wesleyan University 42
West Bank 28, 237
Western Hemisphere Institute for Security
    Cooperation 46
Western imperialism 55–56, 58, 60, 93, 111; see also
    imperialism
Westernization 27, 32
West Germany 17, 89
Wheeler Hall 49
White House 40
Women's Marches 51–52, 90
World Economic Forum 140
Wounded Knee Massacre (1890) 26
Wuxuan 15

Xavier University 46
xenophobia 47-48, 51-53, 75, 77, 86, 100, 106, 118, 124,
    128, 194–195

Yangon 155
Yanukovych, Viktor 114
Yasukuni 164
Yasukuni War Shrine 174
Young Belarus Coalition 120
Young Communist League 46
Young Front 120–121

Youth Human Rights Movement (Russia) 117
Youth Initiative for Human Rights (Serbia) 117
YouTube 63
Yox! (No!) 117
Yudhoyono, Susilo Bambang 145
Yugoslavia 32, 115–116
Yushchenko, Viktor 114

Zagreb 12
Zambia 32, 203
Zapatero, José Luis Rodríguez 98
Zelaya, Manuel 216
Zenawi, Meles 192–193
Zengakuren 14
Zimbabwe 27, 32, 190, 204–206
Zimbabwe African National Union-Patriotic Front
    204
Zolotarev, Yevhen 118
Zomba 198
Zubr movement 117, 120